NO NEUTRAL GROUND

NO NEUTRAL GROUND

JOEL CARLSON

THOMAS Y. CROWELL COMPANY
New York / Established 1834

Designed by Jill Schwartz

Manufactured in the United States of America

ISBN 0-690-58457-1

2 3 4 5 6 7 8 9 10

Library of Congress Cataloging in Publication Data
Carlson, Joel.
    No neutral ground.
    Autobiographical.
    1. Criminal justice, Administration of—Africa,
South.   2. Africa, South—Race question.   I. Title.
Law   342'.68'087   72-14239
ISBN 0-690-58457-1

To Jeanette, whose love and humor and companionship gave me a home and a happy family: no man had a better base from which to work.

To all political prisoners everywhere.

ACKNOWLEDGEMENTS

My work in South Africa would not have been possible without the help and support of many friends there, but to thank them by name here would endanger them. Security police, whether officially on duty or off duty, acting like gangsters would make their lives more difficult. I salute my friends as they continue their work in South Africa. May we meet soon; until then, "sala kahle."

There are many beyond the reach of the present regime in South Africa, and it is impossible to thank all by name, but I mention especially my old friends Jules and Eleanor Lewin; George Lindsay and Peter Connell who brought me support and hope in South Africa, and Tom Reiner whose aid was unstinting. My whole family is indebted to "Henry," who never spared himself and gave his help when it was most needed. Particular thanks are due to Charles Runyon, whose outstanding and loyal support brought me real aid throughout a most difficult period.

Carol Bernstein, Peter Weiss, Betsy Landis, and Charles Mandelstam were among those who befriended me in New

York and gave me a new start in life, making it possible for me to join Tom Franck at the Center for International Studies at New York University.

Many friends know of the generosity and support of co-exiles Mike and Jenny Davis. Throughout the years we worked together and I relied on and always received their ceaseless support. They and their children, Sandy and Mark, gave my family a home when we arrived here. My deep appreciation is especially due to Jenny for all the time and work she devoted to the book. Her soundness of judgment and complete integrity is appreciated and has been invaluable to me.

CONTENTS

NO
NEUTRAL
GROUND

I
LOVE AND
ALIENATION

It is the birthright of every man to see and know the land where he was born. I journeyed far across my land, from the velvet-soft, blue-green vineyards beneath the Jonkershoek mountains and the magical valley of De Doorns, to the wild canyons of the northern borders. It took years and I had not seen it all when I left.

My home was in *eGoli* (City of Gold), Johannesburg, the mining center of the Witwatersrand (Ridge of White Waters). The "rand" and Johannesburg rest on a plateau six thousand feet above the sea, a plateau stretching for hundreds of miles until suddenly, traveling over it, one sees the edge of the escarpment, and beyond and far below, the lowveld, flowing in the sunlight toward the horizon.

As often as I could I would travel far to the north and east of Johannesburg to visit and revisit the lowveld, this land below the escarpment. It is hot, tropical country, rich in green vegetation and blazing with the colors of its flowers. Before descending into this distant world I would stop at the knife edge of the plateau and climbing along the rocks, find a flat one—thrusting into space, its orange face basking in the sun—where I could sit alone. In this remote place, I would search the earth and the air around; I would listen to the sounds and hear the silences. Here, in our machine-mad world, was an old, old earth, unspoiled and balanced in its natural way.

The bushes were rugged and gripped the hard-baked earth firmly. Long, wispy strands of grass grew from clumps lying just above the ground. Trees were short and gnarled, twisting in irregular-shaped branches, time tested in their struggle for survival. It was dry and warm; and sitting there the sun soon subdued all thought. If I closed my eyes I could lie and dream endlessly there. I could feel the earth; I wanted to disappear, sink into it, and be part of it. I have yet to find a land so full of warmth and so rich in beauty as my homeland.

In exile, now, and far away, it is still easy to recall clearly the joy of sitting alone beside a waterhole, silently listening to the sounds of wild game. Waiting patiently, I anticipated and watched the movements of buck, of lion, of elephant or giraffe, or so many other animals. All came down to drink, each practicing a caution long learned; each alert to sounds and smells. The animals approached the water's edge with natural grace and simplicity; muscles moving beneath sleek skin. At last, judging all danger to be absent, the animal's head would reach toward the water, forefeet stretched wide apart. The sudden crack of a branch, a bird's sharp call, would break the silence. The head would jerk, the feet ready for instant flight. The hindquarters would push, the forefeet pull, and in a smooth line of motion the safety of a distant bush or tree would be sought. Then the scene would be empty and but for bird calls, silence would return until once again the cycle would repeat itself. To be left undisturbed in the peace and quietness of this small part of the wild world was real happiness.

My story begins a long time ago—it begins when I decided to break with my past. The luxury of living the life of a white South African was little compensation for the anger and frustration I felt. Neither at home growing up nor at the university did I find any relief from the tensions arising out of the continuing injustices I saw practiced daily by white people against black people. The behavior I witnessed in my own home was little different from what happened in the homes of my white friends, for injustice is the traditional way of life in South Africa. In vain did I try to right these wrongs.

All my friends were white. My school, a small suburban public school, was a "white school." The children and the teachers were exclusively white. Only white visitors came to my home and the homes of my friends. At the movies the audience was all white. The swimming pools and tennis courts were similarly "pure." Until I went to the university I formed no real friendships with any of my peers; not one of them felt about these things the way I did. I also had no opportunity to meet a black man or woman in any situation other than a master-servant one. This was the norm for South Africa and I was part of it.

Once at Johannesburg's Witwatersrand University, I began to meet black students. There were only a score or two—mostly men—but they were my fellow students and I sought them out. They were highly politically conscious people whereas I was politically naive, but I was accepted by them because I was not a racist. Indeed, surprised as they evidently were by my attitudes, they welcomed me warmly. My friendship with these black students deepened. I visited them in their homes, was struck by the wide differences in our backgrounds, and recognized even more strongly the inherent injustices in the basic philosophy of the ruling whites in South Africa.

Soon after World War II, university students were particularly active politically. Besides the representative groups of the Nationalist and United parties, the two major parliamentary parties in South Africa, there were Communist party groups, Trotskyist groups, Anarchists, Christians, Zionists, Socialists, and Revisionists. My black friends involved me in the bustle of student politics, and I discovered that I had the ability to run organizations efficiently and soon became chairman of many student bodies. This brought me closely in touch with the intrigues and petty personal jealousies of the leaders of the many political movements. It was only later that

I realized how much this intrigue and jealousy was the rule, the normal practice of all organized political activity. At the time, as a young student, I was bitterly disillusioned by the factions, the political infighting, and the wasted energy, all resulting from the political differences among my friends.

Meanwhile, throughout South Africa, white racism was growing in power until it took over full control of the country. In 1948, with the election of the Nationalist party, Nazi sympathizers and outspoken Fascists were appointed to high office. The "New Order" moved directly and forcefully toward Fascism, claiming that it was the spearhead of the Western world's fight against Communism. During this period, the splits and divisions among the student groups became even more bitter. Instead of uniting against a common enemy, energies were expended in fighting one another.

Frustrated and angry with my life at home, disillusioned with the politics at the university, I determined to make my own way and my own contribution toward change for the better in the society in which I lived. I wanted to find out more of how the white system was applied to blacks. I wanted to see for myself how the law was enforced. Once I learned the facts I would be able to take my next step.

I remember the day I reached this decision. The Zulu name for my parents' house was *Ikaya Lamatye* (House among the Rocks). It was well named. The house was bedded in and wedged up against red and ocher rocks that had been blasted away to make room for it. The rough-plastered white walls, two stories high, held up a blue-black, high-pitched slate roof. The *kopje*, a stone-topped hill, rose up behind the house and dropped down in rock gardens, stone walls, wild shrubs, and cacti to the gateway below where a wooden plaque carried the house name.

The view from our hill was one of the best in Johannesburg. On that day I stood outside the house just after a thunderstorm had broken. The lightning crackled, whipping the dark heavens with electricity. For over thirty minutes the rain poured down in torrents, then as suddenly as it all began, it stopped. I watched the storm pass westward where the streams of airborne water, defined in channels, were still falling from the low-lying clouds. Far northward a flood of light hit the earth where the clouds had broken and whole patches shone in sunlight.

The scene was never still—light and shadow intermingled. On the horizon the purple mountains of the Magaliesberg, about fifty miles from Johannesburg, moved nearer in the soft afternoon light. Haze and light played tunes of color on the faraway slopes. Below me, the green grass of the golf course glistened in the sunlight. Shafts of light fell on the curved water towers in the east and the sun descended slowly to spill color in all its glorious hues across the sky and shoot the high white clouds with orange and pink. Steam from the many tarred streets rose and disappeared in evening breezes. I walked endlessly on those steaming streets and thought about my future.

I decided to join the civil service and ask to be posted to what were then called Native Commissioners Courts. Since the British Parliament gave self-government to the South African white minority in 1910, these special courts had enforced the laws that applied only to the African people.

The first day I began work, the day I left home, is another memory easy to recall. It was early in the morning when I set out for the bus stop, jumping down the rough rock pathway, a short cut from the house directly to the avenue below. I reached the last paving stone and walked along the sidewalk. Sunrise had been followed by a rain shower and the air was crisp and fresh. Purple jacaranda petals pressed their trumpets to the arched macadamized roadway. The rough-hewn stonework gutters flowed with rain water laden with fallen flowers.

From each side of the street, tall jacaranda trees linked their branches across the road below to make a tunnel of green and purple. The early sun broke through the gray of the morning, hitting drops with light as they fell from the branches above. Reflections sparkled with the sharpness of the light. I stopped to watch a drop form along the center strand of a cluster of delicate little leaves. The crystal-clear drop grew in size as it moved down the strand before falling to earth to lose its form forever.

Above my head I saw the gentle hands of the early morning breeze hold the silken flowers and let them parachute to earth where they came to rest intact and unharmed. I bent down to pick up a purple flower and felt its soft texture and smelled its fragrance. On the street I heard the swish of hard rubber tires as they passed over and popped the petals that had fallen and pressed them flat to the surface. Only the color remained to dull the light reflected off the wet road. There was richness in the sunlight and in the sounds, smells, and colors around me.

Walking along I passed stone walls, fat and solid, sitting on the boundaries of their private estates. The crevices were earth-filled and in them, red geraniums grew. Yellow canary creepers were entwined the length of the walls and green runners spread over the bulging sides. In the rich gardens flowers grew in abundance, red-hot pokers held their vibrant heads high on firm, long green stalks, and cacti wallowed in the sun, their thorns defiantly pointed against intruders.

I reached the bus stop and stood and waited with the sun pouring through my jacket and into my bones. I stood at a "white" bus stop, waiting for a "white" bus, driven by a "white" bus driver. One hundred yards down the road stood a cluster of Africans waiting at a "black" bus stop for their "black" bus. "Black" and "white" buses were all painted the same red and cream. Only a small sign on the front saying *Nie-blankes* (Non-whites) distinguished one from the other. My bus traveled through the white suburbs to the city where I caught a tram to Fordsburg, where my court was situated. The route ran past the old produce market and the Indian bazaars and shops. My stop was at the Indian school and I went through the playground, a narrow street closed to traffic during recess, crossed the open railway track alongside the road, and walked on to the courthouse.

It was on the southern end of a large freight yard that stretched between Johannesburg and Fordsburg. Directly opposite an ash-covered embankment some twenty feet high, was a long, dirty-gray, prefabricated, single-story building. It was built as a temporary structure but has now been in use for nearly half a century. Perhaps one day it will be destroyed when justice is done to it, for justice was never done in it.

Black and gray puffs of smoke rose from the engines shunting freight cars up and down. The court proceedings were constantly interrupted by high-pitched squeals of protest from moving wheels as the cars stopped with a clang of iron on iron. Coal dust and grit covered our courtroom and all the adjoining offices. There was no point in cleaning the windows as they were thickly coated with coal dust and with sand that blew off the hard, dry, orange ground. Actually, there was little incentive to clean the windows anyway as they faced out onto two latrines. The main entrance to the courthouse was through a double wooden door, varnished a dark brown, that opened onto well-worn wooden floorboards, splintered and stained. The bottom half of the walls inside were painted the same dark brown, the top half a dull cream color. A passage led to left and right. It was dark and lit by bare bulbs that cast a yellow light.

My office, a small room about eight by twelve feet, was the second door at the right of the entrance. Heavy mesh wire barricaded the windows. This office remains unchanged today although the yard outside the window has been altered. To-day, a high brick wall topped by a corrugated stretch of roof with barbed wire on top runs from one end of the courthouse to the other. Previously there was no such wall and no bricked-in enclosure. Standing inside the courtroom one can see the prison yard now enclosed by that wall. The asphalt-surfaced floor is divided into cages by twelve-foot-high fences and in each cage men and women, and some children too, are kept. If there are few prisoners they are able to sit on the ground but if there is not enough space to sit, they stand. All wait for "justice" to be done.

It was in this court, and others like it, that the full force of pass laws was felt. The document known as a pass has changed only in form during the one hundred fifty years since it was first introduced by whites. The pass laws were designed to channel the flow of Africans who left their homes to seek work through government labor centers. Today Africans are even referred to in government circulars and by white govern-ment ministers as "productive or nonproductive labor units," serving the white economy. The dependents of these "labor

units" are called "superfluous appendages." Any term will do
so long as the African is depersonalized and dehumanized.
Strictly regimented and controlled, no African can work or go
anywhere or remain anywhere without his pass. According to
the law, every African aged sixteen or over has to produce
proof that he or she "is entitled to be, remain, work, or reside
in" the particular place he is in. Failure to produce a pass on
demand, a pass clearly showing compliance with the law,
results in immediate arrest and imprisonment. Each year a
million Africans are arrested under the pass laws and the
majority of the African population have been arrested at some
time under these laws.

White man's justice at Fordsburg began with the early-
morning "deliveries." The court served more than a score of
police stations. All day and night, policemen—black and
white—were busy arresting pass offenders. Some lucky ones
would immediately pay the policeman and be freed. Others
had relatives or friends who heard about the arrest and
arrived at the police station to pay for an "A/G"—admission
of guilt. Then, they too would be freed without having to sleep
in jail for a night or two. The least fortunate would be jailed
and then would be brought to the Native Commissioners
Court in Fordsburg.

Each morning when I arrived at court policemen were
waiting for me. The prisoners came in police pickup vans or in
old army trucks covered over with wire mesh called *kwela-
kwela* trucks. (*Kwela-kwela* is an African dance step.) When
loading the trucks the police would swing their sticks, shout
"*Kom, kom, Kaffir,*" and hurry their prisoners up the back
steps. The Africans would have to jump to it and almost jump
up into the truck—hence *kwela-kwela* (jump, jump up). Each
policeman had to make these deliveries to me at the court.
First they handed over any "A/Gs" and were issued with
receipts; then they handed over a list of prisoners. We only
checked numbers—names were a nuisance and no one ever
bothered much about them. In South Africa, servants are
renamed by whites because whites only call Africans by
"white names." Almost no whites ever knew the real names
of their black servants.

Having received and checked a list saying twenty-nine prisoners were being delivered, I signed for it. All prisoners had been fingerprinted and the Central Fingerprint Bureau would be consulted if it were necessary to establish the identity of any prisoner. White policemen were normally attended to first. They were often young teen-agers, made men by the authority of their uniform, proud of their white skin and arrogant. All were tanned, the blond men rednecked, the dark men burned brown, and their uniforms were immaculate—the brass buttons shone. They recognized me as a *rooinek* (an English-speaking South African), but they tolerated me and were patient with me. After all, I was one of them—a white man working for the system. My office was a pleasant meeting place for these young men just out of police college and dispersed in stations all over Johannesburg. The conversation between them was easy and friendly. There was no conflict here. They did their job, spoke to friends, and left. The few black policemen stood aside and listened, talking little, waiting.

After the formalities of the delivery had been made, I counted the fines, entered the amount in the ledger, and placed the bags of money in the safe. Then I began making entries in the court record book. On the left I placed the name of the police station, then the white man's name for the prisoner, then the offense—Section 10, Section 12, Section 29, and the like. In court, the junior judicial officer, in my day called a native commissioner and today a Bantu commissioner, but white, of course, would mark down the conviction and sentence next to the name of each prisoner. Generally, offenders would be called strictly in the order of the names in the book to facilitate and speed up the proceedings.

Having completed this paper work, I would take calls from irate white employers complaining that their "boy" had been picked up by the police. (In South Africa as in some other parts of the world, the term "boy" refers to a black male of any age and is used by the whites in a derogatory way.) Protesting that he was a "good boy" or an "old boy," their frustration at not having "Richard" or "John" or "Sixpence" to make the fire or wash the dishes that morning was vented on me. "The police had no right to arrest him." "He was standing in front of the gate of our house." "His pass was in our other "boy's" room, he was not even allowed to go and pick it up." "It's shocking what goes on in this country, a crying shame!" "How long will it be before my 'boy' comes back?" Sometimes, enraged by their smugness and hypocrisy, I would say, "Madam, we have no boys here." At other times I would ask them for the man's full name, which they could never give me. Always I was anxious for them to come down to court and see the process for themselves, but none of them was prepared to go to that amount of trouble for their "boys" or "girls," and I had to be satisfied if they sent their other "boy" with a note and the money to pay the inevitable fine. I soon learned that white people preferred not to see or know what was really going on. They merely wanted to ensure that the method of enforcing their white man's laws should never inconvenience them.

These calls inquiring about servants took me out to the prisoners' yard adjacent to the back door of the court. When I worked there in the late 1940s, this was an open, fenced enclosure backing onto a "tin shanty," a corrugated-iron structure that sometimes sufficed as a prison for the very few night prisoners. Just before I started in at the court, several prisoners had been put into its one large room with some insane men, there being no other accommodation. It happened to be a long Easter weekend. The prisoners were not properly attended to—the whole arrangement was a makeshift one—and four of them died.

Jutting out from this corrugated-iron shanty was a small overhang providing the prisoners with some shade from the sun, some cover in the rain. The open-wire fence was a blessing for it enabled relatives and friends of the prisoners, who had received bush-telegraph messages of their plight, to come to the court, see and talk to them, and to give them help. Formalities were waived for we had no staff or facilities for more regular formal visits. Money was handed through the fence as well as bread and milk and fruit. Talk and laughter flowed freely—no one was ashamed. The law—not the prisoners—was held in contempt.

In my visits to the prison's backyard, I frequently encountered a man called Oom Piet talking to the prisoners. What he was saying was obviously important. The visitors on the outside of the fence had been moved off a distance and the prisoners compelled to stop talking and gather around and listen. At first I did not know what it was all about and whenever I came into the yard Oom Piet stopped talking. I took the hint and decided to learn from afar. I stood in the courtroom casually listening; I questioned the African interpreters and asked the other officials about it. Slowly the picture formed and I learned something of a system that I can never forget.

Oom (Afrikaans for uncle or for a kindly elderly man) Piet's full name was Piet de Beer. He was a chubby, clean, red-faced little man. He bore some resemblance to Winston Churchill and he always waited expectantly when meeting a stranger for this resemblance to be remarked on. If nothing was said he marked the stranger down as "not so educated." I was rated highly as I mentioned it within five minutes of meeting him. Of course he made it painfully obvious; he wore a rose in his buttonhole, a bow tie and spats, carried strange hats, and loved his cigars. Officially his title was "the prisoner's friend" and he occupied the office next to mine. He had been in the civil service a long time. On his wall was a picture of the troop ship *Mende*, which carried a Zulu regiment to France during World War I. The ship was sunk with all hands, and the picture showed Oom Piet and some other whites commemorating the loss of the Zulus who bravely went down with the ship. Other pictures showed local councils of blacks standing in back of seated white officials. The black men, in the English tradition, wore bowler hats and high starched collars and carried umbrellas. As long as the black man "knew his place," Oom Piet tolerated him. He only disliked the cheeky Kaffir and the "won't works," sadly admitting that these were "most of them." There were very few "decent ones," he said.

Each day sunburned white farmers would gather casually in Oom Piet's office. Sometimes the overflow would move into my office. These men, dressed in loosely fitting khaki shirts and pants, some with veld hats, would lounge around, waiting. Dealing with them was only part of Oom Piet's job. He had first to deal with the prisoners in the back. As I was writing up the court book after all the prisoners had arrived, Oom Piet would go into the yard where a table and chair, symbols of civilization and authority, had been placed for him.

He would greet the prisoners and introduce himself— "I am the director of public prosecutions," he would say. In fact, this is a term used by prosecutors in the metropolitan police courts in London, entirely unknown in South African courts, but the title made him sound important. "I have the power to take you to the court or withdraw the charges against you." In truth he had such power, irregular as it was. "I am also the prisoner's friend and I am here to help you—the help I have is work. Now you have a choice, the choice is between going to jail or taking up work. Mind you, if you go to jail you will work. Yes, you will get hard labor, you will be sentenced to work for six months or a year, who knows for how long? It is for the court to decide. Whatever your sentence you will work hard in jail. What will you have at the end of your time in jail? No money and no job. The help that I can give you is work. I can get you a job on a farm. There you will earn three pounds a month for six months. The farmer will feed you, give you blankets, and look after you if you are sick. You will work in the fresh air, eat fresh food, and earn money. Now, which do you want? Do you want to go to jail or let me withdraw your case and go to work?"

The police who were present allowed no one to talk. No discussion or questions were tolerated. Each man had to listen intently to Oom Piet and then make up his own mind. "Those who wish to work stand here behind me," said Oom Piet. First one would go, then two, then more would follow. Women's jeering voices shouted at them from afar. "*Thula* [shut up]!" shouted the African policeman, holding up his hand.

As more volunteers came forward, Oom Piet's beady eyes would count the heads; then, satisfied, he would go inside to greet the farmers in his office. Handshakes were exchanged along with friendly conversation in Afrikaans. A black policeman would come in and report the final total to him—"*twee-en-twentig* [twenty-two]." Then a line of prisoners would move from the prison yard to the garage, while in Oom Piet's office the merrymaking continued. Afterwards, "Carlson, keep this in your safe for me," and Oom Piet would hand me a bottle of Scotch and some boxes of cigars.

In court Willem van Heerden, our police sergeant prosecutor, would be busy writing in the court record book. Twenty-two times he inscribed the letters "W by P/P"—"Withdrawn by the Public Prosecutor." The farmers ready to drive home called their "boss-boys"—tough-looking Africans armed with *sjamboks* (whips) or kerries (fat-headed gnarled sticks)—and they all went to collect their bag of boys, their "volunteers." I watched as they were marched in single file to the trucks and, all pretense at courtesy gone, were roughly ordered to get in. Then the farmers would climb in behind the steering wheel while boss-boys mounted guard in case any volunteers tried to run away.

When the orderly called me for the day's justice to begin, I would turn back and walk with heavy legs to my desk in court. The courtroom was big enough to afford the luxury of a public gallery, one for "whites" and on the other side of the barrier, one for "nonwhites." While Africans packed their side, the white side was always empty. The prosecutor would stand at his desk beside the only dock, a wooden, open-framed structure about two feet wide and six feet deep, and the interpreter would be right in front of it. In the dock would be the first man named in the court book. Squeezed in behind him the second man, behind him the next man, and the next and the next, packed like sardines. The single line would extend behind the dock to the door, down the three steps, along the outside wall of the court, and right around the fences. About six black policemen were stationed at intervals along the line to ensure the smooth, fast movement of prisoners in and out of court, and to maintain order. The prosecutor was ready, the charge sheets in a bundle in his hand. The commissioner would arrive at the door and the orderly bark out "Silence in court!"— *"Stilte in die hof!"* in the two official languages. The policeman hissed orders to the black public gallery and we would all stand. The commissioner would take his seat and say, *"Ja,"* to the prosecutor. The justice machine was about to start.

I saw this scene repeated a thousand times. The prosecutor

mumbled in Afrikaans, calling a name and mentioning a section of the law—all very familiar to him, an old hand. The first prisoner, however, appeared startled when he heard his name spoken in this white man's hall. Except for naming the prisoners, the prosecutor addressed himself only to the commissioner. The interpreter never waited for the prosecutor to finish talking for he knew exactly what was being said. He had used the words a hundred times a day, six days a week, for the last seven years. He shouted gruffly to the prisoner. Unfamiliar with the proceedings, confused and dismayed, the prisoner hesitated. Immediately, the interpreter pleaded guilty for him. The commissioner said, "Six pounds—six weeks." The interpreter pushed the prisoner away and a policeman moved him down one side of the line. He could not ask questions for already the next case was finished and that prisoner was following close behind him. Both prisoners arrived at the door of the court, convicted men. More justice had been done.

All I had to do was stamp each indictment handed to me by the prosecutor and write in, "six pounds—six weeks," or whatever the sentence was. Try as I might I could not keep pace, so I would relax and proceed more leisurely. Once the court adjourned I would have the rest of the morning and the whole afternoon to write in the details.

In my own court, I tried to determine what caused one man to receive one sentence and another man a different one. Each commissioner seemed to have his own secret and different formula, although often the same commissioner would change his pattern from one day to the next. Since the court rarely listened to any evidence or heard any mitigating circumstances, the discrepancies made no sense at all, nor did the system, but who was there to realize that?

All the commissioners tried to get through the morning's proceedings quickly. One week there were even bets as to which commissioner would finish the court roll in the shortest time. I was present the day Gronewald took the bench. He finished sixty-six cases in ten minutes, a record that lasted for some time.

After the court sessions, one of my jobs was to complete

the court records. I had to state how many cases had been
heard and fill in the column rating the time spent on each.
Here I had difficulty. On my first day I generously estimated
that we had spent forty minutes in court. "*Yurrie magtig* [God
damn it]!" exploded the prosecutor, "you can't write that.
You had better go and talk to the commissioner." I went to the
commissioner. "Excuse me, sir, how long did we spend in
court this morning?" "Two to three hours. Put two and a half
hours," he said. The book was filled in accordingly. Often, not
withstanding those falsified books, the prisoners were before
the court for less than a minute.

Every now and again, a prisoner would have enough
courage to interrupt the court proceedings, brushing the
interpreter aside or arguing hotly with him. We would all stop
work. "*Wat mekeer* [What's wrong]?" the commissioner
would ask. The interpreter would exasperatedly explain,
"*Hierdie man wil onskuldig ploeg.*" (This man insists on
pleading not guilty.) The man would maintain that his pass
was in order or that he was not out after curfew hours, or he
would put forward some other defense. Without hesitation,
the commissioner would say, "Right, case remanded for two
weeks. Take him away." He would ask the prosecutor to see
that the policeman who made the arrest attended court in two
weeks' time. Meanwhile the prisoner would sit in jail. If after
two weeks the policeman was not in court, it was unfortunate
for the prisoner because he was then taken back to jail for
another two weeks.

I remember so clearly three young men who all pleaded not
guilty. The police picked them up just before 9 P.M., they said.
They were carried around in a police van until after 11
P.M.—curfew time for all Africans—and only then were they
taken to the police station and charged with being out after
curfew hours. After four weeks in jail, the arresting policeman came to give evidence. He contradicted them and, of
course, was believed. The three were treated lightly, however,
as the commissioner took into account that they had already
spent four weeks in jail and sentenced them to only a further
two weeks.

I remember, too, the small boy who insisted he was only

fifteen years old. He was arrested at the railway station for failing to produce a pass although he explained he was still at school. When he appeared in court, after two weeks in jail, his Boy Scout uniform was dirty and he himself was in tears. The commissioner was lenient—he found him guilty but discharged him with only a caution. Still the boy cried; he said he had no money as it had been stolen from him after his arrest and his home was in Pietersburg, some two hundred miles to the north. I asked "the prisoner's friend" to buy him a train ticket and said I would pay for it.

The cruelties were endless and went on day after day. The most pitiful prisoners were the mothers, brought to court from prison with their babies. When a baby was hungry or just needed comfort, the mother would offer her breast. Diapers had long since been dirtied—none were provided by the prisons. The women would wash them out at the tap soon after arrival at court and stuff them in the wire fence to dry.

The horror of the things I saw appalled me. Every day I returned home not knowing how I could go on witnessing such suffering. One afternoon I went to the editor of the Rand *Daily Mail*, a so-called liberal morning newspaper in Johannesburg. I told him some of my stories and after listening for a while he asked, "Are you a Communist?" I looked at him in astonishment—I thought he was mad. "Go to hell!" I said, and left.

I wondered whether there was any point in confronting the authorities with the situation. I decided to see the chief commissioner. He gave me tea, told me what a great future there was for me in the service, and praised all the very good men working under him. I could not believe he was ignorant of the true situation. If he was, despite all his years in the service, then he chose to be and would certainly not believe what I had to tell him. If, however, he was being shrewd, indicating that I should become like his "good men" and shut my eyes and ears to what I saw, there was no point in discussing the matter with him. In either event he would reject what I said. I drank my tea and said nothing. I went on wrestling alone with my problem.

One day an English-speaking commissioner named Kokkot

took the bench and he too finished the proceedings with great speed. We completed all our work before 1 P.M. and I was asked to phone the prison to send its van to pick up the prisoners. My records showed eighty-one prisoners that day but the guard riding the van swore there were only eighty "tickets"—thin sheets of paper called "prisoners property receipts." We could not let the prisoners go until the numbers tallied.

All was confusion as we checked and rechecked. At last we found the one prisoner who had no ticket. He was knocked about by the police and finally admitted his crime. He went to the toilet, he said, and the only paper he had was his ticket so he used it. The prison guard and one of our policemen started beating him up in the court in my presence. I got up and they stopped and took him outside where the beating continued. I was just starting to go after the commissioner to get him to put a stop to it when he walked in. "I hear one of the prisoners didn't think much of my sentence," he said. At that moment, the man was dragged back into court, bleeding and sobbing. "Good," said Kokkot, "you treated him right," and he walked out. The prisoners were loaded onto the van and taken away.

It was clear to me after nine months, that I could not stay in such an evil place any longer. Previously, although I had begun law school, I had felt no overwhelming desire to be a lawyer. Now, however, it was terribly important for me to return to my law studies and qualify. As a lawyer I could expose the injustices I had witnessed. My experience in that court had seared through me. I had learned for the first time what the law really meant to some South Africans. If I had not been part of the administration of justice and had not observed this aspect of the law in practice, it would have been impossible to have learned this.

My law studies never taught me about the law as it applied to black people or, indeed, to any people. The theory and practice of the law I learned related to the property disputes of litigants involving money claims, or criminal law involving illegal acts committed by "criminals" on the person or property of another person or persons. In the Fordsburg court I learned not only of the law of one class as it was applied to another class. I learned raw politics, raw economics, and their terrible effects on the relationship between black people and white people in our society. It was clear, too, who structured this society and imposed the laws. A small group had power; the mass of the people had no power.

My law studies taught me nothing about the indomitable spirit of the people either, but I first learned something of this on an afternoon that I spent at the great complex of courts known as the Central Magistrates Court in Johannesburg. As the black prisoners waited in the cells below the court, the *kwela-kwela* trucks arrived and lined up to return them to jail. It was at the end of the day's court session when suddenly I heard it and I leaned over the balcony overlooking the driveway where the trucks stood. The deep swell of singing voices came rising up through the courts, through the concrete and stone walls of that whole massive building. It was the song of the prisoners that says, "We are here, we are black, we are in our cells, we wait. We wait for justice. We wait for our freedom, it will come. Now we go to the jail, the jail for all blacks." The air was heavy with the song. The prison guards and police could not quiet those voices. The singing continued—in the cells, in the *kwela-kwela* trucks, back in the jail. That day I knew that the deep, resonant voices of Africans will be heard.

What I had seen in Fordsburg scarred me and I still carry those scars. For a long time, I tried through the avenues of the law and the courts to expose these injustices and to bring about real change. Convinced that if the facts were made known to the public, the public would insist on changes being made, I was determined to obtain the truth and state it, simply and clearly, for all to hear. It was to take many years for me to learn that those who built the system will go to any lengths to prevent the truth being exposed. Those who benefit under the system prefer to be happy knowing nothing of its mechanics rather than be made uneasy and disturbed by the facts. Nevertheless, the truth had to come out, and I set forth with great enthusiasm and vigor to make sure it did.

II
THE DINGAKA
MAN

In a small narrow downtown building in Johannesburg, its eight floors wedged fast between the massive corporate headquarters of the gold- and diamond-mining houses, stood Washington House. It was here that I opened my own law practice in April, 1955. The building fronted on Commissioner Street, named for the mining commissioner who, seventy years ago, traveled around on horseback settling disputed mining claims.

Johannesburg was at that time little more than a mining camp. Then it was discovered that the gold seams ran in the rocks east and west of there in a gold reef at least fifty miles long. From the Witwatersrand came the greatest supply of gold in the history of man. White miners flocked to Johannesburg in search of quickly made fortunes. The Africans who came to *eGoli* were more modest. All they wanted was a chance to work and earn some money.

Today, the picture has changed only on the surface. Ten thousand feet underground gold is still being mined and gold rock brought to the surface for processing. By now, the greater part of southern Johannesburg is undermined with long, dark, narrow tunnels carved through the rocks in all directions under the earth. Above ground, yellow in the sunlight, a half-century of accumulated processed dust marks Johannesburg as the "City of Gold." These old mine dumps stand defiantly against winds that lift a fan of fine gold dust from their surfaces, spreading it across the streets, the houses, the shops, and the factories in a gritty fog. When the wind is gone, the dump remains, untouched, immovable.

From the west, the Golden Highway runs from the highveld slightly above the city. Below, the mine dumps form a framework for the concrete buildings—hard, regular, and ugly in their gray form. By contrast, the irregular shapes of the dumps—pear-shaped, peaked, or long, stately pyramids— glow in the rich afternoon sunlight.

The great majority of the men who work these gold mines are black, and are recruited by special recruiting agents who receive a commission on every head they sign up. They induce the rural Africans to volunteer for mine work and have them sign contracts for six to eighteen months. The agents then arrange transportation to the mines and the African is sent by train or truck to his particular "center."

In the heart of the city is the central railway station. Even today, one often sees the recruiting agencies' boss-boys there, taking delivery of a trainload of migrant black mine workers. The boss-boys are old trusties. Once raw workers themselves, they have had years of experience in the mines and have been promoted to the soft job of shepherding the new recruits from the city center to the mine compound. The contrast between the boss-boys and the new workers, often coming for the first time to the golden city is an obvious one. The boss-boys, looking well fed and confident, are dressed in brass-buttoned, dark navy-blue serge uniforms, peaked caps and shining shoes, whereas the recruits are thin and ill-clad, strangers to one another and to all around them. From the faraway hills and plains, open and quiet, they are catapulted into the noise and clamor of the city by the white man's train or plane. They are seeing streets and sidewalks and high buildings for the first time. Traffic looks as dangerous as shop windows look bright and tempting, but the boss-boys allow no time for diversions. Their job is to get the workers to the mine compound as quickly as possible.

The workers are marshaled into line, then herded and hurried down the streets. The boss-boys enjoy the exercise of their authority and boast of their knowledge of the city in whose ways they are all-wise. When the line is cut in two by a red traffic light, boss-boys stand on opposite corners, bellowing orders to one another and to the bewildered recruits, while the traffic flows between them—hooting, accelerating, and blurring the shouted words. Then the light turns green, the line re-forms, and the men move quickly on to their uncertain future.

Outside in the streets, it is still an adventure and not without joy. In the iron cages slipping down into the mine on steel girders, there is little joy. Packed and crushed together in darkness, the men go down, down, down, into the hot earth. Heart and ears and stomach sink into one, and man is made the size of a pea. The great heat and the noise in the half-light is exhausting and frightening. They had been told nothing of all this, but their contracts bind them to the work all the same.

The thousands upon thousands of rural and urban Africans, searching for work outside the mines, were directed to the large pass offices which then stood close to the mining houses and my own office. In both the central government offices and local municipal pass offices, there are staffs of white officials with black aides. Each official exercises to the fullest all the authority delegated to him by either the central government or the municipality. It is up to the Africans to satisfy all the regulations enforced by these authorities, and to do this, they often spend weeks, months, or even years, going from one official in one building in one area, to another official in another building in another area, in an almost endless walk. The officials accept, as a basic maxim, that "whenever possible and whenever in doubt, endorse the black man out." The general feeling is that there are too many blacks in the urban area, so they endorse hundreds out every day. The stress is on endorsement out—not *to* any place—just out. No official has to direct where a person endorsed out must go;

that is not his problem. His duty is only to see whether a man
has "the right to be, to remain, to reside and work in the area."
The onus in law is on the African to establish any rights he
claims he has, but few officials have the time or inclination to
listen to a black man's explanation. When the white man
makes his decision, it is final, binding, and irrevocable.

In the pass offices, iron-fenced cages separate the human
"labor units" into different categories. Here people stand and
wait endlessly or they go from office to office, from official to
official, carrying papers, messages, classifications, certifi-
cates, letters—to and fro, around and around, each waiting for
his fate to be determined by some white official. It is the
official who decides whether a man may seek work or remain
working; whether a wife may live or continue living with her
husband and children; whether a child may go on living with
his parents or be forced to leave home. The official always has
the power to have the pass seeker in front of him summarily
arrested and imprisoned. The police are ever present and
people continually disappear from the pass offices and their
relatives hear no news of them for weeks or months or even a
year or more. Because of the complexities of the law no
decision is ever predictable. The African never knows what
will happen to him when he visits the pass office.

In my years in practice, besides the ordinary civil and
criminal work all South African lawyers do, I acquired a
reputation of being sympathetic and willing to help people
with their pass difficulties. I learned there were whole laby-
rinths of rules, regulations, and laws, all modified, changed,
and adapted from time to time. I learned never to give up, that
the most important thing was to keep on trying. I could never
be sure whether I would be successful or not, but if I did take
a case, I left no possible avenue unexplored. I used every
known method and some new methods—even irregular
ones—to assist a man and his wife to stay together, to keep
children from being parted from their parents, or to keep a
family together as one unit in one place. Sometimes cor-
ruptible officials tempered the injustice and harshness of the
law, and accepted the bribes tendered to them by the Africans, but too often it was my sad duty to tell a wife that in
order to comply with the law she would have to leave her

husband. I was forced to stand by helplessly as the family was broken up. Too often I had to admit there was nothing more I could do. Too often I was faced with the question, "But if we leave, where can we go?", and I could only hold up my hands and say, "*Angazi* [I do not know]." It was heartbreaking but I, too, was just part of the system and, in the end, even with all my efforts, I could not help.

My own office, situated between the mining houses and the pass offices, was but a tiny break in the link of the chain welding precious gold to cheap black migrant workers. Word of my efforts was bush-telegraphed over a wide area by Africans, and first in tens and then in scores, they sought my advice about their pass troubles. I worked up a system that required constant adaptation and the continual search for new loopholes, for as fast as I discovered them, they were closed by the officials. Although I tried to listen to each case with patience and fresh interest, I was nevertheless frustrated and exhausted by this work and often I would become angry and shout at my clients. Those Africans who heard me shout seemed to understand the reason for my mood; they would remain silent and tolerate my nonsense. Some nicknamed me "He Who Often Shouts," but they would come back another time and I would try to make amends. When I first began the practice of law I did not appreciate the shrewdness and wealth of understanding my African compatriots possessed. I had been aware of their goodwill and tolerance, but as a white South African, I could never have learned what I did without the close, daily contact with my African brothers.

Among those who sought my advice was a man who proved to be one of my most unusual clients. He came from the northeastern Transvaal near Bushbuckridge, one of the most beautiful parts of my country. Rugged, bare mountains break suddenly in the crystal highveld air, and far beyond the mountain range stretch the long, rolling small hills of the lowveld. It is a country of bush, small thorn trees, fat, prehistoric-looking baobab trees that seem to be growing upside-down. The wildflowers, vivid in purples and reds, are yet soft and delicate. The earth itself turns from orange ocher to purple in sunlight that dazzles the traveler passing by.

My client was a man in his mid-fifties. His skin was dark

and his face lined, but his eyes were clear. His dark jacket and
gray pants were well worn, and in his left hand he carried a
small stick around which was tied a gray cloth bag. He came
into my office, put the cloth bag beside him on the floor, and
then reached deep down inside the pocket of his jacket. He
produced a paper pasted onto some cardboard to protect it. It
was brown with age and had been much handled.

I examined the paper. The holder, it certified, was a life
member of the Dingaka Association. In one corner was a
picture of an anteater, one of the symbols of the association. I
looked at the man with great interest; this was the first witch
doctor I had ever met. He wanted me to recognize his status
as such and I did and welcomed him.

"It is this thing," he said. "The pass. I cannot deal with it."

I looked at his papers and found that he had been endorsed
out of the area. He wanted to remain in the city to complete
certain work, but only for a limited period of time. It seemed
to me that such permission should not be too difficult to get
and, after taking all the details of his case, I advised him it was
worth a try and he should come back in two weeks. I went to
work and learned which officials handled "witch doctors" and
other people doing "temporary work" in the area. I found out
that in certain circumstances such "temporary visits" were
permitted. Then it was a matter of finding the best way to
persuade an official to exercise his discretion in favor of my
client. Magically, what I did worked. My witch doctor was
granted permission to remain in the area for nine months.

When he came to see me again, I told him the good news.
His face lit up and he thanked me enthusiastically. Then he
asked if he, in turn, could do me a service to express his
gratitude. He wished to make an offering—a prayer for me.
He was granting me an honor but I quickly said it was not
possible that day since he could readily observe how many
people I still had to see. But I knew as I said it that this was
just an excuse. I was behaving like any white official in the
pass office—I was telling him to come back another day
before refusing him. Ashamed, I added, "But if you come on a
Saturday morning, sometimes there are not so many people to
see me and it could be done then."

He showed his pleasure at this and seemed satisfied. He bent down, picked up his gray cloth bag, wished me *Dumela* (good day), and walked out. I did not think any further about him. About two weeks later, arriving early at my office on a Saturday morning, I was greeted at the door by the witch doctor. He had remembered. I showed him in.

The Dingaka man sat down opposite me. He was very serious, and spoke quietly in very simple words. "Listen carefully and follow me." I nodded and said I would do as he said. He reached down into his ever-present cloth bag and brought out another, smaller black bag and after carefully taking a small tin box from it, he placed the bag on his lap. The tin box was square, painted red and gold; it had once been used for cigarettes but was now empty.

"Do you have a half-crown piece?" he asked. I fished in my trouser pocket and found one. He held out his hand and I passed it over. He felt it carefully and then put it into his red and gold box. As he picked up the small black bag, he began a chant. His body swayed slightly from his hips and his head moved rhythmically sideways. From within the black bag he slowly produced a firm but soft, black-colored ball, about the size of a half a dollar. He stopped his chant.

"This ball," he explained, "is a dung ball. Not just any dung ball, no, not that. I watched as it was made before my eyes. The dung beetle had made this dung ball when the sun was hot and people were sweating. There were many people about but not one of them disturbed the dung beetle."

In my mind's eye I could see his story come alive. I could see the large, hard-covered beetle move jerkily over the dry, cracked earth—the black of the beetle against the orange of the ground. I could see the beetle struggle across the grains of sand and small tufts of short green grass, pass in between the feet of men and women, unharmed, and continue its work.

The witch doctor went on. "The path along which this dung beetle worked was not any path; it was specially chosen. The people who walked it did not walk to go to work or to see relatives or even friends or the sick; there was no bus to catch to make people hurry along this path. The people who passed along this path were walking to and from the shops, shops where people went to purchase things for money and from which they returned with the goods they wanted. It was on this path that the dung beetle made this dung ball."

"I understand," I replied.

He then paused and passed the ball between his thumb and forefinger and then from hand to hand, and began chanting again. Next he placed the dung ball on the silver coin in the tin box. He made another request. "Can you give me some matches?" As I shook my head and said, "No, I'm sorry but I don't smoke," my African clerk, Vivian, held out his own box. The Dingaka man took it.

"Auh!" he exclaimed. "This has a special meaning. This means that this young man will serve you here and you and he will be together a long time."

I smiled, glanced at Vivian, and said, "That is very good."

He lit several matches, placing them alongside the dung ball in the tin. Now he was chanting again. The ball burned slowly, the flames jumping an inch or more above the coin. He held his hands together, gesticulating now and again, and spoke once more, saying, "From wherever the winds blow, from where the sun rises and sets, from the north or the south, the people will come to you." His face showed his concentrated effort as he stared straight ahead.

He continued, "The people will bring you troubles and you will know them; and the people will bring questions and you will search with them; and the people and you too will be satisfied in the work, and there will be much work for you to do."

He remained silent and distant until the flames had gone, and there were only ashes in the tin and over the coin. I met his glance and he thanked me, and I him. "There is one more thing to do and then I will go," he said.

"What still remains?" I asked curiously.

"These ashes, they must be thrown across the door entering your office," and he rose, the tin box in his hand. Across the threshold of my door, he let the ashes fall and again his lips moved, but silently now. He then returned to my desk, handed me the coin, and said, "This you must keep and hold fast." He bent down, put the box back into the black bag and it into the cloth bag. Picking it up, he said, *"Dumela,"* raised his hand, and left.

In the meantime, my office had filled with Africans who had seen and heard some of what had been happening. There was a babble of animated chatter. I was warmed and pleased to have been so honored. This man had performed the best of his service for me and had taken me along on the journey of his people. I was with them and was among them. I knew, as they did, that man's wish to understand the unknown is as old as the earth and there is much yet unknown for which there are still no answers. All this mystery and mysticism is part of Africa and as old as Africa, and Africa, after all, is the cradle of mankind. The magic of the land and the magic of its people is there and it is as hard and enduring as the rock.

III
JOHN LUGOJOLO

His earlobes were stretched in the Zulu fashion to hold flat, round, wooden disks. These denoted the seniority of his status. On his feet were sandals cut from old rubber tires, which being cheap and practical, are worn by many Zulu men. It is not often that one sees African men with gray hair. Although John Lugojolo was only fifty years old, he had gray hair and looked older than he was. A big, heavy man, he still moved lightly and with vigor. Watching me all the time, his eyes searching my face to gauge my response, he spoke quietly and seriously. Only when I knew him better did I learn how in an instant his face could light up when he saw the humor of a situation, how his eyes could sparkle with enjoyment.

When he first consulted me he was afraid of receiving another rebuff. He needed advice and no one had been willing to listen to him sufficiently well to understand his problem.

"What is it?" I asked him.

Carefully he sorted out some letters he held in his large hands. Like most Africans, he had beautiful hands and I watched his fingers take a white paper and unfold it before passing it to me. It was a typed letter addressed to me from a friend at the Mental Health Society. It said that the social welfare officer who was first consulted had concluded that John needed a lawyer rather than a doctor.

When I finished reading it I looked up and met John's stare. "I have read it, tell me your trouble now."

He did not reply but instead unfolded two small sheets of lined blue writing paper and handed them to me. It was a letter signed "John Lugojolo." The writing was neat and legible.

"Is this written by you?" I asked.

"It is my writing" he confirmed. Obviously, John had been to one of the mission schools in Zululand.

Then I read the opening line: "A light has gone out in my head, I cannot see in my darkness."

I was held in the grasp of these words. Nothing I later learned or heard described with more forceful simplicity the truth of John's trouble. Through him I learned the story of the Charlestown Zulu people and the plot to deprive them of their rights to own land.

Charlestown, no more than a whistlestop on the railway line between Johannesburg, the great industrial complex inland, and Durban, South Africa's busiest port, rests in the shadow of the great Majuba mountain. The Zulus, like so many Africans, are people of the land. Their huts are dotted about the many-sided, velvet-green slopes of the valleys that stretch from the foot of the mountain down to the river below.

Clavis township, where John Lugojolo lived, was just outside Charlestown. It was named for the white couple who had developed it. Mrs. Clavis had grown up among the Zulus; her parents were shopkeepers in Zululand. She knew the people and their customs well, spoke Zulu, and was respected by them. When she married, she and her husband came to Charlestown to live and there negotiated a land deal with the town board, represented by a white lady administrator, a Mrs. Evilly. The Clavises agreed to take over a large tract of land that the town board considered useless. Clavis planned to subdivide this land into plots and sell them to the African community. He hoped to make a considerable profit from the sale because the Africans welcomed the opportunity of owning their own land. In exchange, he was to give the Charlestown board a large area of land owned by his wife.

Clavis relied on his wife's good relationship with the Zulu people to gain their confidence and allow him to do business with them. Together they arranged for Gad Maseko, the revered leader and elder of the small community, to call a meeting of the people to hear the Clavises' plan. That Gad Maseko presided was, of course, fortunate for the Clavises because the people were more likely to accept the truth and worth of what was said.

At the meeting, Clavis talked first of the longing of the Zulu people for their own land. He told them he had purchased from the town board all the land from the railway line to the valley of Majuba, and it would be divided up and sold in plots to the Zulu people living there. The price was between thirty and thirty-five pounds, a small fortune in the early 1930s, and about two years' total earnings for the Africans, but in the circumstances, they considered it reasonable. He would allow them to pay in installments—a down payment and further payments every month. Once an agreement had been made, each Zulu would receive a deed of sale and a receipt for the money that he had paid, and would later on have the right to a title deed. But, he told them, everyone who bought a plot would keep it as his own forever; he would be chief and king on his own land.

The Zulus discussed the plan and many agreed it was good and they bought plots. They received their deeds of sale and the receipts for what they paid and they took possession of the land. They built kraals and they went on paying their installments and all was well. They settled down in peace in Clavis Township.

Unknown to them, however, all was not peace between the Charlestown board and Clavis, who had not carried out his part of the land deal. Then he was killed in an automobile accident and Mrs. Evilly found that the board was unable to take possession of the land it was to have acquired from him. As a result, she decided to stop any further sales to the Zulus and to initiate action against them. Without consulting Gad Maseko or anyone else in the Zulu community, she called a meeting. Naturally, only a few Zulus attended.

Some of those who did reported the strange things they heard there to the rest of the people. They reported that Mrs. Evilly said that all the Zulus in Charlestown must pay whatever money they still owed Clavis to her. Furthermore, they must pay her for roads, for light, for water, and for other services.

Someone had asked her, "What roads must we pay for— there are no roads in Clavis. And what is this talk about light? Do you not know that we buy our lights in candles from Ismail Essop's store?" There was much laughter at this, and Mrs. Evilly was very annoyed.

Another said, "What is this talk about paying for water—we get our water from the river and the water is stored in drums. Who represents the river, then, that we must pay for the water we get from the river?"

"There will be taps installed," Mrs. Evilly said.

"When the taps are installed, we will pay for the water we take from the taps; there are no taps now," was their answer.

The Zulus also told Mrs. Evilly that according to their purchase arrangements, they made their monthly payments to the Clavises. Since she was not a party to these arrangements, they could not make the payments to her unless the Clavises agreed.

For a while nothing came of all this, but more meetings were held and Mrs. Evilly eventually brought in the police and the native commissioner and there was much more talk about what the Zulus owed. When two water taps were installed, the Zulus began to pay for that water but they refused to pay all the other amounts demanded by Mrs. Evilly. They kept telling her that they had paid for their land, and kept showing her their title deeds and receipts. The fact that Clavis had not paid her was something that the white men had to settle among themselves; it did not concern the Zulu people.

The matter dragged on for years. Finally Mrs. Evilly lost patience. Unknown to the Zulus, South African law allowed the town board to gain control of their land by a simple procedure. All it had to do was to publish a notice both in the *Government Gazette*, a publication carrying only government notices issued regularly, and in a newspaper circulating in the district that was more likely to be read by the local inhabitants. Mrs. Evilly arranged for such a notice to appear, which said that if all those from whom money was claimed did not pay within a certain time, the town board would take over the land.

The Zulus were as ignorant of the law as of the published notice. They lived peacefully in the area and they remained confident that they could at all times produce proof that the land they occupied was legally theirs. Their confidence was misplaced. After the publication of the notice and the failure of the Zulus to comply with what it said, the court officers moved in to expropriate the land. Among the landowners was John Lugojolo.

At the time John was working hundreds of miles away from Charlestown and knew nothing of what was happening. By bush telegraph, his friends in Clavis sent a message calling him home, but he had changed jobs and was working in another town, so it took a long time to reach him. When it did, he responded immediately. With the permission of his employer, he caught a night train, sleeping on the wooden third-class benches. It was early in the morning and cold when he got off the train and began to walk the remaining distance to Charlestown. The ground was covered with frost and there was still mist about the mountain of Majuba. By the time he arrived, the mist had been swept away, the frost had turned to water, and it was a clear and bright day.

John's home was on the near side of Clavis. As soon as he caught sight of his house he saw something was wrong. The door hung open, there were no hens or chickens about, no cow or donkey. The fences and gate were down. He ran inside but his wife and children were not there. The place was a mess—tables overturned, the bed and several chairs broken, all the blankets gone. Everything was ruined.

His neighbors came in, shouting at him, "Where have you been? Why did you come so late?"

He replied, "What has happened, where is my wife?"

"She's in jail, in jail in Pietermaritzburg for three years."

It was then that the light went out in his head.

The neighbors went away and only Umzinto, Gad Maseko's brother, stayed behind. When the voices outside had died away, Umzinto said quietly, "Take strength, your children are safe. They are well, they are in the house of Vilakazi. The mother of Vilakazi cares for your children. I have your cow and your donkey. Many things the gang of police took. Your wife fought the police. The white man she hit on the head with an iron."

"But why?" John asked. "What had the police to do with me? Why did they come to my house?"

Umzinto replied, shaking his head, "I cannot tell you all. I can only tell you what I know." He waited silently for a while and then left.

John sat for some time, shaking his head in bewilderment, and then he got up and went to learn from the neighbors, from the police, from the commissioner, from whoever could tell him, what had happened to Eliza, his wife, to his home, to everything.

John learned that a black policeman from Charlestown had brought his wife a summons. Eliza had asked the policeman, "Is this for my husband?"

"Yes," he said, "it is for your husband."

"When does he have to be in the court?" she asked. "What has he done?"

The policeman shook his head, "I know nothing about that," he said, "it gives no date for the court. It just says you must leave this place." He seemed uncertain and his confusion led to smiles among those present. Then John's wife asked him, "But how can there be no date for the court? Are you not sent by the court with this and is this not from the court? It must summon my husband there. If you cannot tell the date, how then can I tell him when he is to be in the court. He is away now so when must he return here?"

The neighbors were all in agreement with Eliza. "You must say the date," they echoed, "you must say it." But the policeman said, "No, I tell you there is no date. You had best send for your husband, for you must leave this place," and he left.

The neighbors talked about this and said there must be a

date, otherwise how could one go to court? Eliza, however, was uncertain, so that evening she went to consult Gad Maseko but he was away. When he returned, she saw him and he said, "You had better tell John Lugojolo to come home and come as soon as possible." So the message was sent to call John back, but that was the message that took a long time reaching him.

Two weeks passed and nothing more was heard. Then one morning a truck came with two policemen in uniform and a white man in plainclothes. This white man kicked the door open and went in. Eliza was ironing at the time.

She shouted, "What do you want here? What are you doing here?" He answered, "What are you doing here? You were told to leave. Pack your things now and go. Come on, be quick."

Eliza was angry with this man but he was white so she stood where she was, silently staring her defiance at him. Then he moved toward her and caught her by the arm. Immediately, without thinking and without hesitation, she hit him on the head with the iron she still clutched in her hand. He fell and the two black policemen rushed toward her. She fought, she shouted, she screamed, and madness broke out in that hut.

The neighbors saw a bleeding Eliza being half-carried out to the truck. The white man, too, was bleeding and holding his head. The children were crying. There were only women and old men and children about because the young men of the community were all away working elsewhere. All they could do was comfort Eliza's children. The truck drove off with Eliza in it. Later the police returned, both white and black police, and when they left little remained of what had been Eliza and John's home.

Eliza sent message after message to John. He did not come. She learned her children were safe. She learned too of what had been done to her home, the place to which she had come after John had paid her father, and they had been married—the home where her children had been born. What had happened, she wondered, what wrong had she done? Where was her husband and why did he not come? She heard what went on in court at her trial but she took no part in the proceedings. They were beyond her understanding; she was beyond understanding anything about life any more. She heard the sentence passed on her, that she must go to jail for three years, but she had already received more punishment than such a sentence could inflict on her. She was taken as a prisoner, as a criminal, by train, to a faraway jail.

John was broken by the story he painfully pieced together. Gad told him to go to Newcastle and find a lawyer, so John did. The long walk to Newcastle gave him time to think, to dwell on what had happened and what was to be done. He saw the lawyer and an appeal was made. He went to the court. His wife, however, was not there and he knew that this was not right. He could not understand all the words that were spoken and there was no interpreter to tell him what they all meant. He watched the faces of the judges but all the judges and all the lawyers were strangers to his wife Eliza. They had not even met her; not one of them. He knew there was little good that could come out of this court but he listened to his lawyer who was hopeful about the appeal and said that he, John, must be hopeful, too.

John went to see his wife. He knocked on the big wooden prison door. It had a heavy iron ring and iron bars across the square of glass that served as a peephole. "This is where the thieves and all the criminals are—this is where they keep my wife," he thought. He saw his wife from afar at first; she wore the long khaki dress that is the prison uniform for women. She came in and their eyes met, their mouths silently moving in greeting. What was there to say?

"You have come," she said simply.

"Yes," he said, "I have come now." He spoke slowly. "The children, they are with Vilakazi. The mother cares for them, they are well." Then he said, with his head down, "I have tried the appeal in the court. We will know next Wednesday what the result will be." He looked at her and saw in her eyes there were no words to be said.

They remained together for a few moments until the white matron said harshly, "If you are finished then come, Eliza, it is enough."

Eliza had nothing to say. She put her hand out on the table

and John, too, put his hand on the table. It was a sign—
it was a greeting. Their eyes talked and then they parted.

Wednesday came and John heard the result. The appeal was
denied. The lawyer wanted to go further with the case but
John had no faith and no money and so the matter was
dropped. He returned to his work, depressed and heart-
broken. His employer told him to write everything down and
then sent him with a note to the social welfare officer and that
was how he found his way to me.

John now asked me to see Gad Maseko, so the Zulu elder
came to my office with other men from the Charlestown
community. He wore black trousers and spats, a long, char-
coal-gray jacket, and a gray-and-white-striped shirt. The shirt
had a high starched collar and back and front gold studs. He
kept a handkerchief in his left sleeve above his wrist and used
it frequently to mop his large brow. His hair was white—he
was old now but he was still as proud and dignified as he must
have been throughout the years he led the Zulu people of
Charlestown.

With great charm, and some humor, too, he related some of
the history of the township of Clavis. He gave me details
about people and events that my own research had not
discovered. He told me many personal experiences, and then
we discussed what could be done for those who had not yet
lost their land and how some who had could still demand
compensation for their loss. We agreed on what could be
done. Gad Maseko said he would speak to his people but we
would have to wait and see, since they no longer believed
what the white man advised. I said I understood this and
would wait for their answer. But in regard to John and Eliza's
case, I told him there was no longer any hope. John was
present at this conversation and heard me telling Gad Maseko
that he should now accept what had happened to him and not
seek further aid. Gad agreed with me and advised him to do as
I said.

Over the years John kept in contact with me and would
come to my office every now and again. I welcomed his visits
and always asked him about his wife. Then one day when he
came to see me he was once more very serious. Did I know

that Eliza was leaving jail on this very Friday? I told him how pleased I was at the good news and said he must bring her to see me. He hesitated—he was embarrassed, even sad. He asked me if I could find a place for Eliza to work and a place she could stay. I said yes I would try and then he said, "You see, it has been a long time and now I have found a new wife."

IV
I AM THE LAW

"What do you mean, you don't believe it? It is so, sir," said my clerk Vivian. "These local superintendents think they are God and can do what they want. Anyhow, who is to stop them?"

"Yes, I know that, but he can't behave like a damn fool. He must know he can't get away with it. I just can't believe what they are telling me."

Two men in their late thirties were sitting before me. Benjamin was short and stout. Joseph, too, was short, but very thin, with an elegant handlebar moustache, his narrow features in striking contrast to the round plumpness of Benjamin. It was Benjamin who spoke first.

Turning to Joseph, he asked, "How are we going to convince this lawyer who does not believe us?"

Joseph did not reply—I do not know whether he had even heard Benjamin's question. Upon hearing my words, his face had broken into a beautiful wide grin that said more than the words he now uttered.

"You are quite right," he said. "We find it hard to accept,

too, but that's just why we have come here. What do we do now? That is the question."

His own question at once brushed aside my disbelief and convinced me that the superintendent they talked about was one of the breed who really saw himself as sole lord and master, ruling supreme in one little location and controlling completely the lives of all blacks in that particular ghetto.

Benjamin and Joseph, both the children of squatter parents, were born and grew up on the farm of a white man. When they were in their teens, the farmer sold his farm and the new owner said there were too many squatters there. He gave a number of them, including the boys' parents, trek passes, notices to leave his land.

Forced to leave and seek work elsewhere, the families split up and Joseph and Benjamin worked on different farms. Joseph found a farmer who after a year taught him how to drive a tractor. He asked the farmer to hire his friend Benjamin, who was very good with machines. The farmer agreed and the friends worked together for a further two years. One day, a man who ran a garage at Morgenster, a nearby town, asked the two "tractor boys" if they would like to come to work for him. He offered them two pounds more a month to tempt them, and they agreed.

They worked at the garage for several years, earning five pounds a month, and they saved their money. They both married and obtained houses in Morgenster's "residential area," or "location" for blacks. In these locations, sometimes also called townships, only white officials and authorized whites may enter. The blacks there are tenants on sufferance. They can be "endorsed out" of the area and may lose their right of residence at any time. The white superintendent of the location controls who may and who may not live there.

Then their *baas,* the garage owner, left Morgenster and their work came to an end. For three months they looked around the area to find employment but were unsuccessful. Eventualy, the superintendent gave them permission to seek work elsewhere. Leaving their families, they went to Johannesburg and found jobs in a factory. Soon they were earning ten pounds a month and more when they worked overtime.

They worked hard there for five years and their monthly salaries increased until they were being paid fifteen pounds a month.

Every year the factory closed for two weeks. At that time, taking their savings and their best clothes, the two friends would go back to Morgenster. It was then that the trouble started. The superintendent resented these smartly dressed, idle men walking around his location and he called them to his office. He told them that if they went on working in Johannesburg they could not leave their wives and children to be a burden on him. They argued with him, reminding him that they were up to date in all the rental payments; that they had paid all the school fees, and that, besides, there was no work for them in Morgenster. Also, they said, Joseph has spent some two hundred pounds in improving his home over the years and Benjamin had spent some ninety pounds in doing the same to his house.

The superintendent would not listen. He said emphatically, "You must come back to Morgenster and find work here. You must listen to me. I am the parliament of this location. My word here is the law. When I have spoken, so it must be done. Either you must leave this location with your wives and families, or you must come home and work in Morgenster."

They could see that arguing was no use. In January, they returned to their white employer in Johannesburg and told him of the superintendent's ultimatum. The employer was not unduly upset. He told them that as a businessman he was sure he could deal with the problem and when next in the country, he would call on the superintendent. Meanwhile, in case his "boys" had been offered better salaries anywhere else, he increased their monthly wage by one-third of a pound—he could well afford it.

Sometime later, when their boss returned from his visit to the country, he said he had spoken to the superintendent and had been assured by him that the "boys" could stay on in Johannesburg for another year. When they next went home for vacation, they did their best to keep out of the superintendent's way. Thereafter, each year, in January or February, their white boss would visit the superintendent and come back to say that all had been fixed up. However, after three years, he said he could not fix things any more. He told them they would have to go back and work in Morgenster at the end of the year; there was nothing more that he could do.

Reluctantly, employer and employees parted and Joseph and Benjamin returned with much fanfare to their homes in Morgenster. They had had a whole year to plan their future. They had saved enough money and had made many inquiries and they knew what they were going to do. They went to the local magistrate and applied for business licenses in Morgenster. They were confident they could make out by selling a variety of goods in and around the district. After peddling their wares by donkey cart for some six months, they each managed to buy a small truck and then their business thrived. At the end of their second year back in Morgenster, the superintendent called both Joseph and Benjamin to his office.

"In this location, my location, you must work. I want to see you leave for work after sunrise in the morning and come back at sunset. Each of you must find a *baas* here. There is work for you and you must work for a *baas.* I will not permit all this running around the country with your trucks. You had better sell those trucks and find work or else you and your families must get out of my location."

He would not listen to anything they said. Joseph and Benjamin met that night to plan what to do. It was already December. They decided to act quietly and without fuss. They went to the magistrate to pay the license fees for the following year. Although they said nothing about being given notice, the magistrate told them that he now had to have a letter from the superintendent before he could give them licenses. They had no choice but to see the superintendent again, although they knew there was little hope that he would give them the letter they required. And they were right.

When the new year came their old licenses expired. They decided to seek help and went to see a lawyer who told them they were entitled to take out a license if they could pay the license fee. He phoned the magistrate who told him that the "boys" should come down and see him. They did so and the magistrate quietly took their money and gave each a license.

When the superintendent learned of this he was furious. He told Benjamin and Joseph to get out of the location that very month. But they stayed put. At the end of January when they went to pay their rent, he refused to take the money. Again in February they went to pay rent and again he refused to accept payment. Then he said he was ejecting them from their homes at the end of February for failing to pay their rent. Also he said that according to location regulations, if they did not have lawful work or occupation, they had to leave, and he was thus giving them notice.

It was at this stage that they came to see me and their question was what could they do now.

"Well," I said, "I can tell you, even if I believe your story no court would. You have nothing in writing to convince a court."

"That is so."

"Well," I continued, "perhaps if you write to the superintendent, that might be sufficient to make him see sense. Whether or not he sees sense, you will at least have made an effort in writing and have evidence that you have tried to pay the rent you owe."

They looked at me curiously. Only a white man could suggest that they write letters to the superintendent but I was insistent and so they decided to do what I asked. I explained that they must send postal orders in registered envelopes to the superintendent with a note saying, "Rental for House No. —." Each of them should follow the same procedure. They agreed to do this.

I was reluctant to go to court for them. Although they may not have realized it, the true cause of the trouble between them and the white superintendent lay in their success as local businessmen. They had made more of their life and their future than he had made of his, but they were black and he was white; therefore he ruled over them. Furthermore, they and their families had no way of changing the state of affairs—they had to live in the location under the superintendent's control. There was no other ghetto to which they could go and it would be a serious matter for them if they were endorsed out. All of them would become homeless. Although born in this land they would become displaced persons. They could not return to the place of their birth and they could not lawfully go anywhere else in the land without official permission. I knew they were concerned with the immediate issues—that they had not yet recognized the long-term consequences that threatened them, but these consequences worried me. There seemed little point in winning a skirmish in court with the superintendent if that drove him to even more vindictive action.

Ten days later they were back. They had carried out my instructions and had the papers to prove it—the letters they had written, the registered envelopes, and the postal orders.

"So what happened—how did you get your documents back?" I asked.

They were waiting for my question. Joseph smiled. "Well, the day after the letters were delivered to the superintendent he sent an African clerk to call us to his office. The clerk said we were to call at seven o'clock the next morning." Joseph and Benjamin went to the superintendent's office at 7:00 and waited. Just after 8:00 he arrived and called them into his office, shouting furiously at them.

"You are cheeky Kaffirs! Since when do Kaffirs write to a white man?! Take your fucking letters and don't you ever dare send me letters again or I'll *donder* (beat) you! You better get out of this location at the end of this month or I'll throw you, your wives, and your children out! Now get the hell out of here, do you hear me?" and he dismissed them from his office.

"Well," I said casually, "that's not so bad."

They still thought they were talking to the wrong man. Benjamin said, "But where will I put my wife and children at the end of the month? I have ten children and Joseph has six."

"Listen to me," I said. "I can win a case for you but who will be living in the location after the case? I won't be living there but you will—together with your wife and children. The superintendent will be waiting for a chance to get even with you. That will be bad. If we can get this man to see sense we must try. There is an attorney in Bethal. I will instruct him to see the superintendent, to speak nicely to him, and try to settle this matter without further trouble."

They mulled this over between themselves and reluctantly agreed to the course of action I had suggested. I immediately telephoned the attorney in Bethal and explained the predicament to him, asking him to call on the superintendent and try to arrange a settlement. Two days later the attorney telephoned back and told me it was useless speaking to the superintendent. He said that as soon as he had told him why he had come, he had flown into a rage and insisted that my clients be out of the location by the end of the month. His attitude was that blacks had no right be given a hearing—had no rights at all—and he resented the attorney making representations on their behalf.

I sent for Benjamin and Joseph, who were not surprised at my news. I said I would now write a registered letter to the superintendent and send him all the past rent payments that were due. I would also inform him that I would pay him regularly in the future within the first seven days of each month. Benjamin and Joseph's attitude was now one of resignation. They had gone this far with me so they decided to go a step further. They would wait for one more week.

I wrote the letter and within a week they returned to give me the written notices issued to them by the superintendent, ordering them to leave the location at the end of that month. I found, upon investigation, that the notices were issued under a regulation dealing with the price of eggs in a distant Transvaal village.

They smiled at this, enjoying the embarrassing position in which the superintendent had placed himself. But when I pointed out the error to the superintendent, his reply was sharp and quick. He issued fresh notices under the correct regulations. He was not going to be moved. All my efforts to avoid a court case were unavailing. I told my clients that under the circumstances there was no way out other than to draw up a petition to the court. They were relieved. Smiling, they rubbed their hands and advised me that I should have listened to them all along. Their confidence in me was renewed; although I had waited for so long I was at last prepared to act.

I filed their story in a petition that was taken to the Supreme Court, asking for relief from this harassment. We asked that the notices issued against Benjamin and Joseph be set aside; that the superintendent be compelled to accept the rent that had been tendered to him. We also asked the court to accept that both Benjamin and Joseph were carrying on lawful occupations.

Nothing further was heard from the superintendent, but at the last moment, the afternoon before the petition was to be heard in court, the attorney for the municipality of Morgenster telephoned me. To my surprise he said there would be no opposition to my petition by the municipality and that it would agree to my clients' obtaining all the relief we wanted, provided that the petitions be withdrawn.

I refused to accept these terms but instead stipulated that if they withdrew the notices and accepted all rental payments and did not victimize my clients, I would not ask the court for an order but would merely postpone the matter. Eventually, this was agreed to. Next day we went to court and the only opposition that we received came from the bench. The partiality of the white judges to their functions as upholders of the white law becomes more obvious as the years go on. The judge objected to the fact that the respondent had not replied to our allegations. He was anxious that there be a rebuttal by the superintendent even if there was a settlement. However, in the absence of such representations by the superintendent, he had no alternative but to grant us the relief we sought.

Benjamin and Joseph were able to return to their jobs and stay with their families in Morgenster—they had been proven right. The superintendent was a bully and after this incident he left my clients in peace.

V
INNOCENT
LANGA

In mid-June 1957, Innocent Langa came to my office. His older brother, Nelson, had disappeared and he wanted me to find him.

Five years before, Nelson had come to Johannesburg from a village in Pondoland, south of Durban, and found a job as a municipal street cleaner earning three pounds a week. After about three years, he had sent a message home to his father with a man from the same village, saying, "Innocent must come. There is a place here. There is the work here. They are honest and pay the money. Come and take the job." So Innocent had come to the city, too, and had been working for the municipality and living in the same compound as Nelson ever since.

Each day of the week, except Sunday, they took a garbage can and a broom and swept the streets clean. They started work early in the morning and when they finished early in the afternoon, they returned to the compound. All the men ate in a communal dining room, with tables and benches fixed to the cement floor. They slept in dormitories, divided into units of six concrete bunks. No unit had a door and there was no privacy. These men came from rural areas as migrant contract workers and were sent home at the end of the contract period. Regardless of whether or not they were married or had families, they had to live throughout the contract period in bachelor quarters. The only women they ever had anything to do with were prostitutes and illegal beer brewers. It was a beer seller who had given Innocent the news about Nelson. She had seen him being loaded onto a *kwela-kwela* with other men that afternoon, although Nelson, on his way back from work, was still in his uniform and carrying his broom. He had shouted to the woman to tell his brother what was happening.

Innocent had made inquiries about Nelson's whereabouts and had gone with friends to search for him in the police stations and courts but had found no trace of him, and he feared that Nelson had been injured in an accident or even killed. I knew that Innocent, as a black man dealing with white policemen and white court officials, would be at a disadvantage in making inquiries. I was not surprised at his failure. I had conducted such searches many times before and told Innocent that we would try to find his brother.

I assumed that Nelson had fallen into the hands of the "ghost squad," a group of plainclothes policemen. The ghost squad was developed in the 1950s, when the police decided that insufficient pass arrests were being made, and their disguise as civilians enabled white and black policemen to trap unsuspecting Africans more easily. This was before the days of mass pass raids and mass pass arrest procedures. The police had not yet adopted the technique whereby every area—block by block, street by street—was divided up and every black inside the area stopped and made to produce a pass for inspection.

Tracing persons who fell into the net of the ghost squad was really difficult because the police would tour an area until the *kwela-kwela* was full and then deposit their haul at whichever police station could accommodate the prisoners they had collected. Frequently, the persons arrested were traced to police stations far away from the place of arrest. Our task was made more difficult because the police station that finally accepted all these prisoners rushed their processing through in order to get all their extra paperwork completed. This paperwork included recording the name of the prisoner. If he was lucky, the name entered by the policeman would be the same, or nearly the same, as the name he was known by; but this was not always the case and when an inquiry was later made about a particular prisoner, no trace might be found of him. I did not anticipate this difficulty for Nelson Langa. He had an easy name.

We made extensive inquiries over the course of the next few days but police station after police station denied having any record or knowledge of Nelson Langa. Similar inquiries made to the courts had the same results. We stretched our search area farther and farther from the place of arrest; prison and hospital records were searched, and, finally, inquiries were made at the morgue. No trace of Nelson Langa could be found.

Every two or three days Innocent would come to my office, anxious and expectant, but I could give him no news of his brother. I could only tell him of our exhaustive efforts.

We started at the beginning again. Late one morning I spoke to an official at a court who said quite casually, "You know we don't get all the cases arrested. Many of them go to the Farm Labor Bureau."

"Where is that?" I asked.

He told me it was at the Market Street government pass office in town. As soon as I heard this I felt instinctively that our search had ended, that we would find Nelson Langa through the Farm Labor Bureau. It appeared that the old farm labor scheme I had known in the Fordsburg court, which had been curbed in the late 1940s under public protest, had been reestablished, functioning now as an adjunct to the main government pass office in Johannesburg.

I found the right official at the Farm Labor Bureau, a man named Tom Martin, and asked him to tell me which farm Nelson Langa had been sent to on June 17 or 18. He looked up his records and said, "*Ja.* We sent a boy by that name to this farmer in Bethal," and he gave me the relevant details.

I was jubilant. I had not only found Nelson but had

unearthed a new farm labor scheme. I knew it could not be any better than the previous one. I hurried back to the office and sent for Innocent.

When I told him Nelson was working for a farmer in Bethal he said in disbelief. "How can that be?"

"He volunteered," I said.

"*Aikona* (Oh, no)," said Innocent. "That is not true. He was forced to go there, otherwise he would not go."

"You're quite right, Innocent. I agree with you."

"How will we get him back?" he asked.

"We will have to go to court and ask the court for help to bring him back."

"Yes," he said, "we had better do that."

It was Saturday, June 29. I told Innocent to come back that afternoon. "I will arrange for all the paperwork to be done and for the advocate to come and we will go to court," I said. (Under the dual legal system in South Africa, attorneys can only appear for clients in certain lower courts. In the higher courts, all called supreme courts, only advocates or counsel may appear for litigants but they must at all times be briefed or instructed by an attorney. To get Nelson back we would need to petition the Supreme Court and I would need to brief an advocate.)

My clerk and I returned to the office at 2 P.M. The typist phoned and asked whether she should come in. I asked her to wait as our client had not yet returned. The advocate phoned and I told him the same thing. At three o'clock there was still no sign of Innocent and at four o'clock, cursing him, I canceled the arrangements I'd made, and my clerk and I went home.

Monday morning was July 1 and there was no sign of Innocent when I arrived at work. However, at two o'clock he came in and was met by a storm of words from me.

"Where the hell have you been? Here we find your brother and you don't bother to call."

He protested that I had told him to come at 2 P.M. and here he was.

"Two P.M. Saturday," I said, "not today."

He had heard me say Saturday, he explained, but he could

not believe that I meant Saturday afternoon. What white man would work on a Saturday afternoon and why would I work for him on that day? He had concluded that I meant Monday. It was my turn to be embarrassed.

He gave me a book he had with him and said, "This is Nelson's pass book."

I had assumed that Nelson had the book with him. "Where did you get that from?" I asked him.

"We do not carry the passes with us. The work is too dirty. At the municipality we get a badge and we wear the badge. It has the number on it. It is the pass. Look," he said, and pointed to his badge. He also pointed to Nelson's pass book and the signature in it. "This morning I stood in a line with the others and *Baas* Jack, he signed my book and he signed my brother's book; he signed because we are both working for the municipality."

It was an inspired move by Innocent. This signature on the first of the month by Nelson's employer placed his status as a municipal employee beyond doubt. Whatever contract Nelson had been induced to enter into at the Farm Labor Bureau was illegal as he was still employed by the municipality. Furthermore, there were occasions when municipal and government authorities cooperated for their own mutual benefit and to avoid embarrassment. In this case, the farm labor authorities and the police could ask the municipal officer for his cooperation. They could then argue that Nelson had been dismissed from his employment immediately prior to his contract with the farmer, which would make the farm labor contract legal and easier to sustain in court. Innocent's move had made any such ploy impossible. How fortunate it was that he had not called on Saturday.

Immediately we set about drawing up a habeas corpus petition. It simply stated that Nelson was a laborer in the street cleaning department of the Johannesburg municipality; that he was returning from his work to the compound when he was arrested by the ghost squad and spirited away to work for a farmer under conditions of forced labor. It was not conceivable that he would have abandoned his work at the municipality where he received per week almost the same wage as he had been offered on a monthly basis from the farmer. He had no reason to abandon his work, the wages due to him, his clothes, and all his possessions, and depart in such secrecy and haste that he was unable to say good-bye or leave any message for his brother or his friends. The petition alleged that the only reasonable inference to be drawn was that Nelson Langa had been arrested and sold as a laborer to the farmer.

The petition was read and carefully explained to Innocent. He was told of the seriousness of the allegations. "That's the truth," he said, and without any hesitation signed an affidavit to this effect.

We prepared to go to court early the next morning. Innocent declined to come if he was not needed because he would rather not lose another day's wages. It was late at night when I dropped him at the compound. I went home and spent a restless night anticipating the next day's events. Now that we had a petition to present before the Supreme Court, I could demonstrate that the scheme was illegal and that shanghaiing techniques were used. I was confident that the courts would declare it illegal. They had no alternative. The petition was unanswerable.

Early the next morning I picked up my advocate, Louis Dison. My wife, Jeanette, joined us and we traveled to the capital city, Pretoria, seat of the Supreme Court. The atmosphere was filled with excitement as we checked all relevant details. Did I have enough revenue stamps? Had I phoned the registrar of the court yesterday afternoon? Dison was a tall, thin man in his middle thirties; a very gentle and religious man. He was particularly disturbed by the wholly improper procedures of this farm labor scheme and was as determined as I was to expose the injustices.

We went to the registrar's office and advised him of the urgency of the petition. He suggested we call back in half an hour when he would be able to tell us at what time the matter would be called. When we returned he told us our judge would be Judge Frans Rumpff and that he would hear the matter after the morning tea break. This judge was a recent appointee made by the Nationalist party government. Although I had no doubt where his political sympathies lay, the facts set out in the petition and the strength of the law favored us overwhelmingly.

When the court convened, Judge Rumpff's face was drawn and tense. Obviously he appreciated the implications of this petition. He called on Dison, who, in his usual quiet voice, began his argument. Before he had finished dealing with the facts and long before he had even come to the law, the judge began to interrupt him.

"All these allegations you make are hearsay. They are unsubstantiated," he objected.

"That," said Dison, "is just what the law permits in a habeas corpus petition."

Judge Rumpff was reluctant to accept this and did not want the factual argument to proceed further. Dison explained that as firsthand facts were not obtainable, the applicant, who was the brother, was entitled by law to bring this application. On the facts as stated it was the court's clear duty to bring Nelson Langa to court and ascertain the truth.

The judge was not satisfied. "If these allegations are untrue, what recourse has the farmer?" he asked.

The reply was quick. "Only that provided by the law m'Lord."

"Is that sufficient to protect him?"

"It must be, m'Lord."

Judge Rumpff shook his head. He refused to grant immediate relief and said we must serve the papers first. He scheduled a hearing for the following day and also ordered that the papers be served on the native commissioner in Johannesburg as well as on the farmer, to ensure that the government through its servants gained official notice of these proceedings. The effect of this was to unite farmer and government officials and bring them into court together.

Despite all my confidence, the judge had found a way out. Having the law and the facts on our side was not enough. Furthermore, there were enormous practical difficulties in having the papers served urgently at two places so far apart from each other on the same afternoon. The farmer was in

Bethal, about 150 miles to the southeast of Pretoria. Normally, a deputy sheriff would serve the papers and return them to court. But we could not get the papers to either of the two deputy sheriffs in time. To avoid delay I decided to serve the papers myself.

I arranged for a colleague in Johannesburg to get Dison's copy of the papers and to serve these on the commissioner in Johannesburg while I set out with my wife to Bethal. There had been a rare snowfall that morning and the automobile association reported that the road to Bethal was impassable. There was a biting cold wind blowing and we ran into rain and sleet. Low-hanging gray clouds raced just over our heads. When the tar road ended, the mud and slush of the gravel road stretched far ahead of us. The steering wheel slipped around in my hand as the car slid all over the road, and we made slow progress. Fortunately there was no traffic. After driving for endless hours we finally reached the main road some twenty miles from Bethal. We had not had to stop once for oncoming cars or stray animals and I breathed a sigh of relief when we gained the tar again.

It was late afternoon when we eventually arrived at the farmer's large yellow-brick house. Leaving Jeanette in the car, I knocked on the front door and an attractive young woman in her early twenties invited me into the house. Her father was out, she said, but would be returning shortly. She offered me tea and cake and was very hospitable but her curiosity was intense and I found it difficult to remain polite and avoid answering all her questions. At last her father arrived. He, too, pressed me to eat and drink and the daughter was berated for her lack of hospitality. As soon as she left the room I told the farmer why I had come, gave him a copy of the petition, and explained it to him, advising him of the judge's ruling.

He dismissed it all easily. "You want one of my 'boys,'" he said expansively. "Is that all? You don't need a fuss about that. If I've got him you can have him. What's all this nonsense about court? It's all unnecessary." As he spoke I realized he was more than anxious and very unsure of himself. "Besides, I might not have the 'boy' and the roads have been impassible since four o'clock this morning, so I can't get to my farm to find out."

I told him that Tom Martin of the Farm Labor Bureau said Nelson Langa was on his farm.

"Oh, you know him, do you? He's a good friend of mine. I'll phone him now. He may think it better for me to send the 'boy' back to Johannesburg to him." He picked up the phone and while waiting for the call to come through, he told me that he had erected a prison on his farm and this had cost him $13,000. The department sent all the laborers available on one day each month. When he got through to Johannesburg, Tom Martin confirmed that Nelson was one of the "boys" in the last batch and suggested that he be sent back to Johannesburg.

The farmer then said he would give me a note to the effect that he would send Nelson back to the department in Johannesburg, and when he did, I gave him a copy of the papers and suggested he phone his lawyer. We then started the long, slippery journey back to Johannesburg.

I called Dison as soon as I arrived to give him the news and learned from him that the papers had been served on the commissioner. Both of us felt that in view of the difficulties Judge Rumpff had raised, it would be advisable to brief a senior counsel. Those advocates who have reached the top of the profession are given the title of "senior counsel." An attorney can brief one only in company with a junior counsel and both of them must then act together. Next morning we instructed as senior counsel Issy Maisels, Q.C., and we all met early to discuss the matter before proceeding to Pretoria.

On arrival at Pretoria I learned that the farmer had brought Nelson to court early that morning and had simply dumped him there with no word of explanation. I found him and told him that I had been instructed by Innocent, who believed that he had been taken against his will to the farmer. He stated that this was so, and I told him to tell the court exactly what had happened.

The court convened shortly after lunch. Maisels introduced himself to Judge Rumpff and asked that Nelson Langa be called into court. The judge told Nelson to enter the witness box, and refusing Maisels the right to examine him, he himself put the questions to him.

JUDGE: You have just come from a farm in the Bethal area?

NELSON: Yes.

JUDGE: Can you tell me when you arrived on the farm?

NELSON: This is the third week since I got to this farm.

JUDGE: How did you arrive at the farm?

NELSON: By one of those big troop carriers—an ex-army truck, a covered, enclosed truck.

JUDGE: Before that you have been living in Johannesburg?

NELSON: I was working in Johannesburg before that.

JUDGE: What were you doing?

NELSON: I was sweeping.

JUDGE: Sweeping where?

NELSON: In the streets.

JUDGE: Were you working for the municipality?

NELSON: Yes.

JUDGE: What happened to you?

NELSON: At about three o'clock when I was about to knock off work, some gang, some police dressed in civil clothes came to me. They said to me, "Pass."

JUDGE: Where were you when they came by you?

NELSON: I was in the street on my way to the compound where I live.

JUDGE: They asked for your Pass?

NELSON: Yes. I said to them, "I have not the Pass on me. We don't carry the Passes when we work." They said, "We are arresting you." I said, "Here is my badge with the number of my work and here is the broom that I use in my work." They said, "We have

nothing to do with that. Get on the kwela."
I got on.

JUDGE: What happened to you?

NELSON: The kwela continued with the lot of us that
were in it, passing along the streets arresting people in the same way I was arrested
and put on the lorry and that night we slept
in Regents Park. Next morning we were
taken to Johannesburg. I left my broom
which I had used at Regents Park. We
were taken to the Old Pass Office in Johannesburg. There each one of us were called
out by name and after the names were
called out we were told we were to be
given work. I then spoke and said, "I don't
want to be given work, because I am
working." They said, "We have nothing to
do with that. You are going to be given
work."

JUDGE: Who said that?

NELSON: There was a clerk who took down our
names, he said so. We were told we were
going to be given work and on Thursday
we were put on the troop carrier and taken
to Bethal.

Nelson also told the court that he asked the policeman who
arrested him to telephone his employer but the policeman's
response was, *"Voetsak* (Go to hell)." When Nelson appeared
in court he was still wearing his belt with the Johannesburg
municipality badge on it.

Judge Rumpff then told Nelson he was released and could
go back to where he belonged. He then called on the other
side, who maintained that the police records would show that
Nelson Langa had been arrested for failing to produce his
pass on demand. The judge asked what the fine would be if he
was guilty, and was told one pound or four days to a week in
jail. It appeared to me that the judge's anger was mounting; he
was not in sympathy with Nelson Langa but he was upset by

the incompetence of the state officials which made it possible for us to expose the whole irregular system. Not once, however, did he condemn or comment on the system.

Despite the fact that Nelson was free, it was important and necessary that the court decide whether or not there was just cause in our bringing our petition. I wanted a court finding that would confirm the illegality of the farm labor scheme.

Nelson had shown no hesitation or fear in the witness box. He was firm and direct in his replies and gave the impression that he was speaking the truth. We now needed a full statement from him, giving a firsthand account of the events. Fearing, however, that he might again be spirited away and disappear, I decided to take such an affidavit from him then and there before I returned him to his compound. His statement confirmed all that we had said had happened to him—all the deductions we had made were correct. They had been logical and reasonable. It confirmed that he had been arrested but was never charged. He emphatically denied that he had ever signed any contract. He stated that he was just sold to the farm with all the others who were sold the same day.

It was 1 A.M. and the cold night wind cut through us as we walked to our car and drove Nelson back to his compound. The blackjack—black municipal policeman—at the gate woke up and moved lethargically from his fire. He walked cautiously toward the car until Nelson and Innocent shouted to him in Zulu, identifying themselves. Then his fear disappeared and with a broad smile he welcomed us. "*Sakubona kunjani wena* (I see you, how are you)." By now the whole compound knew about the case of Innocent and Nelson Langa. He allowed us to drive inside where I dropped off the Langas and as I turned to leave the policeman shouted, "*Hamba kahle, yabonga hamba, kahle, n'Kosi* (Go well, go in peace, thank you, chief)."

"*Sala kahle* (Remain in peace)," I replied, and we headed toward home. It had been a long and hard but successful day.

Nelson's affidavit was duly served and filed. Some two weeks later I received almost two hundred closely typed pages of affidavits and supporting documents from some twenty people—officials, policemen, farmers, Africans—drawn and filed by the state attorney. Although the farmer was a private citizen, he was being represented by the state, which was using its funds to pay for his litigation. The kernel of the state's case was a blank denial of all the facts attested to by Nelson and Innocent Langa and an insistence that Nelson had lawfully been arrested for failing to produce his pass and had then volunteered for farm labor in order to avoid prosecution. The state was apparently going to rely on the quantity of affidavits filed and argue that it was impossible for the court to ignore all these documents in favor of the testimony of two black men.

There was an affidavit by the official who "induced" Africans arrested to "volunteer" for work. He said that whenever he addressed these Africans he was very careful to stress, "You are not being sold into slavery on the farm; a man is not to be sold like a donkey." There was an affidavit from the Farm Labor Bureau official Tom Martin, stating that all the laborers he received on a certain day had, by prearrangement, been sent to the farmer in Bethal. On that particular Thursday, Nelson Langa had been among these, and Nelson Langa had volunteered to work on this farm. There was an affidavit from the farmer's foreman. The state even filed affidavits from three blacks, all of whom were present at the time Nelson had been heard to "volunteer." There was an affidavit from the so-called Bantu clerk who interpreted the contract to Nelson, emphatically denying that Nelson was at all hesitant or that he had said he was employed by the municipality.

Finally, in order to clear the record for the government, there were affidavits from important senior officials such as chief magistrates and commissioners, telling of the great demand for farm labor and stating that the enforcement of the pass laws by the police and the farm labor scheme provided the labor required by the farmers.

The chief labor commissioner also disclosed a document upon which the framework of the "voluntary" scheme rested, dated June 14, 1954, and issued by the Department of Native

Affairs, with the concurrence of the secretary of justice and the commissioner of police. It was titled "General Circular 23 of 1954," and was addressed to all officers of these departments throughout the country and to all magistrates. Because of its significance I quote the first three paragraphs verbatim:

PARAGRAPH 1. It is common knowledge that large numbers of natives are daily being arrested and prosecuted for contraventions of a purely technical nature.

PARAGRAPH 2. These arrests cost the state large sums of money and serve no useful purpose.

PARAGRAPH 3. The Department of Justice, the South African Police and this Department have therefore held consultations on the problem and have evolved a scheme, the object of which is to induce unemployed natives now roaming about the streets in the various urban areas to accept employment outside such urban areas.

It set out some ten petty offenses, such as not producing a current tax receipt on demand, for which Africans may be arrested, and instructed police on the procedure to be followed. These prisoners were not to be taken to court but to the labor bureaus where they would be induced to volunteer.

Our case was scheduled for a date early in July. Once again I picked up my two counsel early in the morning and we traveled to Pretoria. We had already planned our course of action. While the other two retired to robe themselves, I walked to the entrance of the Palace of Justice, which overlooks Church Square in the center of Pretoria. Dominating that square is a statue of Paul Kruger, the founder of the Transvaal Republic and its first president. It is enormous and ugly but is a precious idol of Afrikanerdom. Kruger is surrounded by his fighting men who sit at the base of the statue where the struggle of the Boers resisting the English enemy and the black man is depicted.

I was standing and dreaming when Mr. MacGregor, the state attorney, surprised me. I had heard that this man refused to speak English, apparently feeling the need to emphasize his

Afrikaner origin by speaking only that language, so when he
addressed me in Afrikaans I deliberately and rudely replied in
English. Now, however, he wanted to do a deal with me so he
switched to English. He asked me whether I would be
interested in a settlement. Since I had "the 'boy' Nelson," in
order to save time and be rid of all this nonsense, he would
recommend to his clients that they pay the cost of the petition
provided I withdrew the matter from the court. This was more
than generous, he said, what more could I want?

What I wanted more than anything was to expose the
injustices of the system. Though I could not say this to him, I
was convinced that he knew it, and was in fact taunting me as
well as offering me a very reasonable settlement. It was true
that Nelson had been released; what more could I expect from
the court than this?

It was obvious to me that the state was extremely eager to
avoid an exposure of this irregular and improper system. They
were also anxious to continue its operation. While I hesitated,
MacGregor went on talking and in so doing gave me my reply.

"After all," he said, "how can you expect the court to
believe your Kaffirs in the face of all the high officials whose
position and integrity will not be questioned by the court."

My reply was immediate and simple. "You know, Mr.
MacGregor, you do have many high officials on your side, but
there is truth and good common sense on my side. I'll struggle
along."

He walked off in anger.

I reported this conversation to my counsel and they agreed
I had done the right thing.

We were lucky that day. We had been given an English-
speaking judge, one who had been appointed to keep a
religious balance between the judges. He was a Catholic from
the Johannesburg bar.

The atmosphere inside the courtroom was tense. Mac-
Gregor had no doubt reported my rudeness to him and
opposing counsel were angry. They had hoped to avoid an
open confrontation in court.

When court opened Maisels, a tall, thin, and very eloquent
man, addressed the court and drew Judge Faure Williamson's

attention to the conflicting facts, which could not be resolved by the affidavits before the court. We asked that evidence be given in court by the parties to the dispute who could then be subjected to cross-examination. This was the only way the judge would be able to determine the truth.

Immediately the senior counsel on the other side complained that this was unnecessary, irrelevant, and costly. The documents before the court, he said, could resolve the conflict. Judge Williamson stated that he had read the exhibits and was disinclined to agree that they could resolve the conflict. He suggested that a short adjournment be taken so that the parties could get together and try to reach a settlement.

Immediately on adjournment the other side went into a tight huddle. We tried to maintain a nonchalant air. Maisels lit his pipe and slouched down in his seat. Suddenly he turned to me.

"Carlson," he said sharply, "show me the original of that contract that Nelson Langa supposedly signed."

I leafed through my copies of the documents tendered by the state and found that all I had was a blank contract form marked "duplicate copy" in red ink, which the state attorney had given me when he had served his documents on me. I gave this to him.

"No, no," he replied impatiently, "I have that. I mean a true copy of the original."

"Oh," I said, "I haven't got that."

"But you have seen it, haven't you?" he demanded, and I admitted that I had not. I was embarrassed because this was a serious omission on my part.

We were interrupted by the opposing senior counsel, Frans Badenhorst, coming to talk to Maisels. Before he could say anything Maisels said, "Could I have a look at the original of the contract that Nelson Langa is alleged to have signed?"

"Yes, of course," he said, and turned to MacGregor for it. At the same time he told Maisels he would like to have a talk with him.

"Yes, certainly, but just let me have a look at his document," said Maisels.

The state attorney shuffled his papers; we waited and the

tension grew. Eventually he produced a document and handed it to Maisels.

After reading it, he said angrily, "I do not want to have any further discussions. I would like to put this before the judge without delay. With your permission I will ask him to return."

Judge Williamson came in. "Well, gentlemen," he began hopefully, "have you reached any agreement?"

Badenhorst replied that it seemed agreement was impossible.

Maisels then rose. "On a matter of importance and before we go any further into this case, I wish to apologize to your Lordship for my failure to look at the original documents— the contract allegedly entered into by Nelson Langa, marked A 16, page 80, of the documents. Neither my junior nor my attorney have seen the original. We were only served with blank forms marked 'duplicate copy.' Perhaps your Lordship has a full copy in the court file."

Judge Williamson looked through his file and said, "No, I have the same sort of duplicate copy."

"Well," said Maisels, "may I, with permission, call upon my learned friend to produce that contract?"

The judge nodded assent.

The original document was again produced and handed over by the state's counsel. A moment of silence ensued while Maisels perused it. He then pointed out to the court that where the document provided for a signature by Nelson Langa, another signature appeared, the same one that appeared where the employment officer was to sign. It was also the same signature as that of the man who attested to the fact that Nelson had been present, had had the document explained to him, and had signed the document in his presence.

Maisels gave the document to the court usher. "From this, my Lord, it appears that the employment officer, the attesting officer, and Nelson Langa are all one and the same person. There was only one person's signature on this contract and that is the signature of the employment officer. My Lord, it is most improper that this full disclosure was not made."

Further silence ensued while Judge Williamson read the document. He then called on the opposing counsel for an explanation. They were obviously embarrassed but they talked about a power of attorney having been given to the employment officer. That was the best they could do. We came back to the attack and asked the judge to order that evidence be given. It was essential that the employment officer be brought to court for cross-examination. The other side asked for a short adjournment, which was granted.

I could hardly contain my excitement but Maisels was outwardly very cool and very calm. When we resumed, Badenhorst explained to the judge that it was accepted practice for the labor officers to be given powers of attorney by the farmers, who couldn't always leave their farms to sign for their laborers in person. In this case, the Bethal farmer had given a power of attorney to the employment officer to accept on his behalf all the "boys" on every second Thursday. On those days the farmer would send his foreman to the labor bureau to take the "boys" to the farm. Often they were illiterate and there were too many, really, for the staff to deal with, so that once the "boys" had made clear their desire to work, the employment officer, a responsible official, signed for all the parties to the contract.

These details had not been disclosed in the affidavits filed and the answer was far from satisfactory. Immediately Maisels rose and asked the judge if the state could produce this power of attorney. Again there was a silence and a search and we waited.

"Perhaps we should give my learned friend more time," Maisels suggested, but the offer was refused with a polite, "Will your Lordship bear with me for a moment." He was given a moment and another but the document could not be found.

The judge was now annoyed. He said, "But you told me a moment ago that you had it."

"No, my Lord, I said that it was the authorizing power; if I had it, my Lord, I would produce it." His embarrassment was obvious. "We do not have it," he said, "and I can't produce it."

"But you mentioned it and your opponent is rightly entitled to ask for it. Where, then, is it?"

"I do not know," said Badenhorst, "but we have not destroyed it, I assure you. If I did not want to produce it my attorney could have destroyed it and then I would not have mentioned it. We have nothing to hide and we will try and find it."

The judge exploded. "Are you suggesting that a state attorney, an officer of this court, could destroy a document?" His face was red, his three chins bounced at the preposterous submissions being made to him.

Badenhorst tried to explain and became more embarrassed. Meanwhile I had been going through the documents and saw that a list of volunteers had been referred to as well as a form that the interpreter acting for Tom Martin had reported that he had filled in when Nelson volunteered. We asked for these to be produced and they were. On examining them we found there was no mention of the presence of those Africans who allegedly were present when Nelson volunteered, either in the police record or in the bureau record. We also found that the interpreter acting for Tom Martin had filled in a form clearly stating that Nelson Langa had informed him that he was previously employed by the Johannesburg municipality, yet in his own affidavit, he stated that Nelson had never told him about this.

We put this information before the court and again insisted that under the circumstances it was not possible to believe the deponents who filed affidavits on behalf of the state and it was essential to have them appear in the witness box to undergo cross-examination. However, in view of the state's refusal to have the truth tested in this way, we asked the court to draw the only conclusion it reasonably and legally could, namely to believe our case and to disbelieve the state's case.

The other side rose to reply and begged the court's permission to argue the documents on their merits. I was surprised when Judge Williamson acceded to their request. However, they could not get around the inconsistencies. There was no real answer to the arguments we advanced. Maisels then not only asked the court to grant an order in our favor, but asked for an expression of disapproval of this type of conduct by the state through the granting of a punitive measure of costs against them. Judge Williamson reserved judgment on all questions.

We were sure that we had won but it was not clear how complete our victory would be. I could have jigged for joy but was able to contain myself and behave with the solemnity demanded by the occasion. As we drove home, up and down the hilly road between Pretoria and Johannesburg, the afternoon sun sent beams of light along the strands of red Transval grass bent over in the winter's cold. Dison gleefully went back over the events of the day, playing out the various roles, while we smiled at his impersonations and his clowning. Maisels, the man who had worked so brilliantly all day in court, sat relaxed in the back corner of the car, pipe in hand.

I thought I had achieved my ambition at last; the evil scheme had been exposed. This airing would certainly kill it. I had noticed a reporter for the main English newspaper in court and I was sure the story would make headlines throughout the country.

I was right. The case was on the front page of the afternoon paper in Johannesburg. Next morning there were more articles on it. But by the following afternoon the case had been forgotten. There was no response; there was no reaction. It was as if nothing had happened. A week passed and there was no decision from the judge. I could not understand what had gone wrong. I spoke to Dison about it and was told that decisions often take time. More important, I asked, why was the scheme still being continued?

"Before you can break that scheme," said Dison, "you will have to upset the system. You will need to bring fifty such applications, not one. Only then will they sit up and take notice."

Victory, then, was a defeat. All my determination and all my efforts to end the scheme had been unavailing. I realized that it was not sufficient to use the weight of the facts and the laws of the land before the judges of any South African court. The state could ignore our exposure because it knew it would not have a long-lasting effect.

In fact, the judge took eleven months to render his decision. Then he saw fit to blame the whole sequence of events on some "Bantu clerk" who through carelessness had misled the white officers. Technically, we had won the case, although not with the punitive measure of costs we had asked for, but no comment on the system was made; the state was free to continue using it. My disappointment and disillusionment were intense and I began to realize that I, too, was just a part of the system, a system that was in operation daily. While I remained part of it, I would just have to persevere in my fight against it.

VI
THE MAN FROM
GINGINGDHLOVU

One morning, some months after the Nelson Langa case, a colleague and friend telephoned me to ask if I would help an African who had been brought to his office by the man who cleaned his apartment. He gave me no details over the phone—I learned the facts later from Charlie Nyoni himself when he and his uncle came to see me.

The uncle, an elderly man from Zululand, wore elaborate beadwork around his neck, and by his wooden headring denoting his senior status, I could tell he had two wives. Charlie, on the other hand, wore his hair in *isicoco* style—cut in a line right around the head—which indicated he was a bachelor. In the white man's world, however, both these men were reduced to the same status, that of "flat-boys," domestic servants who worked full time cleaning apartments or flats as they are called in South Africa. When they came to see me they were dressed in the uniforms supplied to them by their employers—unbleached calico short pants and loose-fitting tops, bordered with red braid. No jacket, shoes, or socks were issued. Being frugal and practical, too, they made their own sandals out of old automobile tires. They also made knee pads from tires to afford some protection and enable them to move more easily as they polished the floors on their hands and knees.

Charlie had no pass and that was what his trouble was all about. His story emerged slowly and painfully as he was not an articulate man but gradually, in response to persistent questioning, he related the drama of how he had lost his pass and how he had found his way to me.

Charlie earned ten pounds a month. After working without a break for four years, he had at last managed to save enough money to go home for several months. His employer consented to this arrangement and endorsed his pass book accordingly: "Bearer is proceeding home on long leave and will return to his place of employment six months from the date hereof." It was signed, stamped, and dated. In those days long leave after many years of work was an accepted practice, especially among Africans who came from rural areas and were separated from their families while they worked in apartment buildings and in offices.

At the end of his leave period, Charlie returned to his job. His train arrived in Johannesburg on Sunday evening. He walked from the station to a tall office building close by, where his cousin who came from the same area in Zululand and was also a flat-boy put him up for the night. Of course this was illegal but it was common practice since Charlie, like so many others in the same predicament, could find no alternative accommodation until he was given quarters by his employer, usually in one of the many "locations-in-the-sky." These were small rooms at the very top of apartment buildings, alongside the water storage tanks, shared by the domestic servants who worked in the building and out of sight of any of the white residents.

Early on Monday morning Charlie went to the real-estate agent to be assigned to an apartment or office building. He left the building where he had slept, slipping unobtrusively through the service entrance in the basement. Two blocks away he walked straight into the arms of the waiting ghost squad.

Charlie did not recognize them as policemen but even if he had, he was not deliberately trying to avoid the police because he was convinced that his pass was in order. He was employed, was registered, had gone on leave, and was now returning to his previous employer. As he passed the men of the ghost squad, one of them put out a hand and said the one word: "Pass." Charlie ignored him, and blithely continued on his way. The man immediately took him by the arm and said, *"Kom, skelm, pass."* (Come on, you rogue, where's your pass.) A white man joined in and said curtly and quickly, "Pass, pass, pass." Charlie was uncertain of what to do but he decided not to take a chance and he produced his pass—after all, he had nothing to hide. To his surprise, before he could even show it to them, they grabbed him and shoved him into a group of men standing against a wall. He was immediately handcuffed to a stranger. His protests went unheeded, while the ghost squad went on with its work.

Charlie remained standing handcuffed in the street for more than an hour. After many more men were rounded up, the *kwela-kwela* arrived and all the prisoners were pushed into it. Some of the ghost squad accompanied them in the truck as it drove around the city picking up batches of other pass offenders. When eventually about seventy to eighty men were packed inside, the truck headed for Marshall Square, the main police station in Johannesburg. There, all were unloaded and led into a yard surrounded by a high wall with barbed wire along its top. By the time they had been searched, their names entered in the police record books, and they had been put into their cells, it was early afternoon. Charlie sat and scowled at the cold cement floor of his cell. On every possible occasion, he tried to gain the attention of a policeman but no one would listen. He grew resigned to spending a night in jail. The place smelled like a dirty urinal and the blankets were thin and shiny with years of grime and stains of all colors, but worst of all they stank, too. They smelled so bad that he kicked them aside and chose to sit up against the wall, dozing through the night.

In the morning, Charlie and many fellow prisoners were loaded into another *kwela-kwela* and taken to the courthouse in Fordsburg and locked up in the back of the prison yard. Toward midday, Charlie and one other were taken into the prosecutor's office and confronted by three white men and one black policeman. The prosecutor asked Charlie for his pass and handed it, and the pass of the other man, to a short, fat white man. Speaking slowly through the black interpreter, he told them that instead of going to jail they could serve the white man on his farm for six months and they would be paid three pounds a month. He said they had no right to be in Johannesburg because they did not have permission to work there.

At this point Charlie tried to interrupt and he was told: *"Thula* [Be quiet]!" The policeman ordered them to follow the farmer but Charlie spoke up again, asking the black policeman to tell the prosecutor that he had a job and was earning more than three pounds a month. He added emphatically, "I do not want this job on a farm."

The prosecutor replied abruptly, "You do not have permission to work here. You go to the farm or you will go to jail for two years."

The white farmer and the prosecutor took the two prisoners outside to a van parked nearby where a boss-boy was waiting. They were ordered to get in and sit on the floor. Charlie thought briefly about jumping out and running away, but he was afraid. Even if he got away, he reasoned, "What am I to do without my pass book?" He knew that he might then really go to prison for a long time, so he decided to wait and see what happened.

While Charlie was describing the events in the Fordsburg commissioners court to me, I questioned him closely. His answers described all the procedures with which I was so well acquainted. I was convinced that he was an accurate and truthful witness and asked him to continue his story.

He told how they had driven until the sun was halfway down the sky. Finally, they came to a farm gate which the boss-boy opened. The van drove up to a cluster of farm buildings. Charlie could not say where this was—it was new and strange country to him. He said that the farmer was about fifty years old, five feet five inches in height, and bald, except for a fringe of white hair. He was called *Baas* Robert. The van in which they had driven was a blue Chevrolet panel truck with a TDJ license plate, but he could not remember the license number.

When they reached the farmhouse, *Baas* Robert ordered the boss-boy to take Charlie and the other man to the compound. On the way there, the boss-boy demanded Charlie's shoes. He refused to give them up, and for a particularly good reason—one that I was to learn of, later on. He was not afraid of the boss-boy and at that stage, the boss-boy was not prepared to start a fight. Instead, when they got to the compound door he opened it, pushed Charlie and the other man into a room, swore at them, and slammed the door shut. It was dark and smelled like a sewage pit.

As his eyes grew accustomed to the darkness, Charlie saw wooden bunks splintered and broken up, and a pile of sacks. In one corner of the room stood an open half-drum that was used as a latrine; a second half-drum contained drinking water. The floor around the drum was wet, the walls were covered with soot and grit, and near the center of the floor were the ashes of a fire. High up in one corner of the room above the latrine was a small, slightly open window. Charlie sat down but there were vermin everywhere and he was unhappy about staying in any one spot for too long. He found it difficult to talk to his fellow prisoner because the man was a Venda and they did not speak the same language. They sat silently and sullenly until they heard men shouting.

Suddenly the door was thrown open and a group of dirty, sweaty, exhausted men came in. All were dressed in meal sacks, with holes for their arms and heads. They rushed for the half-drum of water, pushing each other aside in their haste, and scooping it up with their hands so that soon the water in the drum was filthy. When they had finished drinking, they looked at the new recruits and, in turn, were examined in astonishment by Charlie. He noticed that some had sores or wounds on their legs or on their heads.

Two of the men were called out by the boss-boys and returned with two buckets of hard porridge and a big tin of black coffee. There were no plates or spoons, and the men who were seated caught their porridge in their laps; others took as much as they could hold in their hands. Charlie tasted a handful of the stuff but when he saw worms in it he threw it away. Others, too, threw their food on the floor and Charlie realized that this was why the floor was so dirty. The coffee was warm and sweetened, and Charlie drank a mugful of it. There were only four mugs and these were shared by all the men. The smells, the food, the men, the lice, all became unbearable. Charlie decided then that he must get away. That night he could not lie down; he sat up and dozed but he was exhausted and eventually he slept for a few hours.

The next morning they were awakened at sunrise and were given porridge and coffee in the same way as the night before. The boss-boys gave Charlie a small, white card divided into thirty squares. He was told that for each day he worked, a square would be signed by one of the boss-boys. On the days he did not work, whether it was because he was sick or because it was a Sunday, or because it rained, the card would not be signed. The other workers told him that if he fought with the boss-boys, they would not sign the card, and that sometimes one had to work six, seven, or eight weeks to have the thirty days of one month signed. That day the boss-boy again demanded Charlie's boots and again Charlie refused to surrender them. He was hit about the legs and the body but still refused to give up his boots. The boss-boy said, "You will work and you will not have your card signed. In a few days you will be too tired to fight, then you will get a hiding and we will get the boots. In the meantime, your card will not be signed."

The work was backbreaking. The men had to dig up potatoes with their bare hands. If they stopped to rest for a moment a boss-boy would strike them with his whip or with a stick. At lunchtime they were given only water, no food. After a short break, they returned to work and continued until sunset. Charlie watched all day for an opportunity to escape but soon realized that this was impossible. Not only were they surrounded by boss-boys but there was also one man on horseback, whip in hand, mounting guard.

On the way back to the compound Charlie remembered the window above the latrine and decided he would try to escape that night, before he got too weak. He waited for the food to be served; he drank some coffee and even took a handful of the porridge and tried to eat some of it. When the others fell asleep he made his move. He got up and edged his way quietly toward the corner where the half-drum latrine stood. Very cautiously, he put his foot on one side of the drum, grabbed the window bar at the top, and pulled himself up. The window was half-open and he found it just big enough for him to squeeze through.

It was not far from the window to the ground. He dropped down on the grass and lay still, listening. All was quiet; nothing moved. He looked around and saw a clump of trees some distance ahead. He ran toward it, stopped, caught his breath, and listened again. There were dogs barking in the distance but still no one came. Slipping through the trees, he came to the end of the plantation and turned toward where he thought the road ran. He could not find a road but followed a path running in between the farms. He walked on and on for many hours. At last the sky began to lighten and he suddenly saw a railway line. Whistling in relief, he followed the tracks and in another hour, he saw the Kendal station and Africans waiting on the platform. He stopped, and behind some bushes, removed his shoe and took out of his sock a pound note he had hidden there. He bought a ticket and caught the next train; exhausted, he slept all the way to Johannesburg. There he went in search of his uncle and told him what had happened. His uncle then took him to the friend who phoned me.

I asked Charlie where he had obtained the one-pound note he had used for his rail fare. He said that at the police station, as soon as he saw the trouble ahead of him, managed to hide his only pound note inside his sock. Charlie's resourcefulness had undoubtedly saved him for the moment, but the problem still remained—what was to be done now? In this case, I had Charlie but I did not have his pass, and it was going to be extremely difficult to prove his story. I told Charlie and his uncle that it would take time to solve his problem; that I would have to make many inquiries. I told his uncle that the safest thing for Charlie to do was to keep off the streets.

I began making inquiries immediately. The personnel

officer at the firm of real estate agents for whom Charlie
worked confirmed the date on which Charlie was due to return
and the date when he was last discharged. He also gave me
Charlie's reference book number. Armed with this information, I visited the court. At first I was unable to find any trace
of Charlie but I kept after it and eventually the clerk of the
court found the record of Charlie's case, which indicated that
he had appeared in court, that the charge had been withdrawn,
and that he had been told to report back to his employer. The
record had been completely falsified. I was well aware of the
uphill fight I would have to convince a judge that the officers
of another court had acted so fraudulently.

The only recourse was to find this "*Baas* Robert" to whom
Charlie, in his own words, had been "sold." Using the Kendal
railway line as a center point, I plotted a twenty-mile radius on
a map and drew a circle, inside which I was certain one could
find *Baas* Robert's farm. I telephoned all the police stations in
the area and asked whether any employer had reported
Charlie's desertion. The answers were negative. I let a few
days pass and again telephoned the police stations, asking
sergeants on duty to search their records, but still no one had
reported Charlie's desertion. Obviously, realizing he had
gained Charlie illegally, *Baas* Robert had not reported Charlie's escape.

That weekend I went to see a colleague who had, before
taking up law, been a farmer in the Kendal area. Drawing on
his memory, he suggested who *Baas* Robert might be. The
description tallied with that given by Charlie and the location
of his farm was in the area bearing TDJ automobile license
numbers. I rushed home jubilantly, certain that I had the right
man. I searched the Kendal telephone book, found *Baas*
Robert's telephone number, and immediately called him. Not
surprisingly, he was very hostile. He admitted abruptly that he
had employed Charlie—he had obtained him after the "boy"
had been sentenced at court. He said he had not bothered to
report his desertion—there were so many desertions farmers
often did not report them.

It was true, he said, that he had had Charlie's pass book but
he could not return it either to Charlie or me because he had

already returned it to Johannesburg and I could now make inquiries at the pass office there—they would have it. He told me Charlie was a criminal and declared he was not prepared to give me any further information. In fact, he said, it was an impertinence on my part to bother him on his weekend with such nonsense. He then hung up.

Elated as I was at having traced Charlie's employer, I was aware that I had reached another dead end. There was now no legal way to get Charlie's pass book. It had been my hope that once I knew who the employer was and had confirmed that he had the pass book, I could make a legal application to have it returned to Charlie, for it had been fraudulently and dishonestly taken from him at the outset. However, with the pass book in the hands of some pass office I could no longer do this. What could I do for Charlie now?

There seemed no way out of this case and I was frustrated and angry. Try as I might, I could find no way of providing any legal relief for him in the way of court action. The only thing left to do was to take Charlie's deposition and send it on to the commissioner of police for investigation. I called Charlie in and advised him of the position and he agreed to this procedure.

I realized the significance of the allegations that Charlie would make in his statement and I expected a storm to break over our heads. I was confident that Charlie would be able to convince a court he was telling truth. I was equally confident I had enough evidence to convince a court that what Charlie said was true. We completed the statement and sent it to the commissioner of police and we waited—but nothing happened. Two weeks passed and I heard nothing. Meanwhile, Charlie was getting uneasy and anxious. He was wasting his time; he could not work, he had no pass. I told him I was doing all that was legally possible and there was no other way out except to wait, but I realized how unhelpful my advice must sound to him.

A week later a letter arrived from the chief of police of western areas, Johannesburg. I was advised by his office that the complaint was being attended to and I was given the name of the man conducting the investigation. I could not believe what I read. The man in charge of the investigation was, in fact, the very same prosecutor who had sold Charlie to *Baas* Robert in the first place. No sooner had I received this information than he telephoned me. Reluctantly, I agreed to see him and we met that afternoon in my office.

Sergeant Bezuidenhout was full of charm. He had brought all his documents with him and he told me he had already conducted and completed the investigation. According to the court record, he said, Charlie had been prosecuted. The charges had then been withdrawn and a farm labor contract entered into by Charlie and the farmer. Everything was in order.

This was the third variation of the story that I had heard. I was, for the moment, speechless, when he said to me, "You know, of course, that Charlie is an agitator and that he just wants to make trouble. There is no truth in his story. In fact, I could prosecute him for leaving his local area without the permission of his chief or the local commissioner before he came to Johannesburg. However," he continued, "I'll tell you what I am going to do. None of us want all this trouble. You have been decent and you have reported this matter to the police. I too, will be decent. After all, you are one of us."

I was seething with anger but he held up his hand and said, "Listen to me. If your Charlie pays ten shillings and swears that he lost his pass, I will see that he gets a new pass and this will be the end of the matter."

Furiously, I told him I did not wish to deal with him and ordered him to leave my office. Then I called in Charlie and told him what the prosecutor had said. Charlie hotly denied the official version of the story, and I told him that somehow or other, I would bring all the legal assistance possible and we would fight to get his pass back.

Then Charlie said, "Let me pay the ten shillings and get my pass."

I did not expect this, and although I accepted his reasons, I felt angry and disappointed with Charlie and told him he should think over what he wanted to do and come and tell me the next day. I went home sick with the knowledge that the system would again escape attack.

When I arrived at my office the next morning, Charlie was waiting for me. He had his ten shillings in his hand so I did not have to ask what he wanted me to do. I brought him into my office and in his presence I telephoned Sergeant Bezuidenhout. When I told him who I was and what it was all about, I added, "Charlie is prepared to take the ten-shilling course. Will you arrange for him to get his pass?"

"Ja," he replied, *"nou praat jy soos'n regtige kérel."* (Now you speak like one of us.)

He told me to go down and see a Mr. Esterhuizen at the main pass office. So Charlie and I went to the main pass office. Esterhuizen greeted me warmly and offered me tea and biscuits. He insisted on bringing a chair for me so that I could sit down while he asked Charlie questions and completed innumerable forms. Then, forms in hand, he led us past the long lines of waiting black men.

Charlie was given preference everywhere. He had his picture taken; he had all his papers filled in; he paid his tax; he paid his ten shillings. In forty minutes he had his duplicate reference book papers and was ready to resume life as usual. I had to thank Mr. Esterhuizen, then we left the pass office. Charlie went off, pass in hand, and I returned to my office, angry and disgusted.

Charlie's case left me with deep-seated frustrations, and so heightened my growing doubts about the effectiveness of my actions in bringing about changes in the system, that I seriously considered giving up trying. Long after the case, I happened to be in Zululand. On an impulse, I drove to Charlie's home at Gingingdhlovu. Northward from Durban, the broad road unfolded from Amazimtoti to Umhlanga Rocks. The sea flowed into magical little bays; the hills fell into sand dunes toward the water. The signposts carried the musical Zulu names of the towns along the way—Empangeni, Matubatuba, and Amatikulu. I sped up an incline and descended again through the heavy green foliage that wrapped both sides of the road through the hills. The road narrowed and laced the seashore. I followed it and around a corner I saw the sign: SHAKA'S ROCK.

The great military genius and Zulu leader, Shaka, will one

day feature large in the history books of Africa's schoolchildren. He was a master of battle and his conquests stretched across southern Africa. He conquered all the black nations he confronted as well as the might of the British and the Boers. Ask any British soldier at which battle the greatest number of Victoria Crosses were awarded, and he will tell you Isandhlwana. Like Caesar before him, Shaka was knifed by his jealous rivals. After his death, the mighty power of the Zulu nation crumbled and its final defeat is celebrated every year by whites in South Africa.

I came upon Shaka's Rock on a dark, gray afternoon. As I stopped the car the rain began to fall. I walked around the hill to the sea; the tide was high and the sea dark green. Low-lying dark clouds were blowing in toward the land and the horizon was blurred in mist. I walked down the pathway at the base of the huge cliff toward its edge. Then the path turned sharply, leading under an archway of rock, and through it I could see a cauldron of wild water pierced by dark, jagged rocks thrusting sharply out of it. Churning backwash faced inflowing sea and each crashed against the other. A short lull brought another crash as currents pulled the water around. Above me was the Execution Rock. Once, Zulus sentenced to death had walked proudly over the edge of this precipice to be battered against the rocks by the violent waves before they joined their forefathers.

Behind me the ocean unrolled itself all along the beaches to the north, and the little bays stretched out their sands. The waves that made their way past the rock ridges out to sea dropped peacefully onto the beaches. Directly in front of me, only fifty feet away, great green rollers moved in a solid wall, contemptuous of the rocks before them. Then, up and up they rose, sucking in the backwash, until finally, breaking fiercely, the heavy rolls of white water bellied over to crash on the rocks obstructing their way. Back the water flowed; and the next wave mounted higher and higher and, as it broke, crashed against the rocks and flew up in white spurts, only to be drawn down and back into the next wave. The bubbling white water that fell on the other side of the rocks came down into the calmer pools below. The backs of the rocks were black and gnarled and impassive. They gave protection to three fishermen, small figures drenched in seawater, each one holding his rod before him as reason to stand and face the sea. The scene was repeated again and again. Still all remained the same and only time gave way.

Cold and wet I walked back. I dried myself and had some tea. My flesh tingled with the salt spray and I was warmed by the protection of the car windows around me. I drove westward towards Gingingdhlovu. Before me was another sea—the vivid green of the sugarcane fields—the long bright stalks reaching to the hills and mounting them. Gusts of wind bent the cane, which moved forward and back in undulating rows.

Suddenly a bright ray of sunshine hit the sand and ocher rocks through which the road was cut. The light beneath the clouds spread out across the cane and once again the sea moved in changing colors and shapes. Far on the western hills, the clear blue sky showed itself behind the clouds. The land bounced in valleys and hills up into the distant mountains. Once more I stopped and got out of the car. I listened to the breeze and caught the sound of insects. Far down, a family of Zulus walked toward their huts—round, chocolate-brown, and grass-roofed. Groups of huts clustered on level ground upon the hills, and valley followed valley. The sun cast its light vividly as it descended. Red and orange blazed up into the clouds above the horizon. It grew still, except for birds overhead, homeward bound. The air was invigorating and peace descended. Was this the secret Charlie knew? Whatever madness was beyond, here there was peace.

VII
A SECOND
CHANCE

Nearly a year and a half went by without any significant cases arriving at my office. It was just as well, as I felt little enthusiasm for handling them. Charlie's reaction—his unwillingness to litigate—and my inability to stop the farm labor system left me with considerable cynicism about the value of my role as a lawyer. I contented myself with my civil and criminal practice and the never-ending stream of pass cases.

Every success on behalf of an African family was of major significance for the people directly affected. I was gratified by the warmth that they expressed toward me. Certainly, there was satisfaction in finding solutions for such people, but each case was just another bead in a chain that I knew I could go on making endlessly. The help I was able to bring them alleviated individual suffering but it did not change the system that daily wrought more and more violence on people's lives.

In the late 1950s I moved my office nearer to the center of town. It was here that Josiah Noko came to ask my help. Despite everything I already knew, I found his story almost impossible to believe, but his seriousness, his intensity, compelled me to listen to what he told me. Josiah was middle-aged but looked younger. He was well built, had a round face, and wore spectacles, and was well able to make himself understood. For many years he had worked as a chauffeur to a multimillionaire in Johannesburg. He was fond of his job and the status it brought him. He enjoyed the smart clothing that his employer provided. He loved the luxurious cars he drove and he relished driving an important man to important places. This happy state of affairs was only possible because Josiah's employer ignored the pass laws. Josiah was a Rhodesian by birth; his employment could not be registered and was, therefore, unlawful.

The African states on our borders are not as rich as South Africa and there are few jobs available, so poor black peasants are forced to look elsewhere for work. On the other hand, South Africa's mines and farms are constantly in need of cheap black migratory labor. Consequently, the South African government encourages black labor coming in primarily as mine or farm workers. It does not usually grant such Africans permission to work in any urban area and they are termed "foreign natives." However, in both rural and urban areas, such men are often employed without permission. Their employers simply do not register them as they are required to do under the pass laws. Both employer and employee risk prosecution but prosecution of white employers under these circumstances is very rare. Invariably, only the employee is prosecuted.

Josiah took the risk of this unlawful employment as his alternative was to work in Rhodesia where he could only earn two to three pounds per month in contrast to the twelve pounds a month the millionaire paid him.

I asked him how he had managed to escape the pass laws for so long and he told me, "I always carried five to ten pounds cash with me. That was my pass." However, one Sunday afternoon his luck ran out while he was waiting at the Sophiatown bus terminal. It was his day off and he had been gambling and lost all his money. He had also had too much to drink. When he arrived at the bus stop, he said, "This policeman—he came up to me and asked for my pass. He was a black policeman from Marshall Square Police." Josiah had his savings book with him which showed a credit but he had no cash, so he was forced to go with the policeman to the police station. He said he wasn't too worried at the time because he was sure he could find someone to bail him out. At the police station he was put into a cell. The food and the stink in the cell made him sick all night but he hoped to go to court the next morning where he was sure he would find someone to turn to for help.

"To my surprise, next day there was no court nor was there a court the next day or the next. Really now I began to worry. I became more sick, there was no friend I could find, there was no knowing what would happen to me and I became afraid. Each day the room was filled with more prisoners. We sat, we talked and we did not know what fire was being prepared for us. Then one morning we were ordered into a covered van and we drove for some hours. When we were unloaded from that van, I read the sign. This was the 'Nigel Farm Labor Bureau.' Here too I knew that if only I had the money I could buy my way out. We slept at that place that night with many others. Next day, early in the morning, we were called out and told we were going to work on the farm. I told the official I was working already but he said, 'Wherever you work you don't have the permission; we will get you the work.'

"There were many others from Rhodesia and about twenty of us were lined up in the prison yard. The officials brought in a short fat man wearing a big broad belt around his belly. I could see this one was a rough one. He and the officials walked past us. The fat man looked very carefully at us. He would feel a muscle of one's arm; punch another in the stomach; look inside another's mouth; and finally he pointed to six of us. Within half an hour we were loaded on the back of his van and his two boss-boys who carried hippo whips sat with us."

On arrival at the huge farm, said Josiah, he and the others with him were locked up in a corrugated-iron building. He estimated that he was no more than fifty miles from Johannesburg. The five other workers who had come with him were also "foreign natives," whose homes were far away from South Africa. Later, Josiah was to learn that, in fact, all the workers on the farm were similarly "foreign natives"—some from as far away as Tanganyika (now Tanzania) and Northern Rhodesia, (now Zambia). It appeared that this farmer specialized in employing men whose whereabouts, in the ordinary course of events, would not be known to their relatives so far away.

Josiah went on to tell me a story that was so ghastly that I, who had heard so much about working conditions on farms from Charlie Nyoni and others, found it to be unbelievable. He described the death of several of the workers on the farm. All of this, he insisted, was happening within fifty miles of the most modern city in Africa.

At first I thought he was exaggerating but I soon realized that there was so much detail, so many incidents, so many names given, that he must be speaking the truth. He told me the name of the farmer was Potgieter and described him fully. He had a good word for Piet, one of the farmer's sons, but he told me of another son who had murdered his brother-in-law, had escaped from prison, and was living on the farm. At the time I found this story incredible; later, it, too, was substantiated. He told me of the local police captain who regularly drove out from town to visit the farm in his blue Mercedes; while he talked to the farmer, the workers would load the trunk of his car with half a sheep, potatoes, and other farm produce. It was clear that what happened on the farm was done with the connivance of the police.

Worst of all were the stories of brutal assaults by the farmer, his sons, and the boss-boys, stories he repeated again and again.

Of his first day at the farm, he said, "When I arrived at the field I saw Potgieter sitting on the hood of his Ford car, watching all the workers in the field. Soon after I started working two of the boss-boys, Abram and Philip, approached me and asked whether I had any money. I said no I had not. They beat me all over the head and body with the knob-kerries which they carried. My mouth started to bleed, I fell to the ground, and one of them kicked me all over my head with his booted foot. All this time Potgieter was there—I saw him when I got up again. I also saw that the two boss-boys beat up the other new workers also and then they just beat everyone as they walked among them.

"These beatings occurred regularly and I noticed that whenever Potgieter arrived at the place where we were working, and honked his horn, the boss-boys immediately started moving among us and hitting out at anyone within striking distance with their knob-kerries. At the same time they would shout to us to work faster. Potgieter would also shout, '*Slaan hulle dood.*" [Beat them to death.]

"At first I wanted to retaliate when I was beaten but the ones that had been there longer than me warned me not to do so. I was told that one of the boss-boys had killed a man in November, hitting him over the head with a knob-kerrie. The dead man's grave was pointed out to me.

"I have seen it happen that when my fellow workers who were beaten or who had fainted for want of water on a hot day, were lying unconscious on the ground, the boss-boys Abram and Philip passed water into their mouths and invited us to urinate in this manner to revive the unconscious men. At other times, those who had fainted were further beaten even by Potgieter himself who came and said they were only faking and did not want to work.

"Plans for escape were discussed continuously among the workers and I never gave up hope of being able to escape. My first attempt failed and I was picked up the day after I left the farm. In that attempt thirty-four managed to escape but I and one, Leonard, were found by Potgieter's son. I was taken back to the farm and Potgieter beat me with a knob-kerrie. He hit me in the small of my back and one blow behind my neck and I fell to the ground. Potgieter's son saw this assault on me as well as the boss-boys and some of the other workers. He called me a baboon and told me I could do nothing to him. I was on the farm of Potgieter for about four months. I never received a penny for the work I did—I never saw any worker being paid any money. At last in March my opportunity came to escape and I was successful. A number of others escaped at the same time as I did."

Josiah identified by name many of his fellow workers who had been assaulted, most of whom were now in Johannesburg. He told me of one worker, a small, slight man—a Muslim by faith—called Musa Sadika, who had been beaten almost out of his senses, and predicted that this man was likely to die as a result of the beatings he had received. He told me he had gone to see Musa Sadika's wife, Dorkus, in Alexandra Township, just north of Johannesburg, and had told her about her husband, but she was afraid to do anything as she and her family were living there without the necessary permission. Her children had been born in the township and could claim some kind of right to remain there, but if she made her presence known to the authorities she was afraid that she would be sent out of the urban area and parted from her children. Even if her husband came back, the family might be broken up. Ultimately, however, after Josiah had told her of the terrible things happening on the farm, she had asked him to seek help in rescuing her husband. Josiah now asked me whether I could help.

I advised him that it was possible to make an application to court but before I, as a lawyer, could do this, he would have to bring me substantial evidence in the way of a number of witnesses to convince me beyond doubt that what he said was, in fact, the truth. If he could do this I would not hesitate to act. However, I said, what he told me was so incredible that no white court would believe it unless we could bring strong corroborative evidence. I knew that Josiah would have difficulty in finding witnesses because once they left the farm, they were in South Africa illegally and would be exposing themselves to a further spell on the farms, or, at best, jail or deportation, if they came forward to give me evidence. Josiah, however, promised to try.

He first brought in Dorkus Sadika. He had convinced her that it was possible to help her husband, so she risked the journey into town to see me. She had little hope that I could do anything because she looked on me as just another white man and part of the white man's law—the law that had separated her from her husband and placed her and her family in jeopardy. Almost in tears, she related to me the miserable life she led and what she had done after Musa had disappeared.

She told me that Musa had come to Johannesburg from Nyasaland (now Malawi) in about 1936, when restrictions on immigration were very lax. After paying the *lobola* (dowry) of fifty pounds to her guardian, Jacob, they married in 1940 and had two children. Musa made ten to fifteen pounds per month as an herbalist.

One day in October, 1958, Musa had gone to visit relatives in Evaton, a town near Johannesburg. He never returned. She inquired from friends and relatives of the family but no one knew where he was or what had happened to him. She had inquiries made from the South African police in Alexandra and at the jail in Johannesburg and she sent her friends to the Native Commissioners Court in Fordsburg and other courts. She even tried several hospitals but her husband had disappeared without a trace. She concluded that he had been killed and not until she met Josiah did she know what had actually happened to him.

By taking in washing, by doing some sewing, by brewing a little liquor, she had managed to survive and support her children outside the law. I promised to help her to the best of my ability but as I had told Josiah, this help was dependent upon my being furnished with further evidence. She was fearful that I would go to the police and ask them about her husband. I assured her I would not do this. I extended my sympathy to her and in the end she thanked me and began to believe that I might be able to do something for her husband.

Josiah promised me that the other witnesses would come to see me within the week. He knew how urgent a matter this was because if Musa died at the farm there was little point in going to court to ask for aid because by then he would be beyond help.

I decided that if Josiah brought the witnesses I would take their statements, draft the affidavits myself, and have them signed before I saw counsel; then if I could convince counsel, I thought it was possible that the court, too, could be convinced.

I wondered whether the farm labor scheme would finally be

stopped if the court was convinced. I wondered what would happen if, when I made a habeas corpus application, the farmer's reply was that he couldn't produce the body because Musa was dead. That would cause a sensation and perhaps that in itself would be a severe enough condemnation to bring the scheme to an end. But I was not sure even of that.

Fortunately, perhaps, lawyers cannot worry about the long-term results of their actions. They have to act for the immediate future —for results that can be seen at the end of one's nose. The immediate objective of a habeas corpus application was to help Musa Sadika and then hope for some long-term good results. There was no point expecting them; there was point only in doing whatever I could do and keep trying. I had to answer to myself in the end and from myself I could not escape. It was fruitless pondering further whether the action was worthwhile or not—it just had to be taken if the evidence supported it. I could not live with myself if I refused to try.

One by one, Josiah brought in his witnesses who came despite the dangers they faced in seeing me in the city when their papers were not in order. Although they exposed themselves to the law, they did not hesitate to act in support of their comrades who were still suffering on the farm. There was Robert Ncube from Southern Rhodesia—a square man with a moustache. He had already found a new niche in life, a new employer who rightly thought highly of him although, of course, the relationship was again unlawful. He had obtained his employer's permission to see me and he in turn asked me for a note to take back to convince her that he had not been loafing. In fact, from his own statement, on the farm he had even earned the respect of Potgieter. The farmer had offered him ten shillings a month more—even a pound a month more —if he would only remain on the farm. It seemed that Robert was the only worker who had received any money from Potgieter. Nevertheless, Robert had refused to stay and was the only one permitted to leave the farm after he had served there for nine months—what a six-month contract amounted to when only working days were counted and thirty working days made a month!

In his affidavit, Robert said: "Over and above the assaults, which was the most terrible thing about the conditions on the farm, the living conditions were worse than anything I have ever experienced in my life. I was once arrested for a Pass offense in Johannesburg and spent 2 months in the jail there. I would rather spend a year in jail than spend a month on Potgieter's farm."

Robert further stated: "After I had been there about four months I noticed one day a boss boy, Tumela, who was only about 16 years old, beating one of the workers who was cutting firewood. After the assault I noticed this man's nose was bleeding a lot. The man sat down and his nose continued to bleed and he was left there until we were locked up at 6 o'clock. The following morning he was unable to get up and work. He was shivering all the time. He did not work for 3 days and on that Saturday morning he died. The boss boy, Philip, told 4 of the workers to carry him into the room where the dead are kept and the body was left there until Monday morning. On Monday afternoon about half past four, I and seven others, including Philip, carried the body and buried it on the farm. There were other graves where we buried him. I never saw a doctor or the police come to see the body before it was buried.

"About two months after the death of the first man that I buried there was another death on the farm. A worker that I knew by the name of John, died in the fields. It was about midday. The boss boy called us together and I saw John's body on the ground. Boss boy, Philip, told some of the workers to take John's body and put it on the trailer—then all of us got on to the trailer and boss boy, Abram, drove it back to our prison. When we arrived there boss boy, Philip, told George Dube and some others to take John's body and put it in the room for the dead. This was on Saturday. On Sunday I saw Philip and George Dube making the coffin. When the coffin was finished I assisted George and boss boy, Philip, to put the body in the coffin. After that Philip selected some others for the purpose of burying John. I was not present when John was buried. Again, no police or doctor examined the body before it was buried.

"Before I had finished my first month there I tried to escape with some other workers but I was caught and brought back to the farm. When I arrived in the field the son, Jan Potgieter, ordered me to lie down on the ground and then told boss boy, Stephen, to beat me up. Stephen hit me on the back with his knobkerrie; I could not count the number of blows I received. I screamed loudly but he only stopped beating me when I started to cough blood. I coughed blood for a week after the assault. I still went on working. After that I never tried to escape again. In all, I worked there for 9 months and at the end of 9 months I was paid 14 pounds."

George Dube, mentioned by Robert in his affidavit, also came to see me. He confirmed the account of John's death.

"After I had been on the farm for just over a month," he said, "there was a new arrival by the name of John. I spoke to him and he told me he came from Alexandra Township. Two days after he arrived, it was on Saturday morning about midday, he was assaulted by boss-boys, Abram and Philip. Abram was walking up and down the line of workers and striking them to get them to work faster. I was slightly in front of John and saw Abram strike John on the back of the head with a knob-kerrie. John fell backwards on to the ground and Abram struck him again. Abram then called Philip and they tried to get him up by holding John under the armpits. All the other workers stopped their work and looked on. We saw John's head rolling on his neck. Abram and Philip signalled to us to come to them. When we came John was lying on the ground. I went over to him — I tried to close his eyes but they would not close. I realized he was dead. Philip then started to tell us that John had died because of the heat. He told us to take John's body and put it on a trailer. The other workers put John's body on my back and I took the body and put it on a trailer. The trailer was then taken by a tractor and all of us returned with the body to the prison. John's body was then placed in the room for the injured and the dead and we were then locked up.

"On Sunday morning Philip called me and gave me a hammer and some nails and told me to look around for some planks for a coffin for John. I made the coffin and later helped

Philip place John's body in it. I and Philip then carried the coffin to a grave which had already been dug up by other workers on the farm. John was then buried. There are other graves at the place where John was buried. When the incident was discussed by the workers later I was told that John was not the first one to die on the farm.

"John's body was not examined by any doctor after he died. The police were not called to examine the body. Had anyone examined the body either that Saturday or the Sunday morning we buried him I would have known about it because the body was in the room which was kept for the injured and the dead and to get into that room anyone must come through the door to our prison."

Altogether, I saw almost a score of witnesses who told me substantially the same story. I took down all their statements but decided that it was not necessary to have their affidavits filed at this stage. Three affidavits were signed and when all this was complete I telephoned George Bizos, an advocate at the bar, and made an appointment to see him.

"Well, Joel," said George, when I walked into his office, "what trouble have you brought up now?"

I was probably sharp with him for I was still upset by what the witnesses had told me. I refused to give him any details. I wanted the papers themselves to convey the shocking story and did not want to prepare him for it. All I told him was that these papers, in my opinion, supported bringing a habeas corpus petition to court. However, I wanted him to read them and come to his own conclusion.

"Right," he said, "then I'll take them home, read them, and phone you this evening."

I went home and waited impatiently through the lovely, sunny, peaceful afternoon. The autumn leaves were bronze-colored and flowers were everywhere. Cosmos, a small white and light-purple daisy, grew profusely in all the empty fields. I strolled down to the little park near our house for a while and watched white children enjoying themselves in their white park, and white tennis players enjoying themselves on the white tennis court in the sun.

At last, soon after 6 P.M., George phoned. His tone was

serious and he asked me to come to see him right away. He
agreed that we should act immediately but thought the
allegations were so serious that a senior counsel should be
brought into the matter. The judges would possibly treat
senior counsel with more respect and take more account of
what he had to say. I agreed with him and George arranged a
consultation with Maisels for Monday. We also briefly discussed the question of putting these allegations to the police. I
was against this course of action as I knew from past
experience that the police were not to be trusted.

Early on Monday morning we met in Maisels' chambers. He
lit his pipe, using the matchbox to shield the match above the
pipe—a risky procedure indeed. Then he drew the flame
downward by sucking strongly on the pipe stem. I was
reminded of all the pipe smoking in the Nelson Langa case.

With a twinkle in his eye he said to me, "Who are you going
to fry this time, Joel?"

I smiled and George briefly explained the issues involved.

"Well," said Maisels, "let's see the papers," and I handed
them to him. He read and reread them, lighting his pipe again
and again, and we remained silent until he had finished. He
then threw the papers on the desk and said, "Damn the
bastards."

We discussed in some detail the procedures we should
adopt. We decided to serve the papers on the farmer before
proceeding to court; I was to go to Heidelberg to serve them
personally. I did not want to take this journey on my own so I
took my clerk with me.

On the way I thought I would call at the office of the deputy
sheriff and ask him to serve the papers. I knew this was a risk
as it was possible that the farmer had influence with the
deputy sheriff as he did with the police and this could delay
service. My suspicions later proved to be fully justified. The
deputy sheriff, in fact, acted in this matter for the farmer as
his attorney. However, I called at his office. As good fortune
would have it, he had to attend a funeral that day and could
not serve the papers. I was compelled to proceed on my own
but he did send a junior clerk from his office with me. Later
this clerk filed an affidavit on behalf of the farmer. However,

at the time I was happy to have another person with me since I was not eager to confront the farmer without a number of witnesses.

We left Heidelberg on a sunny afternoon and traveled along a wide dirt track that was in very good condition. Potgieter owned three adjoining farms of about ten thousand *morgan* (one *morgan* equals about ten acres). His huge house was in the middle of all his land. As far as the eye could see, and in every direction, all the land belonged to him. Next to the house were at least six garages for the many cars he and his family owned, and not far away was his John Deere Tractor Agency and Repair Shop.

We stopped near the house and began walking toward it. A huge, fat man in khaki trousers and khaki shirt and carrying a hippo whip, whom I recognized from the descriptions I had as the farmer himself, came up and spoke to me in Afrikaans. *"Ja, wat soek julle?"* (What do you want?)

I asked him whether he was Petrus Johannes Potgieter and he said he was. As I began explaining the nature of the papers that I wished to serve on him he interrupted me and said, *"Kom binne."* (Come inside.) Without waiting to see if we followed he turned around and walked into his house. Reluctant as I was to go with him, I had to if the papers were to be served. Inside, he called to his sons and two responded. They were both well over six feet tall, well built, and also dressed in khaki clothes. One carried a *sjambok* and the other a little stick like a military baton. As briefly as I could I explained my business to them. Then I left the papers, and with as much dignity as possible, I made a quick retreat.

Once in the car we shot off and I drove as fast as I could for the next twenty miles. Only then did I relax. On my return to Johannesburg, I reported to both George and Maisels that the papers had been served and I completed the necessary affidavit of service. We were due to go to court on the following day.

The legal work was completed and I was determined now that the farm labor scheme, its corruptness, and its illegality should be totally exposed in order to end it once and for all. I had been given a second chance. My experience in the Nelson

Langa case had taught me that exposés could not be left to the haphazard whim of a casual newspaper reporter. Therefore, as soon as I could, I went to see a friend and professor of mine. I had kept him informed of what I was doing over the years and he was quite familiar with the background of these applications. We arranged a meeting of four or five influential persons. One was a senior colonial service officer, whose government was supposed to look after Africans who had come from that territory and were now in South Africa. He was concerned that many of the workers on the farm came from his colony. Another was an alert and brilliant journalist. Two others represented churches and one was a retired but knowledgeable politician.

When we met I explained to them what the affidavits revealed and gave them a full picture of the farm labor scheme. I pointed out the urgent need to expose the scheme so that the public would realize its implications and horror and put an end to it. After a lively discussion they all agreed to do what they could. The reporter, although himself a conservative man, working for an even more conservative newspaper—the largest single daily newspaper in the country—appreciated the illegality and injustices perpetrated in this scheme and was sure that his paper would publish the facts. I stressed to him the importance of being accurate and having no exaggerations of any kind whatsoever in any articles. It was sufficient that the facts speak for themselves. He promised to follow the proceedings closely so as to ensure such accuracy; he could, of course, carry no story until the matter was mentioned in court.

Next day, Maisels, George, and I went to Pretoria separately. Dorkus Sadika and my clerk accompanied me. When we arrived at the court we waited outside the main entrance, anticipating that if Musa Sadika were brought there, he would be taken through that entrance, but we saw no sign of him anywhere. About thirty minutes before court was due to open three Africans appeared. Two seemed to be guiding the third. I walked Dorkus past them casually, asking her to take a close look to see if she recognized her husband. We passed them without any reaction from her and walked back again. She told me her husband was not one of them. Another fifteen minutes or so passed and no one else entered. I urged Dorkus to have another and closer look at the three men who were still standing nearby. I was sure that the man in the middle must be Musa Sadika. He was shorter than the others and answered the description that I had. She went up to him and searched his face carefully. She spun around with her hand at her mouth and gasped, "It's him, it's him—I did not know him. What have they done to him?"

I made a mental note of her words and watched Musa. He did not dare move or speak even though he had just seen his wife. Then I walked up to him, and the boss-boys warned me away. I brushed their movement aside, determined to establish whether Musa was being guarded or whether he was, in fact, a free man. I told his wife to speak to him. As she approached him again the three began to move away, but we followed them.

I asked, "Are you James Musa Sadika?"

The guards said, "You are not allowed to talk to him."

"Who said so?" I challenged as aggressively as I could.

"We have been told," they said. "Only the court can speak to him, you cannot speak to him."

"I don't care what you have been told, here is the wife of this man—she will talk to him."

Dorkus hesitated and the guards started off again, taking Musa with them by the arm. Dorkus was now in tears. I tried to comfort her but she was inconsolable. I immediately went and reported to Maisels and George what had happened.

When the court convened, the judge appeared to me to be very subdued. I was sure it was a result of reading the affidavits. They would subdue most men. Maisels informed him of the events outside court and asked that Musa Sadika be called and permitted to talk to his wife. Judge L-Snyman called Musa into the witness box.

He presented a pitiful sight. In his meanness, the farmer had not even had the sense to put him in new or clean clothes. Musa was dressed in shabby overalls and a filthy, torn khaki shirt. He scratched himself continually and he could not stand still. He was obviously frightened and confused. There was an open wound on the top of his head and the raw skin stood out against the blackness of his hair. His dejection and fear were so apparent that no evidence was really necessary, but the judge pursued his questioning.

"Is that your wife in court?" he asked through the interpreter.

"Yes," Musa said hesitantly.

The judge then tried to explain to Musa the nature of these proceedings and the protection that he, the judge, could afford him, if what was in the papers was true. However, we doubted that Musa understood. Finally the judge asked him whether he wanted to talk to his wife.

"Yes," said Musa, and the court then adjourned.

After Musa had spoken to his wife alone she came to me.

"He is afraid," she cried, "he says they have told him this morning on the way here from the farm that if he said anything about not wanting to return to the farm or said anything bad about the farm, tonight he will die. He would never see the sunrise again. He believes their threats." Sobbing, she told me he wanted to go back to the farm because he was afraid. "He will not listen to me," she said, in despair.

I decided that I should speak to Musa myself and was allowed to see him. I knew that I only had a few minutes with him. I knew also that Musa was ruled by fear and that there was no time for reason or persuasion. I had no alternative but to shock him into telling the court the truth.

"Musa," I said, "Potgieter is powerful, a very powerful man. You understand that." He agreed and I went on. "Although I am young, yet I am more powerful than he—do you hear me?" He did hear me but he doubted that what I said was true, that I was more powerful than Potgieter. "It is I who called Potgieter to bring you here; he did not want to bring you here and when you came here he did not want you to speak to your wife. Is that not so?" He agreed. I went on, "Nevertheless, you are here; you have spoken to your wife. Potgieter is angry but he has had to do what the court ordered." Pointing to Dorkus I said, "She was afraid to come here for she lives illegally in Alexandra Township but I brought her here in order that you could both be together. I have power that will protect you. I have heard you are an herbalist. Is that not so?"

"Yes," he said, "that is so."

"Then you will understand something of my power," I said. "This power brought you to court so you can tell the court the truth. You must tell the court today whether you want to go back to the farm or whether you want to go home with your wife. The court will make an order for what you want." I dropped my voice to a soft, quiet tone. "You will go and tell this court today the truth—you will tell the court whether you really want to go home with your wife or not and if you do not tell the truth I will follow you in the lie that you tell. You cannot suffer from the truth, you will suffer from the lie. Do you hear me—do you understand me?"

"I hear you," he said, and he began shaking and sobbing. I knew then that I had broken through his fear of Potgieter.

We went back into court and Musa was called into the box and sworn in. Hesitantly, but convincingly, he told the court he wanted to go home to his wife and so it was ordered. Musa was released and the court once again adjourned.

The first battle had been won and I was exhilarated. I took Musa and Dorkus home with me and called a doctor in order to get a medical report on his condition. I also called a cameraman to take pictures of how he looked.

The doctor in his affidavit said:

"On examination I found:

"A) The subject was in a filthy condition and continuously scratched his body

"B) He was thin and showed signs of weight loss

"C) There were numerous scars on the back of the head

"D) A pustular rash of the back and the arms

"E) Typical dermatitis of pellagra of the legs, forearms and face

"F) His gums showed severe pyorrhoea

"G) His general muscle tone and skin turger were suggestive of severe malnutrition

"Continuing my examination, I found the scars present were of different stages, varying from recent to some months old;

"A) Seven were seen on the head, each about $1/2$ inch in diameter (others may have been present under the hair)

"B) Fourteen roughly circular scars on the upper back, each about $1/4$ inch in diameter

"C) There was a 3 inch linear scab postero-medially on the right upper arm.

"D) A two-inch scab on the right elbow where there was also a circular scar $1/4$ inch in diameter

"E) There was a half inch linear scar on the left ankle

"In my opinion, the examination and findings are consistent with repeated severe assaults with blunt instruments. The linear scars on the arm and left ankle are consistent with assault with a possibly thin sharp instrument. His nutritional state suggest severe deprivation of food in recent months."

Musa bathed, was given clean clothes, some hot soup, and was put to bed. The next day we took a statement from him in which he confirmed the assaults and the forced labor conditions.

Arising out of the allegations in the petition, that in the past six months two farm workers had been assaulted and died on the farm and were buried in great haste before the police or any doctor examined the bodies, the Heidelberg police now contacted me and asked me to accompany them with my clients to the farm to point out the graveyard. They wanted to exhume the bodies. I did not trust them but was obliged to accede to their request. I visited the police and made arrangements which we considered necessary.

It was important to protect my clients, most of whom were living and working in the area without official permission; to ensure that they would not be subjected to any harassment or intimidation, I accompanied them to the police station. I also wanted to know from the police who was going to conduct this investigation. I was not prepared to have anything to do with an investigation undertaken by the captain who owned the blue Mercedes.

During my consultation with the police I learned the truth of another of Josiah's allegations. The police told me that Potgieter had a son who had "got away with murder." One of

Potgieter's daughters had married a local boy who was "no good." After the marriage he slept with a "Kaffir-maid." When this was discovered, Potgieter's son shot and killed his brother-in-law. He was arrested and charged with murder but pleaded insanity. The local court referred him to a nearby mental institution and he was subsequently committed there. The case was then dropped and some months later the son was released and allowed to return to the farm. There was no fantasy in Josiah's story. More and more he was proving to be horribly correct in all he had told me.

Early Saturday morning the police called for my clients and myself and we were driven to the farm. It was not difficult to see graveyards. We saw the telltale mounds of earth in a number of places. My clients pointed out a particular grave which they said was that of one of the men whose death they had witnessed. The police proceeded with the exhumation and eventually a makeshift coffin was brought to the surface. It was almost falling apart and it smelled horrible. Hurriedly, it was put into the back of a police van, which drove off immediately. After five months in the ground, in a makeshift coffin, it seemed unlikely that any conclusive evidence would be found. I wondered what purpose would be served by having a postmortem examination at this stage.

In fact, the postmortem result was inconclusive. It was only many years later that I learned the real truth about this episode. I was told by one of the persons present at the postmortem examination that, in fact, the police had exhumed the wrong body. There was a second corpse buried two feet under the top body and that was the body that we were seeking. Reflecting on how I had been hoodwinked, I realized that burying two bodies in the same grave was ingenious and no murderer could think of a better place to hide a body.

The press had heard about our grisly mission and had followed the police cars to the farm. While the coffin was being brought to the surface, reporters rushed onto the farmer's land and before he could order them off, they had taken a number of pictures. They also followed the van carrying the body to Heidelberg. The next day, the exhumation, the petition, and the supporting affidavits were splashed across the Sunday newspapers. During the next week, a great amount of attention was focused on the farm labor scheme. Wives and mothers, whose husbands and sons had disappeared, came in a continuing stream to my office. Some of those who had been arrested were boys of twelve or thirteen, not even subject to the pass laws, and too young to be officially employed, but the scheme was operated ruthlessly and recklessly in order to satisfy the farmers' thirst for cheap labor. Sometimes, it was sufficient for me merely to make a phone call to a farmer and he would deliver the man I wanted to my office within twenty-four hours of the call. No farmer appeared to be prepared to defend his actions in court.

The state, however, was still not deterred from continuing the scheme though it was clearly illegal. I continued to make one habeas corpus application after another, so as to repeatedly expose the scheme in court. Each story had its own horror and led to one sensational exposure after another. Newspapers, reporting these issues, had recognized the implications of the scheme and often used their own initiative in exposing it. One reporter had found an old lady who had a son on a farm and he went there with her one Sunday afternoon. The farmer at first refused them permission to see the son, but they persisted and, finally, were allowed to look for him. The reporter, who told me the farm was named *Straffontein* (Place Where a Beating Is Administered), described the conditions he saw. "I have, in the course of my journalistic career over many years investigated living conditions in notorious jails, slums and refugee camps in the Far East, England and Africa, but I have never before seen human beings living in more squalid surroundings and in such abject filth and misery as those I encountered when I entered that room. That Sunday was a bitterly cold day and the men had gathered some wood and had lit a fire in the room. There was no open window and the room was in semi-darkness. The smoke was so thick that it was almost impossible to see from one end of the room to the other. Sacks were scattered on the floor which was filthy as were the walls. The stench of dirty bodies, smoke and general filthiness was overpowering. There were about 30 men in the room, sitting in groups on the floor; they looked gaunt and ill and were inadequately clothed. Some sat head in hands on three rickety, sack-covered wooden benches."

The reporter demanded the son's release. When the farmer refused, he brought the mother to me, and we were successful in freeing her son.

Armed as I now was with an enormous mass of facts, I decided that the time had come to make an appeal to the two parliamentary ministers concerned. I wrote to the minister of justice and the minister of Bantu affairs, requesting a judicial inquiry into all these allegations and calling on them to abandon the farm labor scheme. Later, I released my appeal to the press and this itself made the headlines. The deputy minister of Bantu administration dealt with the matter in Parliament and simply denied that the farm labor scheme existed.

I was determined to establish the truth, so I readily accepted his challenge. Often working twenty hours a day, I proceeded with each and every case that was brought to me. By this time, the farmers themselves had lost confidence in the scheme and feared the exposure. Usually, as soon as I filed a petition, they would surrender the worker named. When they protested to the authorities, the government assured them that in any litigation it would act for them and provide free legal services.

I was forcing the judges, one after the other, to face the facts they read in the papers placed before them. The few farmers who opposed these petitions refused to give evidence when called upon to do so. All of them feared the witness box. At last one of the judges suggested that the government set its house in order. He did not go so far as to condemn the officials or the farmers but he did draw attention to the illegality of the procedure.

One day the chief rabbi of Johannesburg, who had been approached by a group of Jewish farmers, asked me whether I would address a meeting of farmers in the Bethal area. He himself agreed that what was being done was immoral, but he could not guarantee my safety, so I refused. He thereupon called a meeting at his house in Johannesburg and some forty or fifty farmers attended. They told me all of their difficulties and hardships and asked me to listen to their side of the matter. They assured me that if I wanted any "boy," I had only to phone and that "boy" would be delivered to my office without delay. I would get what I wanted, they said, and they would be spared court action and scandal.

I listened to them patiently and then turned to one of them and said, "Tell me, how many of these men have you got working on your farm?"

"Twenty-eight," he said, "but if there is any particular one you want you can have him."

I told him I wanted every one of his laborers acquired under the scheme. When he objected I said, "Right. If you do not want to give me all your labor, then don't give me any of it. I will take it anyway. For each man brought to court will give me the name of another to be rescued and so a chain reaction will set in."

The farmers were convinced that I would not see reason and I knew that they saw nothing wrong in what they were doing. But I urged the chief rabbi to make them see the light. I assured him, and all of them, that I would wait only until Monday before taking further steps.

On that very Sunday afternoon I received an answer. Two truckloads of poorly clad, dirty Africans were unloaded onto the driveway of my house.

"You wanted them, have them," said the farmer.

My house became a kind of farm labor welfare office. My wife and her friends set up a soup kitchen serving bread and gallons of hot soup. Piles of clothing were donated, too. At times as many as five lawyers, typists, interpreters, and many other volunteers were working all over my house. People sat everywhere. Statements were taken, typed, translated, and sworn to. Petitions and affidavits were dictated right onto the typewriter. There was no time for changes, no time for error, and no time for any new drafting. The house became a crazy habeas corpus factory.

After the affidavits were signed, white volunteers would drive the Africans home, running the risk of entering the townships without permission of the authorities. Any African whose statement we still had to take would sleep somewhere

in my house. This was quite illegal but there was no alternative. At all times I had to ensure that no one was picked up
again by the police to disappear once more on the farms.

Now the paper headlined the news: JEWISH FARMERS
SURRENDER FARM LABOR. At home and all over the world, the
brutal farm labor conditions were written up in the newspapers. Many churches and women's organizations joined the
fight. The powerful African National Congress, then still a
lawful organization, called for a boycott of potatoes, the crop
grown on many of the forced labor farms. The government
suffered much adverse publicity at home and abroad.

Then the court ruled in our favor in the Potgieter case.
Although Potgieter denied the allegations made against him,
he refused to testify in court. We, therefore, asked for a
judgment in our favor and finally succeeded in obtaining it.
Musa Sadika, however, never recovered from his ordeal. He
can be seen in the streets of Johannesburg today, carrying a
pass he made himself, wearing a full-length white cotton robe
and a Muslim red fez on his head. He sings and chants and
talks nonsense; he holds out his hands for alms. He himself is
quite harmless but the harm done to him is permanent.

I refused to let up on the pressure and the government
could find no way of stopping me. The minister finally
announced in Parliament that the farm labor scheme would be
suspended. Telegrams, letters, phone calls, and messages of
congratulation poured in. Even the ministers of the pro-
government Dutch Reform Church applauded me as a Christian hero. I had made many friends; I had also made many
enemies.

My jubilation was short-lived. Within weeks the government passed an amended Prisons Act of 1959. Under the act,
short-term offenders were processed quickly through the
courts and then sent to the farms. The act specifically
provided that such farms were considered to be prisons. It
was made a criminal offense to publish anything concerning
prison conditions without the prior consent of the prison
commissioner.

Some six years later, a leading English-speaking morning
newspaper, the *Rand Daily Mail,* its chief editor, Laurence

Gander, and one of its ace reporters, Benjamin Pogrund, dared to expose brutal prison conditions. Their exposure, in turn, led to their being prosecuted by the state, and the litigation lasted some five years. Eventually, prison sentences were passed on many of those who informed to the newspaper and its staff members, and the editor and journalist were convicted. The paper suffered a severe financial loss.

The state was determined to uphold and protect the system. Nevertheless, the exposure of the farm labor scheme had not been without some success. It inspired further opposition to the government and supplied undeniable facts about injustice and racial oppression. It added one small stone to the avalanche of opposition that was to sweep down on the government in the next few years, and which looked for a moment as though it might be great enough to sweep aside the bastions of racism built up over the long years.

VIII
WINDS OF
CHANGE

At the beginning of 1948 the Nationalist party came to power in South Africa by a narrow majority. It has remained in power continuously since then and still governs the country. Its platform was *apartheid* and *baaskap*. *Apartheid* is the policy of enforced separation of black and white people in every sphere and the prohibition of any integration of the races. *Baaskap* means "keep the white man boss." The Nationalist party gained its direct support mainly from Afrikaners, Dutch-speaking white voters, but all whites —English or Afrikaners —enjoy the privileges and power that the doctrine of white supremacy gives them.

The Afrikaners have always considered themselves the civilizing force in the country, having trekked inland by ox wagon, carrying a gun in one hand and the Bible in the other. They are devout Calvinists and the teachings of Calvin and of the Old Testament are still the mainstay of the religious beliefs of those who attend the various Dutch Reform churches in South Africa. During World War II, while a combination of English-speaking and Afrikaans-speaking white people backed General Jan Smuts in joining the allied forces at war with Germany, the bulk of the Afrikaners remained staunch in their support of the Nationalist party and were sympathetic to the Nazis. In 1942 Balthazar John Vorster (presently prime minister of South Africa) said at a Nationalist *strydag* (an exclusive party gathering): "We stand for Christian National-ism which is an ally of National Socialism. You can call it the anti-democratic principle of dictatorship if you wish. In Italy it is called Fascism . . . in Germany National Socialism . . . and in South Africa Christian Nationalism."

Vorster has never repudiated this statement of his beliefs. During World War II Vorster, together with the present chief of the security police, General Pietrus Johannes Van den Bergh, was interned as a pro-Nazi sympathizer. In 1942, Dr. Hendrik Frensch Verwoerd, prime minister before Vorster and the great apostle of *apartheid,* was found by the courts in South Africa to have disseminated *Zeesen* (enemy) propaganda.

After World War II, while the rest of the world moved forward to accept the principles of racial harmony and integration, South African whites moved the other way. Immediately after coming to power in 1948, the Nationalist party accelerated the entrenchment of *apartheid.* It reconstituted the base of power to ensure everlasting white domination. It removed from the voters' roll those few remaining black voters having any kind of common voting rights. Parliament was reformed, as were the courts, and the constitution was drastically altered and, in 1961, made a republican constitution. The police force and the military were taken over by Nationalist party supporters who now are the senior officers in both forces. These men all opposed South Africa's entry into World War II and sympathized with the German cause. The country has now been made a white fortress against the threat of a black takeover.

Fear of a black rebellion dominates the politics of the minority white population. Every effort has been made by the ruling whites to split and divide the majority black people. Great emphasis has been placed on the tribal allegiance of each ethnic group and each of these has been separated into "its own separate residential area." At the same time, great efforts have been made to unite all whites. Afrikaner politicians begged the English-speaking whites to strike an alliance with them and unite against *die swart gevaar* (the black danger).

In the early 1950s various black organizations, struggling to bring unity among the government's opponents, joined radical white organizations to protest the unjust and discriminatory racial laws by a passive resistance campaign. They adopted Mahatma Gandhi's technique. Gandhi, after all, had spent the major portion of his earlier life in South Africa, where he first developed the ideas on passive resistance that he later took to India. Deliberately breaking the law and seeking imprisonment, thousands of blacks were arrested. The government then passed new laws giving it vicious new powers against anyone breaking the law by way of protest. Punishment included long prison sentences and savage whippings and it broke the back of the passive resistance movement.

In the late 1950s the government, which had increased its strength in each election, decided to extend the pass laws to African women. Africans already knew too well the sufferings inflicted on all of them by the application of the pass laws to African men. They knew that pass laws for women would lead inevitably to more fines and more imprisonment, and would result in more families being broken up. This extension of the *apartheid* laws led to a period of increasing African militancy and opposition to white rule, both organized and spontaneous.

In 1958 the African National Congress (ANC) organized nationwide demonstrations against the application of the pass laws to women. Thousands of women were arrested throughout the land and witnesses spoke of those arrested being beaten up by the police. Indeed it is the hallmark of South African police activity that white police indulge in excessive violence and brutality while carrying out the white man's law. In Johannesburg, the police arrested some two thousand African women who were charged and brought before the courts. Nelson Mandela, president of the ANC and now serving a life sentence on Robben Island, asked me to be one of the attorneys representing these women. Unable to cope with the number of prisoners, the large open spaces of the magistrate's court were hurriedly converted into makeshift courts, so that the hundreds of women, squatting on the polished linoleum floors of the central passage of the court building with their babies, could be charged. In the cells in the basement, hundreds more were charged before magistrates in other makeshift courts. Confusion and disorder went hand in hand with the inadequate and crowded facilities. Most of the trials were rushed. To clear the courts and the prisons, the junior judges fined the women five to eight pounds and allowed payment in installments in order to clear out as many as possible and so ease the congestion in the cells.

At the same time, riots occurred in many rural areas. In Zeerust, in the western Transvaal, hundreds of men and women were arrested. The police called in the army and the air force to help them handle the massive protests, and thousands of Africans fled across the border into neighboring Botswana (formerly Bechuanaland). In the northern Transvaal area, in Sekhukhuneland, rioting Bapedi tribesmen and women rose in opposition to the government and again hundreds of people were arrested.

Cato Manor in Natal, a black ghetto outside the large port city of Durban, was also involved in bloody riots. The conditions in the ghetto were among the most appalling anywhere and a typhoid epidemic had broken out. Only when this happened did the predominantly English-speaking municipality decide to act. As part of its cleanup operation, it ordered that action be taken against women who brewed beer at home for their menfolk, a Zulu tradition. The police were instructed to search for and destroy all liquor in homes and thousands of gallons of beer were destroyed. In retaliation, the women raided and destroyed a white-controlled municipal beer hall (from which the municipality profited and which made it object to the competition of the "home-brewers"). Police rushed to the scene and attacked the women with clubs and batons. The African men, returning from work and seeing what was happening, came to the rescue and attacked the police. Massive rioting followed and resulted in twenty-five buildings being gutted by fire and seven others being seriously damaged. Police then used submachine guns and killed three men and injured fourteen. (In earlier riots here there were 142 deaths and 1,087 people injured.)

In response to the rioting the municipal authorities suspended all services to Cato Manor, including sewage facilities and water supplies, for a period of seven weeks. Later, a commission of inquiry condemned the municipality for its suspension of vital services and found that the root causes of the riots were the dire poverty of the Africans and the poor housing conditions.

Riots also occurred in Pondoland, north of the Transkei, where Africans rose in rebellion against the white regime's imposition of "the betterment scheme," which resulted in forcing Africans off the land and compelling them to "seek work" on white farms, and in the fencing of land, in the culling of cattle, and in the forced removal of whole communities from their ancestral homes. The government responded by passing an emergency law, Proclamation 400. It was to remain in force only for the state of emergency but, in fact, has remained a law ever since it was enforced in 1960. In terms of these regulations, which applied throughout the Transkei, the minister of Bantu administration was empowered to prohibit any person from entering or being in the Transkei or from leaving it. The proclamation authorized the control of meetings, the restriction and control of all statements whether verbal or written, and the extension of the powers of state officials or a chief or headmen. The chiefs and headmen were given special powers to summarily try and penalize people and the native commissioner and police officers were given the power of arrest and detention without trial. A person so arrested and detained was not permitted to consult any legal adviser.

Despite these regulations, in June, 1960, heavily armed police, aided by helicopters, clashed with several thousand tribesmen in a valley adjoining Ngquza Hill, between Bizana and Lusikisiki. Tear gas and smoke bombs were dropped and police vehicles approached from two directions. The Africans raised a white flag and walked toward the police who then opened fire. The tribesmen fled but were pursued into the bush. Later the justice minister told Parliament that six Africans had been shot dead. Subsequently, a constable at the inquest told the court that eleven Africans had been killed. Pondo spokesmen stated that the true number was thirty. When an exhumation was ordered during the inquest proceedings, it was found that three of the eleven bodies exhumed had died as a result of bullet wounds in the back of the head. The inquest magistrate found that two policemen had fired submachine guns and said police action was "unjustified, excessive and reckless." Later, when dependents of those killed sued for damages, the justice minister passed an Indemnity Act (Act 61 of 1961), which was retroactive and made it impossible for the relatives to proceed with their actions.

African resistance increased and was met by even more violence by the police. The rule of the white man became a reign of terror. Cato Manor once more became the scene of riots. Still intent on destroying Zulu beer, a score of policemen on a liquor raid were attacked by a crowd. Finding themselves cut off and outnumbered, the police took refuge in a house. The white policemen, who were armed, barricaded themselves in a front room of the house. The black policemen, who are not permitted to carry guns, positioned themselves in another room. The mob broke in and killed four white and five black policemen and seriously injured the others. Massive arrests were later made but this did little to still the desire of the police for vengeance.

My frequent contact with the police and prison officials made me sharply aware not only of the mounting tension between the races but also of the hatred and fear white police have for blacks. A prison major told me in conversation that in his view the justice minister should have ordered the air force to bomb Cato Manor and kill every "Kaffir" in it. "The trouble," he said, "is that life for the black man today is getting too easy and too good." White policemen were obviously itching to use their guns on black men and they soon had the opportunity to do just that.

Opposition to the government, and particularly to the pass laws, had been growing apace. Black organizations had used the facts disclosed in the farm labor habeas corpus applications to assist them in their campaign against the pass laws. In 1959 the ANC had called for a potato boycott, as it was mainly the potato farmers who used the farm labor scheme. This boycott was partially successful; sales dropped and potato prices fell on the open market, but the farm labor scheme went on. However, the Africans were encouraged by the success of the boycott weapon and decided to use it more often and more effectively.

On December 12, 1959, the ANC held its annual conference, and a call went out for a boycott of all South African goods. A decision was also made to fight the pass laws and March 31, 1960, was designated Anti-Pass Day.

On December 20, 1959, the Pan African Congress (PAC) also called a conference. The PAC had been formed a year earlier by Mangaliso Robert Sobukwe and his followers, who broke away from the ANC. It was opposed to *apartheid* and to multiracialism and its slogan was "Africa for the Africans." Its December conference adopted resolutions calling for a "status campaign," demanding that Africans be shown courtesy by whites. It also decided to launch "decisive and final positive action" against the pass laws under the slogan "No Bail, No Defense, No Fine."

In February, fourteen black and white organizations joined together and produced a pamphlet condemning the pass laws. These organizations made representation to the Johannesburg City Council and presented it with a memorandum. A silent antipass demonstration was staged on the steps of the Johannesburg City Hall.

On March 18, Robert Sobukwe, president of the PAC, announced at a press conference that his organization planned a campaign aimed at the abolition of the pass laws and that this campaign would commence on March 21. Members were being called upon to leave their passes at home and to surrender themselves for arrest at the nearest police station. Should the police refuse to arrest them, their instructions were to go home and return to the police stations later in the day. The slogan "No Bail, No Defense, No Fine," would be strictly adhered to. After serving their jail sentences, the campaigners would again offer themselves for arrest. Sobuk-we stressed that the campaign would be peaceful and would be conducted in a spirit of nonviolence. He said, "If the police are interested in maintaining law and order, they will have no difficulty at all."

Sobukwe further stated that this was all part of the PAC's aim to attain freedom and independence for all the Africans in the country by 1963. He called on the ANC to support the PAC campaign.

The secretary-general of the ANC wrote to Sobukwe saying that his organization could not support the PAC campaign. He termed it sensational and said that the people were not properly prepared for it and it had no reasonable prospect of success.

Nevertheless, prepared or not, the PAC went into action. On March 21, at a number of police stations in widely scattered areas, the demonstrations went off according to plan. Sobukwe himself and a number of companions presented themselves without their passes at the Orlando police station in Johannesburg and they were arrested. At various other police stations throughout the country, the police refused to arrest volunteers and persuaded them to go home. However, at Evaton some ten thousand Africans gathered outside the police station and demanded to be arrested. The police refused and when the people became excited, they called in military aircraft, which dived low over their heads and dispersed the crowd.

Early that same morning between five and ten thousand Africans marched on the municipal offices at Sharpeville, a black ghetto serving a huge steel and coal industrial center some thirty-five miles south of Johannesburg. The crowd was noisy and excitable but it was not hostile and it was not armed. When it arrived at the police station the police called for reinforcements, and armored vehicles, mounted with machine guns, were brought in. The security police officer in charge at the time stepped into the crowd and arrested one of the African leaders in front of everyone. A scuffle took place—stones were thrown—and the Africans surged forward. Two police officers tried in vain to speak to the crowd over loudspeakers but they could not make themselves heard. Suddenly, and without warning, two white policemen opened fire although no orders had been given to fire. Fifty other policemen followed suit, using service revolvers, rifles, and machine guns. The crowd wavered for a moment and then broke up. On March 22, it was officially announced that 69 Africans had been killed and 178 wounded, of whom 40 were women and 8 were children. Subsequently, the evidence showed that firing continued even after the people began to flee, and some 155 people were shot in the back.

The tragedy of Sharpeville shook the whites into a realization of the fear and hatred flowing through the land. The repercussions were so great that they almost overwhelmed the powerful white regime—it floundered and nearly fell. The then leader of the ANC, Chief Albert Luthuli, a Nobel Peace Prize winner, called on all Africans and others in South Africa to observe March 28 as a day of prayer for the Africans killed at Sharpeville and at Langa, near Cape Town, where demonstrations had also resulted in African deaths by the police. In addition, the ANC called for a stay-at-home strike. Meanwhile, on the stock market in Johannesburg there was panic—and capital fled the country. Rioting and unrest spread throughout South Africa. The government declared a state of emergency and called up police and army reservists. Clearly shaken by the events, it announced on March 26 the suspension of the pass laws.

Many in South Africa and beyond its borders doubted whether the government could succeed in holding the rebellion in check. Sitting on my verandah at home during the long weekend following the mass stay-at-home called for by the ANC, I thought I was living in the time of revolution. African resistance was so widespread, I was sure it would succeed and topple the government. I had assisted my wife in laying in a stock of food and purchased gas cookers as I fully expected the electricity supplies to be cut off.

Throughout the country, however, the government had been organizing its forces to oppose the resistance. The African organizations, unable to mobilize as effectively or as efficiently, and being quite unprepared, did not sufficiently respond to the events following the tragedy at Sharpeville. The police, backed by the armed forces, acted with speed and decision. The ANC and The PAC were made unlawful organizations. All the known leaders who could be found were arrested and detained under the emergency laws indefinitely and without trial. In addition, mass arrests were made all around the country. The blacks were unarmed and did not foresee the confrontation that then took place.

By April 4 the government was in sufficient control of the situation for the deputy commissioner of police to announce the reimposition and reinforcement of the pass laws. The ANC and the PAC made known their decision to work as underground movements although many of their leaders had either been arrested, had gone into hiding, or had left the country. A new form of struggle for the black resistance movement had begun.

Although I expected to be arrested during the state of emergency, I was left alone. Perhaps the reason for this was that I was not involved in any organization and was, therefore, probably considered to be ineffective. No doubt, the police also knew that their leaving me untouched would prompt many people to wonder whether I was to be trusted. Actually, I was uncommitted and a member of no organization. I desired independence and I was determined to use my own judgment before taking any action. This was never accepted or appreciated by any of the committed party politicians. As expected, I was considered suspect by some and, by others, unreliable.

I had rejected the white rulers and their way of life and now I was not trusted by the activists among the white opposition groups. Furthermore, I knew that any black man who did not know me would regard me as just another white. Not only was I not a member of any political group but I practiced no religion and did not identify with any group whatsoever. My own decision made me a lonely man.

In June, 1960, in the middle of the emergency, I went overseas. I had been wondering whether I could still play a useful role in South Africa or whether it would be better for me and my family to leave the country and seek a new life elsewhere. As an English-speaking South African, and one whose parents had come from the United Kingdom, and from Ireland, I went to England to see if there was a place for me in that society.

Soon after arriving in London I found that I would have to requalify and take up articles with a lawyer. Only after three to five years could I be admitted to the bar in England and be able to practice and earn a living there. While going about the process of requalifying I found that I could earn only between six and eight pounds a week. I did not have enough capital to provide for my wife and family for more than a year and so it was impossible for me to think of practicing law in England. I could probably do much better in commerce but I was not enthusiastic about becoming either a businessman or acting in some kind of managerial capacity. I had already acquired the habit of living to serve some useful purpose or a cause of my own choosing.

I began to have serious doubts as to whether I should leave South Africa at all. Having made my inquiries in London I decided to devote the rest of my time there to lobbying against the *apartheid* policies of South Africa.

Before I left South Africa I had posted some of my farm labor papers to an address in London. Many of the farm laborers came from British protectorates and I now took these papers to members of the British government. I accused them of not being as energetic in looking after black citizens as they were in looking after white British subjects. The allegation was denied. I supplied details and was told that the matter would be investigated. I spoke at a Labor party meeting in the House of Commons and met Joshua Nkomo, a Zimbabwe leader. He and I sat up all night in the gallery of the House of Commons while the subject of Rhodesia was debated. Among others in London I met that grand radical leader, Thomas Fox Pitt, chairman of the Anti-Slavery Society. I worked with him in preparing copies of the farm labor affidavits for general distribution in London.

On my way back to South Africa I spent some time in Geneva working with the International Commission of Jurists. Later that organization produced a book, "South Africa and the Rule of Law." It published many of the allegations concerning the illegal farm labor scheme and its horrors.

Once back in South Africa I had finally to face the decision of whether or not to leave. While I was in England, my wife Jeanette had sold our house in preparation for a possible departure. Within weeks we would have to look for a new place to live. When I thought back over my overseas trip I recognized that I loved South Africa. Furthermore, I felt that I could still play a role in helping to change its way of life. There was obviously more purpose to my life here than anywhere else and so I decided that we should stay where we were. I remained steadfast in my refusal to associate with any groups and declined an invitation to join the Liberal party. (In any case I wanted immediate majority rule and no lawful group advocated that.) I decided to go about my business as a lawyer and continue to do what I could in that sphere.

The years to come were full of resistance and upheaval. Following the declaration of a state of emergency, Parliament passed successive security laws that, one by one, eroded what little was left of the rule of law in South Africa until the police state became firmly established by 1967. The establishment allowed dissident groups to be dealt with by mass arrests or by the police using what the courts termed excessive force against them. Sympathizers of blacks, especially attorneys who frequently defended blacks accused of various offenses, were dealt with by organizations such as the Ku Klux Klan, which harassed and intimidated them. In May, attorney Rowley Arenstein was attacked by the KKK at his house in Durban.

Despite the government's contention that the African political movements were inspired and activated by Communists, the courts in trying many of the opponents of the regime found that this was not so, nor was it true that the opponents of the government were determined to overthrow the state by violence. The most significant of such trials began in 1956 and became known as the Treason Trial. It involved defendants who were acquitted and recharged time and again until finally, on March 24, 1961, the presiding judge adjourned the hearing, stating that he and his two fellow judges required a few days to consider the arguments so far advanced by the defense. On March 29, all the accused in the four-year treason trial were once again acquitted and discharged on a unanimous verdict. It was found that the alleged policy of violence attributed to the ANC, and the fact that it was inspired and moved as a Communist organization, had not been proved. The prosecution had failed to show that the accused had personal knowledge of the Communist doctrine of violent revolution or that they propagated this doctrine.

Nevertheless, the ban on the ANC and the PAC remained. Despite the fact that Nelson Mandela was sought by the police, he escaped their net time and again while he led the underground ANC. He became known as the Black Pimpernel. In October, 1961, his writings and speeches were banned from publication or dissemination anywhere in South Africa. Eventually Mandela was arrested in August, 1962.

Over and above the arrest and trial of Nelson Mandela, numerous other leaders had been arrested or placed under house arrest, banned, or banished under severe restrictions to remote country areas. These included Africans, Indians, and whites. Subsequently, the government listed all the people banned and those listed were declared officially to be Communists. It was irrelevant whether or not they were indeed Communists—the government considered them to be so, and so they were Communists.

Many African leaders chose to remain as lawful opponents of the regime, but many others were convinced that working within the law would not bring any basic change. So the opposition was split up once more. In both urban and rural areas, African leaders prepared the people to leave the country to train as guerrilla fighters and to return to participate in the liberation of their homeland.

In December, 1961, *Umkonto we Sizwe* (Spear of the Nation) was formed as an independent body by the military arm of the ANC. It stated that it would carry on the struggle for freedom and democracy by new methods; that violence would no longer be met with nonviolent resistance only. It planned attacks on government installations, particularly those connected with the policy of *apartheid* and race discrimination.

In the middle of that month, their first sabotage action was carried out. Simultaneously in Durban, Port Elizabeth, and Johannesburg, bombs went off in the offices of the Bantu Administration Department. One of the bombs that exploded in Johannesburg killed one of the African saboteurs and seriously wounded another, Benjamin Ramotse. A month later Ramotse was brought to trial but escaped when released on bail. He conducted guerrilla activities on the borders of South Africa for the next eight years before he was kidnapped from Botswana and brought through Rhodesia to South Africa to be tried finally in 1970.

In July, 1963, the police raided a home at Rivonia, outside Johannesburg, and arrested seventeen persons. Subsequently, eleven men appeared in court in Pretoria on charges of sabotage. This was the trial of the "National High Command of the African National Congress and its military wing, *Umkonto we Sizwe.*"

Arising out of the acts of sabotage, the government passed a number of laws giving the police supreme power to control the underground resistance movement. One of these laws became known as the 90-Day Detention Law. It enabled the police to arrest persons whom they said had committed acts of sabotage or had information about subversive acts. Persons so arrested and detained were held incommunicado, in solitary confinement, and denied access to lawyers, priests, or wives. No limit was placed on the power given to the police over the persons, minds, and bodies of the detainees.

I was living in South Africa in a time of turmoil. While the eruption occurred, I remained on the fringes. Despite my sympathy with the rebels I did not join them. I saw my role as a lawyer giving whatever assistance I could when called upon. I did not think that political action within the framework of the law was very effective and I was not enthusiastic about joining any lawful organization. Nevertheless, my wife, Jeanette, joined the Black Sash organization, a legal and active civil rights group made up exclusively of white women, and I worked with her whenever I could.

In my office there was the daily stream of pass cases, which kept me in touch with the reality of the black man's way of life. For a while I stood by and watched the whites gain control; I saw their determination to maintain the whole system intact. A series of vicious security laws were passed and brought into full force and effect. The response of the blacks was one of anger and great bitterness. Violence seemed to be more inevitable than ever as resistance to any basic change was built into the system.

IX
A CHILD OF FEAR

The violence of the police and the acts of sabotage of the black resistance movement swirled around me. While I did what little I could professionally, I concentrated more on building up my practice. I wondered whether I was being seduced into the way of life of white South Africans. My test came soon enough.

Toward the end of September, 1963, I received a long-distance call from a colleague, asking me whether I would take over the investigation of the death of a man in detention on behalf of the widow. It was the first known death under the 90-Day Detention Law. Originally an attorney in Pretoria had been instructed but he no longer wished to handle the matter.

The cruelties of the detention law, particularly the solitary confinement of political detainees and the fact that they were held incommunicado, had already been condemned by many leading South Africans of all races. The English press had been strong in its criticism of the law and some lawyers in the bar councils had attacked it. I was not surprised by the announcement of a detainee's death. Instantly I appreciated the political significance of working on such a case and the possible confrontation with the security police. This made me hesitate and I told my colleague I would call back the next day.

That night I talked to my wife about the decision I had to make. Jeanette was cool and perceptive and saw the issue clearly. We both knew I could not refuse to act, for this would be the first conscious step of abandoning what we believed in. We would not accept the "white" way of life in South Africa. Next morning I telephoned my colleague and told him I would act in the matter.

Looksmart Solwandle Ngudle was forty-one years old and an ANC leader in the Cape Province. As this organization had been declared "unlawful" his membership in it and support of it constituted a crime. The police believed Looksmart had organized a Cape branch of the ANC and its military arm, *Umkonto we Sizwe.* He was detained by the security police on August 19 in Cape Town. Nothing further was heard of him until September 20 when an item in a Cape Town newspaper reported that he was dead. The commissioner of police was quoted as stating that Looksmart had hanged himself while in detention. Although no date of death or other information was given, the commissioner did say the detainee's wife, Beauty Ngudle, had been informed of his death on September 15.

Mrs. Ngudle denied receiving any such information from the police. It subsequently emerged that while she was working in Cape Town, the police had called at her home in the Transkeian tribal reserve and informed Looksmart's mother, who sent a message to the family in Cape Town telling them the terrible news. Looksmart's wife then went home and asked the authorities to send the deceased's body to the reserve for burial. The local police told her the state refused to do this because it was too expensive, but would supply a railroad ticket for one relative to go to Pretoria to attend the burial there. It was decided that the mother should be the one to go.

On arrival at Pretoria, she found her way to the prison but the prison officials she saw denied all knowledge of Looksmart and she was unable to get anywhere with them. The next day she returned to the prison and fortunately talked to a

prison guard who took the time to listen to her and to look at
her railroad ticket. He promised to make inquiries and told her
to come back on the next day. Back she came and was told
abruptly that she could not attend her son's burial because he
had already been buried. When she asked where he was
buried so that she could visit the grave, she was told that was
not allowed because it was a pauper's grave and was un-
marked. She then asked for her son's clothing and was curtly
told, "There are no clothes." No one was sympathetic and she
could find out nothing more. Sadly she returned to the
Transkei reserve and told her daughter-in-law what had
happened. They both believed that Looksmart had been killed
by the police and secretly buried.

My first task was to find out when and where Looksmart
had died and then investigate the circumstances surrounding
his death. As the security police had detained him for
interrogation, I began my questioning at security headquarters. The chief security police officer referred me to
another security officer who passed me on to a third man. In
all, I spoke to about a dozen officers. All claimed they had no
knowledge of the matter, and my inquiries there proved
fruitless.

I next applied to the magistrate's office in Pretoria. Here
there was more courtesy and more cooperation but a complete lack of any information about the deceased. We pored
through records and court files but could find no trace of the
deceased. The magistrate's office advised me to search the
prison records but the difficulties of this course of action were
immediately apparent. Unless I could provide the prison
officials with details of the date the deceased entered a prison
and when and where he died, they would not be able to assist
me. This was the very information I had failed to get from the
security police.

I decided nevertheless to approach the office of the commissioner of prisons. I spoke to a brigadier who knew about
the matter from reading the newspapers, he said, but had no
information other than that. Unless I was able to supply him
with the very information I was seeking, he could not assist
me. He referred me back to the security police.

I now turned to the attorney general. He was polite,

apologetic, but unhelpful and referred me back to the magistrate's inquest (coroner's) court or the security police.

So I returned to the security police. I accused them of inefficiency and alleged that they were unconcerned with what happened to a prisoner whom they had detained. My rudeness and aggressiveness brought some responses. I was now told that if I contacted a certain prosecutor at the magistrate's inquest court, he would know all about it. I immediately approached him but he was dumbfounded and denied all knowledge of the matter. I insisted that he check with the security police right away and give me the information I required. He asked me to call back later.

When I returned he told me he had established that the security police had sent Looksmart's papers to his office but they had not arrived. When they did, they would in any event be handled by a special prosecutor and not the regular prosecutor. I was advised to approach that prosecutor later. When I did so, he stated he had some knowledge of the matter but was awaiting further instructions from the attorney general. He offered to give me a copy of the postmortem report. I then wrote him and asked him for the date of the inquest hearing. I submitted that a full and complete disclosure of all the facts relating to Looksmart's death should be made in the interests of the relatives of the deceased and in the interests of the departments concerned.

While waiting for the date of the hearing I decided to make some further inquiries of my own. By this time a number of persons originally detained with Looksmart had been brought to trial and I interviewed them in prison. I was entitled to do this in my capacity as attorney for the widow. I learned that at the time of his arrest Looksmart was a healthy, active man.

I vividly remember the scene at Pretoria prison when I was visiting the prisoners there. This was at the time following the mass arrests made by the security police to break the back of *Umkonto we Sizwe* and *Poqo,* the militant arm of the PAC. A number of political leaders had been arrested and were now awaiting trial. In addition, hundreds of members of these organizations were also in prison. The guards were in a state of confusion, clearly bewildered by the competence and

North of Johannesburg into the Transvaal, the highveld or plateau stretches for hundreds of miles.

The land below the escarpment—the lowveld of the northeastern Transvaal.

For whites only. (Above) a bus stop in the center of Johannesburg; (below) the "white view" from Cape Point.

Above) a *kwela-kwela* truck; (below) the cages outside the courtroom where prisoners await trial. Both of these pictures were taken at Fordsburg, secretly and illegally, which under the Prisons Act constitutes a criminal offense.

Magical little bays along the road north from Durban on the Natal coast.

Charlie Nyoni's homeland, Natal. In the distance are Zulu huts.

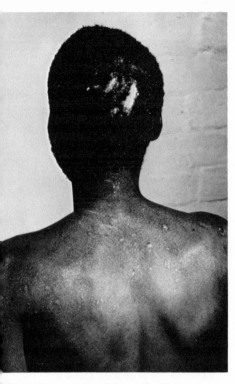

The last picture of Look-smart Ngudle before his death, taken two weeks before his arrest.

Within hours after Musa Sadika was re-leased by the court, pictures were taken to record his physical condition.

Jason Daniel Mutumbulua.

The author made these tracings of photographs of the body of James Lenkoe, which the court allowed him to see for only a moment. According to the security police, Lenkoe hanged himself.

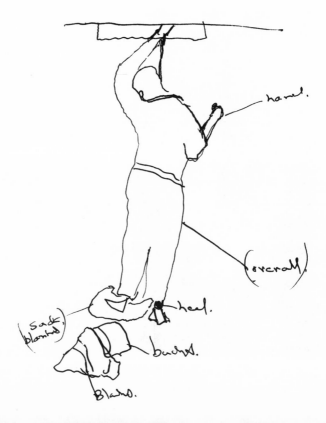

Gabriel Mbindi.

The author about to surrender his passport to the security police after being served with a notice to do so from the minister of the interior.

Chapman's Peak at Cape Town.

The author with his children, Gabrielle, Jeremy, Meredith, and Adam, at Cape Town.

intelligence of these black political leaders. They were not subdued or intimidated by the detention they had undergone, nor by their present incarceration in prison. Furthermore, black and white political prisoners mingled easily together, a strange sight for the guards to witness.

One morning I watched Nelson Mandela being brought from his prison cell to the consulting rooms. Mandela was recognized by the African, Indian, and white prisoners as the leader of the resistance movement. The PAC leader, Robert Sobukwe, was at that time already in prison following his surrender to the police in March, 1960, during the anti-pass campaign. When his prison sentence expired, the government had enacted a new law to keep him behind bars. As Nelson Mandela walked down the corridor and crossed the high-walled quadrangle with guards behind him, he carried himself proudly. Ordinary prisoners ceased what they were doing as he went past, some saluting him. When he saw me he smiled and came toward me. "Hello, Joel," he said, and extended his hand in a friendly greeting. We had a few words together and then he went to his consultation and I went to mine. I was warmed by this contact.

Interviewing these prisoners, who had so recently come out of detention, I used the same method in taking their statements as I had used in the farm labor cases. I took down every detail of their daily life in detention and of the interrogation procedures. I interviewed each man separately and out of all the many details, a pattern began to emerge.

More than a score of prisoners told me that the security police regularly tortured the detainees to force them to give information and sign statements. The electric shock method had been used on many of them. Some could still show me the burn marks on their fingers and toes. They said that after they had indicated to the security police their refusal to talk, they were ordered to strip. They were then told to jump up and down, raising their knees high, until they became exhausted. They were beaten if they stopped. Some were manacled and put in a squatting position, their hands placed over their knees and a broomstick inserted behind their knees and above their elbows. A burlap bag was put over their heads with the cord drawn around their necks and electrical wires were attached to different parts of their bodies. They were repeatedly shocked and it was, they said, excruciatingly painful. Many fainted and when they came to, lying on the floor, water was being thrown on their faces. Then the procedure was repeated all over again. Some defecated and were made to clean up their mess before the torture resumed. Others, I was told, were driven mad by the torture and some had been transferred to prison hospitals or mental homes.

When I had finished these interviews, I had a mass of evidence showing convincingly that the security police used torture as a standard procedure during their interrogations. If it was possible to expose these unlawful and terrible practices in court I was determined to do so, but I knew that the white judges would do everything in their power to avoid such an exposure. They would lean over backward to assist the security police.

There was another difficulty that had to be carefully considered. I could offer no real protection to the witnesses who gave sworn evidence about security police torture. All of them could be redetained at any time and be subjected to further torture. There was nothing I could do to prevent this. Furthermore, if the inquest court ruled that their evidence was not true, then this ruling could be used against them in their own trials, which they still faced. They had absolutely nothing to gain by giving evidence and could be severely compromised by so doing. But when I explained these difficulties to them, courageously, all but only one elected not to give evidence.

Some of the witnesses were able to give me firsthand accounts of the circumstances surrounding Looksmart's interrogation on the very day of his death. They had seen him when he came out of the interrogation room, looking very sick, with his face swollen. He had warned them that he thought he was going to be killed that very day. Other witnesses told how they had been taken by the security police to a strange room in a building close by. A drawer was pulled out and they were stunned by the sight of Looksmart's body. The security police warned them that unless they talked they would land up in a drawer, too.

It was obvious to me that this was not just an inquiry into the circumstances surrounding the death of Looksmart. I saw this death as the first of many to follow. The extraordinary powers the law gave to the security police and the absence of safeguards to protect detained persons, was an open invitation to them to take whatever action they wished. They could abuse their powers and get away with it. Looksmart's death was the inevitable result of this uncontrolled immunity.

Once again my problem was how this condition was to be exposed, so that if the authorities refused to amend the law and permitted the security police an unrestricted exercise of their powers, they could not escape their responsibility for the deaths that would inevitably occur. I had no illusions about the likelihood of the law being changed or restrictions being placed on the security police, but exposure would at least force the public to recognize what could and did happen. Although I did not expect the vast majority of whites to be much concerned, it was a question of putting the horror on record.

There was also another aspect that, for the short term, had a real chance of success. The security police, like torturers everywhere, preferred to keep their procedures a secret, and so far, they had enjoyed the protection of prison walls. Even in South Africa, torture was officially outlawed, and the immediate effect of the exposure might be to put a brake on these unlawful actions, at least for a time. Recognizing the importance of this inquest, I decided to face the inquest magistrate with both junior and senior counsel, hoping this would facilitate the airing of all the evidence.

For my senior counsel, I chose advocate George Lowen, Q.C., an elderly man who had escaped Nazi persecution at the eleventh hour and had come to South Africa. In Germany, he had established a reputation as a fighter for civil liberties. He requalified in South Africa and after years of effort attained a senior position at the bar, where he was highly respected by his colleagues. He was a dapper, cultured, and courteous man with a sly, impish sense of humor. Methodical and thorough, he had no legal tricks to learn. He was a shrewd tactician, accustomed to command, but in working up his case he did not stint himself.

My junior counsel was Ernest Wentzel. Together we explained to Dr. Lowen the real significance of these inquest proceedings, proceedings that normally would not interest him and would be handled by the most junior lawyer. He indicated his acceptance of the brief by giving me instructions as to what was to be done, including arrangements for consultation with senior pathologists. He entered into the matter with all that enthusiasm and vigor for which he was well known. We were delighted to have him as our leader.

The date of the inquest had been set for October 23. I arranged for a consultation with one of South Africa's leading pathologists, Dr. Hillel Shapiro. I also arranged for the attendance at the hearing of the widow and other relatives, who lived a thousand miles away. A week later, the special political prosecutor telephoned to tell me that the hearing date had been changed to October 31. I was not consulted about this—I was being informed of it. I was not going to allow this kind of relationship to be established and I objected to his discourtesy. However, he made it quite clear that whether I liked it or not, the inquest would be on October 31. I realized then that we would have to fight on every issue. I instructed Dr. Lowen and Dr. Shapiro of the new hearing date and postponed the family's visit.

Five days later, the senior magistrate in Pretoria telephoned me and told me that there was a further change in the date of the hearing. "The matter will proceed tomorrow," he said.

I guessed that now that I was involved in matters that concerned the security police, they had tapped my telephone. I assumed that they must have learned of some of the disclosures that we intended to make at the inquest and were determined to try to avoid them. I was equally determined to defeat them on this.

I told the magistrate that his "request" was unreasonable and impossible to meet. We argued heatedly and I alleged that efforts were being made to hinder me in carrying out my instructions on behalf of the widow. Eventually, he made a concession and set the date for three days hence.

I rejected this too and asked him point-blank why the matter had to be rushed. "What is the real reason for the change of date?" I asked. I pressed him on this and at last he admitted that it was something beyond his control, that he was acting on "instructions from higher authorities."

"What higher authority?" I asked. "I will make representations to that authority if you just tell me who it is."

"No," he said, "I cannot, but I do know that the attorney general has specific instructions that the inquest must proceed by not later than October 21."

My further protests were unavailing.

One important mistake I had made in talking to the magistrate was in telling him I could not even advise the relatives in time, nor have the chance to consult with them fully. The security police would appreciate this piece of information, which, no doubt, the magistrate passed on to his "higher authority."

Dr. Lowen, Wentzel, and I discussed all this and were in agreement; we had to oppose the hearing on October 21 and prepare our argument. I set out in an affidavit all the difficulties that had been placed in my way by the security police and the other authorities. In addition, we had learned that the state pathologist's postmortem report had serious shortcomings. Using these facts as our basis, we prepared substantial argument in favor of a postponement.

I also prepared a petition to the Supreme Court that I would use only if it was necessary to interdict the inquest magistrate from proceeding should he decide to go ahead on October 23. I was determined to highlight the irregularity of the state's procedure and the indecent haste that had suddenly become necessary for them.

The night before we went to court we worked until 3 A.M. Next morning, when Wentzel and I arrived at the house of Dr. Lowen at three minutes past eight, he was already pacing up and down the street. Cane and briefcase in hand, homburg hat set at a jaunty angle, he looked as though he had had ten hours' sleep. Glancing at his watch he protested, "You young men who can't be punctual," and we set off on the journey to Pretoria.

Pretoria is just over thirty miles from Johannesburg and in those days there was no expressway, just a two-lane road that

twisted around the rands and down into the valleys. The drop
in altitude between the two cities is some thirteen hundred
feet. I had been driving to Pretoria for twenty years and was
familiar with every turn in the road. I enjoyed driving fast and
knew that my responses were quick and alert, but my
confidence was, on the whole, not shared by my colleagues.
As a rule, only the brave—and those younger than I—drove
with me. This time, George Lowen—much older than I—who
was sitting in the front seat beside me (he could never take a
back seat in anything), kept slyly urging me on.

"Joel, you haven't overtaken that one yet."

His words were met by groans from the back seat where
Wentzel rode. Wentzel was a bright young man who had acted
in many political cases. He had, himself, been detained under
the 1960 emergency regulations and had been released on a
legal technicality. He then chose not to take advantage of it
and after his release he surrendered to the police again. He
was in prison throughout the emergency and was released
without charge. His reminiscences of his stay in prison were
told with wit and were exceedingly funny.

When we arrived at court in Pretoria, to our surprise we
found that the security police had made a hurried two-
thousand-mile journey to the Cape and back to bring Looksmart's widow to court, in order to defeat one of the objections I had made to the magistrate over the phone. And they'd
gone even further. In typical fashion, they had induced the
widow to sign an affidavit saying she had never instructed
me to act and had never met me. The implication of this was
that I was an agitator, falsely representing that I was her attorney.

However, while Dr. Lowen was most indignant at this, I
was not upset. I had expected this kind of behavior from the
security police and as soon as I had heard of the change in date
of the hearing, I had called my colleague in Cape Town who
first instructed me in the matter on someone else's phone. I
told him of the possibility of my authority to act being challenged and asked him to obtain a general power of attorney.
This he had done from both the widow and the eldest brother
who was the legal guardian. I arranged for him to send these
powers by special delivery to the office of my Pretoria corre-

spondent. I anticipated that if all went well the letters would arrive the morning of the hearing and had asked the office in Pretoria to deliver the letter to me at court as soon as it arrived.

The hearing began before Judge R. T. A. Muller. Dr. Lowen rose to say: "I appear, your Worship, together with junior counsel, Mr. Wentzel, both instructed by my attorney who is acting on behalf of the widow of the deceased."

Before he could go further the prosecutor interrupted and challenged our right to appear. He advised the court that on information supplied to him by the police, I had no instructions from the widow and he informed the court of the affidavit that had been obtained from her. I watched the door of the court anxiously. The prosecutor finished his argument and there was still no sign of the messenger with the letter I was expecting.

Dr. Lowen angrily rose to question the right of the police to interfere with our client. He said the prosecutor and the court had no right to question my good faith. "What is the state afraid of in this matter?" he demanded.

As the prosecutor rose to object, I saw the door of the courtroom open to admit a young man holding a letter in his hand. He searched the courtroom for me. I went to meet him, and heard the prosecutor say, "Counsel has no right to make these allegations when I say he has no right to act in the matter." I opened the envelope and there was the general power of attorney I had asked for.

Quietly, I went up to Dr. Lowen and whispered, "It's all right, George, show the bastard this."

Dr. Lowen rose gleefully to announce our first victory: "Your Worship," he said, "I said before it was an impertinence to question my instructions. I have here a general power of attorney, signed by the widow and the deceased's eldest brother, the widow's legal guardian, instructing us to act in the matter. My word should have been good enough for the prosecutor and I have shown I acted properly. Now I call upon him to show whether the police acted properly in interfering with our client, and inducing her to sign an affidavit. It seems to me that all these steps are taken to stop the court from hearing the truth."

Ignoring the prosecutor, Dr. Lowen then began a lengthy argument in support of the postponement. I had very little doubt that we would now succeed. My affidavit was handed to the court along with a note on the serious errors on the postmortem report, and we advised the court of the nature of the evidence we hoped to be able to call. The prosecutor did not really advance any substantial counterargument other than to submit that it would be in the interests of the state for the matter to proceed forthwith. The magistrate rejected the prosecutor's submission and postponed the hearing.

Clearly we had won the first round. The state's action was exposed as improper and stupid, and attention was drawn to the possibility that it had acted in this way because there was something to hide.

Back in Johannesburg we worked very hard on the pathological evidence and on the admissibility in law of the evidence of torture of other detainees. We had to show the involvement of Sergeant Petrus Albertus Ferreira, of the security police, and the others with him, all of whom had been named by our witnesses as the ones who had inflicted the torture on them. After scrutinizing the evidence of more than a score of witnesses with great care, we were satisfied that we could indeed prove this.

The pathological evidence of the state was nonsense but it still was a cause for concern for it had been filed in a formal postmortem report before the court. We could break the security curtain and prove the detailed events leading up to Looksmart's death, but we could not prove how Looksmart died. All we could show was that on the probabilities, he did not hang himself.

Our pathologist, Dr. Shapiro, impressed me as a very sound, knowledgeable, and articulate man. He inspired our team with great confidence in his ability. His conclusions about the state postmortem report convinced us that we could show it could not justify a finding of suicidal hanging. From the report, it was impossible to determine whether the body was hanged before or after death. There were facts in the report consistent with a simulated hanging. Furthermore, as a result of my research, I could show that the state pathologist was unreliable as a pathologist and as a witness. In a previous case involving asphyxiation where he had given similar evidence, the court had rejected his conclusions entirely and found him an unsatisfactory witness. However, even if this court rejected his report and his evidence, we had to ask ourselves—as the court would ask us—what were we proposing as a reasonable and probable cause of Looksmart's death? We had to answer the question, How did the deceased die and who killed him?

We had much evidence as to the irregular police behavior but I knew that the court would accept nothing less than specific evidence in support of allegations directly relating to Looksmart's murder. While we could establish a course of conduct and could give specific evidence about what had happened to each of the detainees who was still alive, we were seriously handicapped by not having a postmortem report of our own. We could not prove what I believed to be the real and immediate cause of Looksmart's death.

I was certain that the security police had gone too far in applying torture and had killed Looksmart. A hanging had then been simulated. Before anyone could be instructed in the matter, however, Looksmart had already been buried for over a month. There appeared little likelihood to me of our obtaining an exhumation order and permission to conduct a second postmortem examination. In any event, we were unlikely to find any evidence on an examination of a body that had been buried for so long. We could show that Looksmart did not die in the way the police said he died, but we had no witnesses to bring to court to show how he did die. This was the dilemma we had to face. I knew that the state, not bound by truth or justice, would use any method that came to hand to prevent us from telling how Looksmart Ngudle had really died, but we had to try to do just that.

The state moved faster than I expected. The day before the second hearing the afternoon newspaper carried a banner headline: DEAD MAN BANNED. To my utter astonishment, I read that Looksmart had been banned by a notice published in the *Government Gazette* that morning. This prevented anyone from repeating anything Looksmart had said at any time.

Anyone contravening this ban would be criminally prosecuted.

We worked far into the night trying to decide what action we should take. The banning notice not only affected what Looksmart had said but also would affect the evidence of some of the witnesses we intended to call. We could not possibly proceed because if we continued on we would expose these witnesses and ourselves to prosecution. The authorities were making the inquest a farce. We decided to simply put our case to the judge and then leave the hearing.

At court, Dr. Lowen explained to the judge that the inquest was not a court of law but only a coroner's inquiry. The act banning Looksmart prohibited publication of any statement made by the deceased prior to his death and made it a criminal offense to present such statements at the inquest. Since there was no escape from the law, we would have to withdraw from the proceedings.

Thanking the magistrate for his attention, Dr. Lowen picked up his homburg hat, his cane, and briefcase, turned to Wentzel and myself, and said, "Now we will walk." Showing courtesy to the court but contempt for the proceedings, we walked out.

I could not explain our withdrawal from these proceedings to my Cape Town colleague on the telephone without speaking to the security police at the same time, for by now all my calls were being monitored. So the day after the walkout, I had to drive the two thousand miles round trip for an hour's conversation with my colleague.

Prime Minister Vorster, then justice minister, criticized Advocate Lowen in a blistering, personal attack, labeling him an agitator. Our walkout had obviously angered him. He then stated that he would indemnify the widow's lawyers and our witnesses from prosecution so the inquest hearing could proceed. We agreed to go back into court. We had decided to avoid trying to prove the particular incidents of Looksmart's death but instead, to demonstrate that if Looksmart did hang himself, he did so as the result of the conditions of detention under the 90-Day Detention Law.

It would be our submission that these conditions were such

that any reasonable man would be driven to suicide. We had consulted psychiatrists and psychologists on the effects of sensory deprivation and on the mind-breaking techniques that were then being used in various parts of the world. A number of American experts, Professor Lawrence E. Hinkle Jr., Dr. Harold G. Wolff, Dr. A. D. Biderman, and others had examined the effects of solitary confinement on American soldiers captured by the Chinese in the Korean War. They had published their findings and submitted them to a special conference called to study the implications of the use of such techniques. The conclusions the conference reached had been published and proved invaluable to us.

Looksmart had been detained under the General Laws Amendment Act, which provided for successive ninety-day periods of detention. Under this law, the security police could arrest and detain any person indefinitely and hold him in solitary confinement and incommunicado. All visits from relatives, lawyers, priests, or any friends could be barred; all reading material was prohibited with the exception, in some cases, of the Bible: no writing material was permitted. Exercise in the open air was given to some and not to others, and the maximum time permitted was one hour per day. Food rations varied considerably; some detainees only received bread and water, others were given corn meal and a few pieces of meat. The food supplied to white prisoners was a little better.

The purpose of the 90-Day Detention Law was to create conditions that would induce the detainee to talk, to give information about himself and others, and all or any of their activities. Skilled teams of security police subjected the detainees to continuous interrogation for days and nights on end. In addition, many detainees alleged that they were assaulted in brutal ways and subjected to various kinds of torture. Even if the court would not allow evidence concerning the systematic use of torture, a procedure the security police would undoubtedly deny, there could be no denying that the law permitted indefinite detention of prisoners in solitary confinement.

We now sought evidence from experts on the effects of

such treatment on detainees. Although efforts were made to
have either Professor Hinkle or Dr. Wolff or Dr. Biderman
attend the inquest proceedings, this could not be arranged.
Many experts in South Africa were anxious to avoid any
involvement and confrontation with the security police, but
some were prepared to advise us privately on the conclusions
they had reached. A team was formed and we learned much
from them.

It has been found that individuals who spend even a few
days in solitary confinement can suffer various bizarre experiences: hallucinations, distortion of motivation, depression, a
change in intellectual ability, distorted social relationships,
and paranoid symptoms. Confinement alone without any
physical assault or torture is an extremely severe form of
treatment and can be expected to produce dramatic changes.
The type of change has been examined carefully and can
actually be accurately predicted over a period of time.

Initially on arrest, there is fear and uncertainty. After one to
three days in detention, there is bewilderment and discourage-
ment, followed by overalertness, expectancy, rejection of
food, and attempts at fraternization. After three to ten days,
there is anxiety, sleeplessness, compliance, increasing loneliness, boredom, fatigue, and weight loss. After ten days to
three weeks, there is increasing dejection, repetitive acts,
intense fatigue, constipation, craving for companionship,
humiliation, and loss of all self-respect. After three to
six weeks, there is despair, inactivity, filth, soiling, mental
dulling, loss of discrimination, muttering, weeping, need for
companionship, and the detainee is highly suggestible and
easily grasps at any help. The American authorities Hinkle
and Wolff maintained that a typical subject would require
twelve weeks (nearly ninety days) from the time of incarceration to final "confession." The distinction between
truth and fiction cannot be demarcated. They said that a
skillful interrogator utilizes the prisoner's need to talk and
craving for human association by discussing with him
apparently innocent details of his past life. This cements a
bond of companionship between the two that can be one of
his most effective tools.

Armed with this information, we decided to show in the inquest—if the court had the courage to hear our evidence—that if Looksmart did hang himself, he was driven to it by the security police and by the law expressly permitting such conditions to exist. We thought it best to abandon the attack on the state pathologist as it was impossible for us to prove who specifically caused Looksmart's death.

Our own strength was severely shaken when George Lowen suffered a serious heart attack and his doctors would not allow him to continue the case. Fortunately, we were finally able to replace him with Advocate Vernon Berrange, a man who was regarded as probably the most brilliant cross-examiner in South Africa. When we returned to the inquest proceedings, the prosecutor called the police and prison officials. During cross-examination of these witnesses, Berrange obtained the following facts concerning Looksmart's death:

He was arrested in Cape Town on August 20, 1963. He died during the night of September 4–5. He was detained in solitary confinement in a cell twelve feet square and slept on a coco mat, about one inch thick, on the cement floor. There was no stool, table, or bed in the cell. He had nothing to read and no writing materials and spent twenty-three to twenty-three and a half hours of each day in this cell doing nothing. For half an hour and occasionally one hour, he was allowed out for exercise. He received cornmeal three times a day and a piece of meat once a day.

He, like the other detainees, was taken to Compol, security police headquarters in Pretoria, for interrogation, where at least four men went to work on him. According to these interrogators, Looksmart was questioned by teams of two or three men over a period of five days, night and day. After a period of questioning, and before another team took over, a "linkman"—in this case Sergeant Ferreira—would attempt to gain Looksmart's confidence by acting sympathetic. He offered Looksmart an indemnity from prosecution for his leadership role in the ANC and *Umkonto we Sizwe* activities, an end to the interrogation, protection for his family, and secrecy about the disclosures he had made. All he wanted

Looksmart to do was admit what the police already knew and make a statement involving his friends. If he did not, not only would his treatment continue, but he himself would be hanged for his part in opposing the government.

According to the security police this is how Looksmart was ultimately induced to make a statement. They admitted that he showed himself to be a leader, facing adversity with courage. One officer said that although Looksmart was an outstanding man, "suddenly he became a child of fear." This, he said, was his experience, and it was a common one among interrogators—that "suddenly a brave man becomes a coward." Looksmart had repeatedly denied the allegations put to him but at last his interrogators said he decided to tell all. When asked by Berrange to produce the statement that Looksmart had made, the security police said it was only a verbal statement; no policeman had bothered to take a single note about the statement or to get it into writing. After their lengthy efforts to force Looksmart to talk, and in breach of standing police orders which required notes of such interrogations and their results to be made in the policeman's notebook, he had been returned to prison without any record of that statement's having been made.

We submitted that the real reason that the police had no notes of any kind about Looksmart's decision to talk was that the statement he gave was only about what he himself did and he had refused to implicate his friends. Then, rather than face further police torture, he had hanged himself. We submitted that the police were not satisfied with confessions by the detainees incriminating only themselves; what they really wanted were statements implicating others. The detainees could then be compelled to give state evidence against their friends or family. Thus it was that the majority of witnesses used by the police in political cases were detainees who had been broken.

The police admitted that this had been the purpose of Looksmart's detention. Sergeant Ferreira stated openly that they wanted Looksmart to sign a statement implicating his friends. Major Fred van Niekerk confirmed that Looksmart was considered to be an important man—a key figure—and was interrogated time and again at security headquarters "to get him to talk." This is how the record of that cross-examination reads:

Q. The purpose of the deceased being brought to Security Headquarters time and again was to try and get him to talk?
A. Well, that's the reason why he was questioned.

. . . .

Q. If a detainee, this man or any other, on being interrogated after he had been detained, says—"I am not under any circumstances prepared to give you any information whatsoever," do you leave him alone or do you take further steps?
A. Well, he's got to be asked again.
Q. And again?
A. Yes.
Q. And again?
A. Yes.
Q. And again?
A. Yes.
Q. And again?
A. Yes.
Q. I see. The idea being to wear him down, I suppose?
A. I make no comment.

. . . .

Q. I'm interested in having an answer to my question. Are there repeated interrogations for the purpose of wearing him down?
A. No.
Q. Well what are they for?
A. To extract information from him.
Q. But he had already told you 2 or 3 times he won't talk.
A. Then he'll eventually let go.
Q. Oh, he might eventually let go?

A. Yes.

Q. But the idea to keep on questioning him is to see whether he will change his mind?

A. Yes.

Q. You don't like to use the expression "for the purpose of wearing him down?"

A. No.

. . . .

Q. All right. For the fourth time—well, supposing you had a case of a suspect who was detained because you, the police, genuinely believed he could give certain information and if in fact your belief was wrong and this man couldn't give information, would you keep on questioning him over and over again—a simple question Major.

A. The question is whether we genuinely believe that he could give information?

Q. Yes, I'm putting it on that basis. I'm not putting it on any other basis.

A. I would question him, yes.

Q. You would? Over and over again?

A. Yes.

Q. That would be a dreadful thing to happen to a man, wouldn't it, if in fact you were wrong.

A. Yes.

Q. It would be; and all that that man would be able to see as far as his future is concerned, would be an endless vista of imprisonment coupled with repeated questioning.

A. Yes.

Berrange then informed the court that we could produce some twenty witnesses who would testify that after a time in solitary confinement, they were taken to Compol for interrogation and were tortured. Eleven of these witnesses would testify that the electric shock method had been used on them, and would describe what this entailed. This evidence was put to the interrogating officers, who denied all knowledge of any such method ever being practiced at Compol.

The court then allowed us to call one of our witnesses, a detainee who had been kept in solitary confinement on bread and water and had never been allowed to leave his cell until he was taken to Compol, where he was tortured. At this stage the prosecutor objected, saying this kind of evidence was inadmissible and irrelevant to these proceedings. After argument, the court allowed us to finish with the evidence of the witness, but thereafter we were called on to produce argument to satisfy the court as to the relevance and admissibility of further similar evidence.

Berrange submitted the evidence of torture and brutality that each witness would give if he was allowed to testify, and he read into the record what each witness would say. In addition, we asked an expert assistant to the coroner—a professor of pathology at the local university—to examine the fingers of a witness in a prison in Johannesburg. We stated that if this were done, the electrical burn marks, which were still apparent on his fingers, could be recorded now before they disappeared. The assessor, the judge's expert advisor, did examine the prisoner and described for the record the lesions he found.

Long arguments ensued on both sides. Our submissions alleged that a number of detainees held at the same time but in different police cells, had been subjected to substantially similar treatment, and this indicated a system that should be investigated. The prosecutor stubbornly maintained that all of this was irrelevant to these proceedings and the evidence should not be admitted.

At length, ruling on the issue of our witnesses, Judge R. A. T. Muller said: "On the occasion of the last hearing, counsel intimated that he intended calling a number of witnesses, most of them 90 day detainees, to testify that they were, putting it mildly, ill treated by the police. He intends asking the court to come to the conclusion as an irresistible inference, from that evidence, that the deceased committed suicide as a result of such treatment.

"The prosecutor states that he in turn is able to call witnesses, if necessary, to refute any allegations of ill treatment and dispel such accusations.

"The question of relevancy of this evidence arises. We are not sitting here as a tribunal investigating the general circumstances of detention of 90 day detainees—that is common cause. We are here in accordance with the provisions of the Inquest Act to investigate the circumstances and cause of death of the deceased only."

He then ruled that our evidence was inadmissible and our witnesses would not be permitted to appear.

As a junior judicial officer, it was too much to expect that he show more courage—in fact, his attitude throughout had been correct and courteous. Subsequently, in similar proceedings, magistrates were more carefully chosen and we were never to experience such courtesy again.

As a result of the court's refusal to accept the testimony, we refused to participate further in the inquest. Once more we walked out. The inevitable finding by the court was that Looksmart died as a result of suicidal hanging.

The record showed that torture and sensory deprivation could be practiced at will by the security police, but now, they were confident that they could defeat all efforts to expose the truth by manipulating any proceedings within the legal framework. They could create conditions in detention that would drive any reasonable man to commit suicide, and when men died, the cause of their death would remain a security secret. Only when many such victims died might there be an outcry against these conditions. Acceptance of deaths in detention would soon become a part of the white man's way of life in South Africa. Then who would remember the "child of fear?"

Although I was reluctant to come to the conclusion that court proceedings were useless as a forum for exposing injustices, it seemed to me more and more that the doors of justice were closing. And yet, I realized I could not live in South Africa and tolerate the injustices that I saw every day without trying to stop them, and for me, there was no valid way of doing this other than through my work. I decided again that as long as it was possible for me to continue, I would go on doing whatever I could within the framework of the law. Nevertheless, I could see that the security laws were placing a severe restraint on lawyers' ability to move freely, if indeed at all, in their efforts to demonstrate what the true state of affairs was. To maintain the law and order of the whites, the security laws had to be enforced above all other considerations, and "sacrifices" would have to be made. Who would make those sacrifices and what those sacrifices were would only be determined by the few in authority.

I saw no other way out. I had to commit myself to a continuing struggle against these unjust laws. It was important to try. The fact that one did not succeed was often itself an indictment of a society that permitted the kind of failure we had endured in the Looksmart Ngudle proceedings. But the record would stand and judgment on our success or failure would be made at another time. I knew now it was not enough to condemn the regime. One had to participate actively in opposing the system. I looked forward to my next clash with the security forces.

X
THE TRIAL OF
THE NAMIBIANS

In March, 1967, I received a letter from a London lawyer informing me that he had been given instructions to act in regard to the arrest, detention, and unlawful interrogation of certain Namibians. He gave me their names and said that these persons had been arrested in Namibia (the former mandated territory of South West Africa) and then imprisoned somewhere in South Africa where they were being kept in detention. He alleged that they had been brutally assaulted while under interrogation by the South African security police. He complained, too, that in contravention of all normal standards of legal practice, these people had not been brought to trial but were being held secretly. He asked me to act in the matter—to make inquiries, attend on the detainees in jail, and act for them when they were brought to court.

The London lawyer was unfamiliar with the extraordinary nature of South African security laws permitting secret arrests and detentions. When I replied to him I explained the provisions of our law, but I assured him I would do what I could about these people. I could, for instance, ask for information, but I was not entitled to demand it. I would only receive that information which the security police saw fit to give me. Regarding the accusations he made of police brutality, I advised him that I could not make this allegation or comment on it as I had no specific information about it. Knowing that by now my mail was under constant police surveillance, I dared not comment more fully on this in my correspondence with him or take him into my confidence and tell him of my own awareness of police brutality.

I wrote to the chief of security police in Pretoria, asking if the South West Africans named in my letter were being held and if so, under what law. As was my normal practice, I sent the letter by both registered and ordinary mail as I had learned from experience that the security police did not always reply to letters sent by ordinary mail and frequently denied having received such letters. Registered letters had to be signed for, and more often than not, did elicit some response. I sent a copy of this letter to the London lawyer.

In acknowledgment, he again expressed great anxiety about the welfare of the detainees—he was, in my opinion, quite properly reluctant to accept the far-reaching provisions of South African law and he persisted in asking me to make further inquiries. I welcomed his impatience. His anxiety gave me further reason to write again to the security police. Eventually I received a reply from them in which they simply confirmed that they held in detention the men I had named in my letter. At least I now knew officially that these men were being held.

I made a copy of their reply and forwarded it to the London lawyer. By return of post I received further instructions to take action on behalf of these men. Again I had to explain that there was nothing I could do until the men were brought to trial. Nevertheless, I wrote regularly to the security police, asking what progress was being made in bringing them to trial and requesting that I be advised should any of them appear in court so that I could appear on their behalf.

In fact, I had become aware of the detention of scores of South West Africans in Pretoria prison long before I received the letter from London. In the course of acting in another matter in 1966, I had visited the prison and had, by accident, walked down the long prison passages in which the detainees were held. Chalked on the door of cell after cell were the letters "SWA." Momentarily unobserved, I had been able to pause at the door of one such cell and lifting the peephole, had peered through and I will never forget what I saw.

The cell was about ten feet by seven feet. A man was sitting on an upturned bucket—his knees crossed and his arms folded on his chest. He was dressed only in underclothes and wore no socks or shoes. I watched him stare unblinkingly at the opposite corner of his cell. The light was on and for the thirty or forty seconds I was able to watch him, he did not move at all. He sat and stared. I understood that this was how it was in detention. Day after day after day; days would merge into weeks and weeks into months. There was no telling time or the passing of it. That unfocused stare haunts me to this day.

I passed through corridor after corridor and saw more of the "SWA" cells. I realized, with horror, that these must be people from South West Africa, yet no one outside the prison walls knew that they were there. And it was almost a year before anyone outside the prison sought relief for these detainees. Without instructions of any kind I had been unable to act. I had stumbled upon my knowledge in the course of my duties and I was not, by law, entitled to disclose the information to any person.

Incredibly, it was simple for the security police to hide the arrest of hundreds of South West Africans. The remoteness of Ovamboland, in the northern area of the territory where the men had been arrested, helped the police maintain a wall of silence screening their actions. The families of the men were helpless—they knew only that their men had disappeared. In Pretoria, where the men were brought, no one knew these strangers. Even fellow prisoners could not understand their language, and their detention preserved their anonymity. Now with this letter from London, at last something could be done for these prisoners. Inquiries might at least hasten their being brought to trial.

Throughout 1966 the South African government had constantly vaunted the peace, security, and economic stability that prevailed throughout the country. Ironically, it was throughout that same year that the security police were secretly arresting the Namibian guerrilla fighters. In May, 1967, a few weeks after the last arrests were made, the government suddenly introduced the Terrorism Act into Parliament. This was done against a background of repeated ministerial statements about "terrorist attacks on South Africa's borders," which whipped up almost unanimous white support for the new law to preserve "peace and quiet, law and order." Thus, this act was supported by the whole opposition party and only one member of Parliament, the brave Mrs. Helen Suzman, voted against it. Outside Parliament, all the churches, lawyers organizations, and other "liberal" bodies, remained silent. Only the Black Sash, the women's organization, protested.

Unknown to the country, the act was designed specifically to bring to trial those Namibians already held in detention, for whom I had received instructions. That this was so was soon made clear. The act was promulgated in the *Government Gazette* of June 21, 1967. With remarkable speed, within five days, including an intervening weekend, thirty-seven South West Africans were brought to trial after having been served with a very long and complex indictment drawn up under the new Terrorism Act. The Terrorism Act was itself retroactive to June 21, 1962, and this retroactivity, was applied to the thirty-seven Namibian defendants. The indictment had been typed, schedules prepared, and annexes completed and put together before the Terrorism Act became law. The passing of the act by Parliament was only a formal rubber stamp—the action had produced the permission!

The Terrorism Act provided that the security police could arrest and detain any person on suspicion of terrorist activities. Such detention was for an indefinite period and was designed specifically for the purpose of police interrogation. Detainees could be held in solitary confinement and held incommunicado. There was a specific prohibition against detainees' receiving any visitors, whether from family, friends, or priest. Detainees were also specifically not permitted to consult with or receive any advice of any kind from any lawyer. Furthermore, the act provided that no information of any kind could be furnished about a detainee except with the minister's consent. Finally, the jurisdiction of any court of law was specifically excluded to prevent relatives and others, such as lawyers, from obtaining relief from a court of law. Thus, the validity of the actions of the security police were placed beyond question in a court of law. There was no provision for the detainee to be seen by anyone without the prior approval of the security police, who were also given sole and absolute control over the persons detained. The conditions of detention were left to the discretion of the security police. The law was silent on how and where, and under what conditions, detainees could be held. As a token gesture, however, the law provided: "If circumstances so permit, a detainee may be visited by a Magistrate once a fortnight." There was no determining what circumstances permitted or did not permit such a visit.

The act defined a terrorist in such a way that anyone the police wished to arrest at any time or place, could be arrested and detained as a terrorist. A terrorist under the act was anyone who did any of the following: "Section 2 (2) (F) . . . To further and encourage the achievement of any political aim including the bringing about of any social or economic change by violence or forcible means, or by the intervention of, or in accordance with the direction or under the guidance of, or in cooperation with, or with the assistance of, any foreign government or any foreign or international body or institution. . . .

"(H) . . . To cause substantial financial loss to any person or the state. . . .

"(K) . . . To obstruct or endanger the free movement of any traffic on land, at sea, or in the air. . . .

"(L) . . . To embarrass the administration of the affairs of the state."

The law obliged the detainee to prove his innocence beyond reasonable doubt. It further provided that once charged, the attorney general could issue a certificate prohibiting any court from granting bail. The attorney general could also determine what court could hear the matter and where and when that court would sit. Should any defendant succeed in being acquitted, the act provided that the defendant could be redetained and charged again for the offenses arising out of the actions he had already been charged with. Furthermore, the act provided a guilt-by-association clause, joining all defendants together and holding all of them responsible for any criminal action of any defendant or of any named member of the organization to which the defendant belonged.

The act altered the common law rules relating to the production of documentary evidence to permit the court to accept evidence against the accused which in ordinary practice, courts would refuse to accept. The act also provided that on conviction the court must sentence a man to not less than five years and the maximum penalty was death.

If there was any argument about the nature of the South African regime, the Terrorism Act proved beyond doubt that it was now a police state. The security police were given absolute powers above the courts, above the law, and above any individual. In law, the only person to whom the security police were bound to answer was the very minister who had provided for and authorized these complete powers being given to his secret police.

When the thirty-seven South West Africans were charged under the Terrorism Act and brought to trial, they appeared before a Pretoria judge. Among the thirty-seven were the defendants I had been instructed to represent. True to form, although the security police had been informed that I was acting for certain of the defendants indicted, they kept their court appearance a secret from me. They went further and did not inform those defendants that I was supposed to be acting for them. Instead, both the security police and the judge tried to persuade the thirty-seven to accept state legal defense, an offer the defendants politely declined. The case was postponed to a special court in Pretoria on August 3.

I learned about my clients' appearance in court in the early edition of the afternoon newspapers. The press carried banner headlines, setting out in detail the serious allegations made in

the charge sheet. It seemed clear that the security police
intended to use the trial to demonstrate how necessary the
Terrorism Act was and as an occasion to parade their powers
and the success of their work. Thus, the reason for the state's
efforts to provide the defendants with state counsel, a move
that would ensure that only the security police could make
political capital out of the show trial, which was designed to
demoralize and inhibit the black opponents of the regime.
Black organizations and violence posed a real threat to the
security of the state and the security police were anxious to
demonstrate that failure and imprisonment inevitably followed militant black action.

I sent a copy of the afternoon newspaper, describing the
charges and the names of the defendants, to my London
solicitor. Next morning I drove to Pretoria and sought entrance to the prison. I signed the legal practitioner's visiting
form, gave the names of the five men for whom I was acting,
and asked for permission to see them for the purpose of
consultation. When the prison orderly came back, he told me
there was no trace of these men. I knew what his difficulty
was. He had been looking for ordinary "decent" criminals,
men who were charged with theft, robbery, rape, or murder;
my clients were obviously not among these. Eventually he
asked the nature of the charges against my clients and I told
him.

He exclaimed: *"Agh! Die terroriste? Daardie mense."* (The
terrorists? Those people.)

"Ja," I replied, and he went off to fetch them.

Within a few minutes he was back with the men I wished to
see and we were put in a little office on the ground floor of the
prison building. This was the office often used by lawyers to
interview ordinary criminals and I had no reason to believe
that it was bugged. This good fortune, I knew, would not last
long, so I moved swiftly to take full advantage of the
occasion.

We were strangers to each other and they had little reason
to trust me. I needed to win their confidence quickly. Checking their names against the names in my letter I introduced

myself to them one by one and shook their hands. Ascertaining that at least two of them could speak English, I explained the source of my instructions and showed them the correspondence that had passed between myself and the London solicitor. I saw that they were still suspicious of me. One of them took my letters carefully in his hand to read them. I felt impatient, not because I did not wish him to see the correspondence, but because I knew I only had a few seconds to spare. I curbed my impatience and told them that I understood how they must feel at seeing a complete stranger who could not even speak their own language. Then one of them said he had heard of me, and in a few minutes I felt I had established some rapport between us and I promised to do my best for them.

We were just beginning to relax when the interruption I had been expecting came. Colonel Aucamp of the security police appeared to stop me from seeing these men.

Glaring at me from small, steely-blue eyes, he demanded rudely, "What are you doing here, Mr. Carlson?"

Leaning back in my chair, I looked at him and quietly replied, "I am consulting, Colonel."

"You have no permission to consult with these men," he shouted, "you have no right to be here—who allowed you to see these men?" He looked as though he might seize me and physically throw me out.

I saw those clients who could understand the exchange listening carefully; the others watched this first encounter between their lawyer and the security police.

Standing my ground I replied, "Colonel, you can object to my consulting in this room, I am prepared to shift to another room, but as the attorney instructed, I am entitled to, and will, see these men."

Angrily he repeated, "You have no right speaking to these men."

Again I replied, as coldly as possible, "I have every right to speak to men for whom I have received instructions, and the security police are well aware that I have received these instructions."

Reluctantly he gave way, blusteringly taking the line of retreat that I had left open for him. "You have no right to see these men here—go upstairs."

I agreed, and smiling at my clients I told them I would see them upstairs.

The colonel then tried another ploy. As an afterthought, he turned to the defendants and asked them whether I was, in fact, their attorney and whether they wished me to act for them. This was to be the test. I hesitated at the door, awaiting their answer—for they had not yet formally adopted me as their lawyer. My confrontation with the colonel had convinced them. They showed no hesitation in confirming my right to act for them. The colonel then ordered the prison orderlies to take the prisoners upstairs and he marched off, flushed with embarrassment. The first round was ours.

We met again upstairs in a room I came to think of as the "milk bar"—it was a soundproofed room, divided in two by a wooden counter. Above the counter prison bars stretched up to the ceiling; below were hollow wooden panels. On my side were three steel poles, each supporting a round wooden seat. On the prisoners' side there was just a concrete floor. In the very long consultations to follow, the prisoners took turns standing at the counter for their interview, while the others sat on the cold floor.

After the five prisoners had been brought in, the doors to our consulting room were closed. There was a long, narrow open window immediately to my right, at which a prison orderly stood. He was supposed to be within sight but out of hearing. Whether he heard our consultations or not was irrelevant for I was sure that the room was bugged. During one later consultation our suspicions were confirmed when we found the telltale wires that had been accidentally exposed by some careless repairman. We learned to consult on important issues in this room without speaking intelligibly. On this first occasion I passed my whole file of papers to my clients and suggested that they take their time and read everything. As the first man finished reading, I passed him a note I had written on a pad I had brought with me. My note read: "Be

careful what you say in this room—the police hear everything—it is bugged."

He asked for my pen and in turn wrote his own note, which
he passed back to me. It said, "Thank you. Yes, we know of
this." I was impressed with his alertness; it was obvious that
his spell in detention had not dulled the quickness of his
response. His next message shook me—"You must do something about Herman—he is going off his head—he needs a
doctor urgently."

My response was not so quick. I knew the objections that
would be raised to a psychiatrist's seeing one of the defendants, and the difficulties that would have to be overcome.
The security police would see this as a move designed by me
to show that their treatment had driven a prisoner mad.
Nevertheless, I promised that I would do what I could.

The next appeal followed immediately—"Will you let our
relatives know that we are here. They do not know that, nor
do they even know that we are alive and well." I made notes
of the names and addresses of their relatives and undertook to
write immediately.

Their final request surprised me. "Since we have been
detained we have not once had a church service and we have
not been visited by any priest. Can you arrange to have a
priest call and conduct a service for us in prison?" I remembered how the newspapers had painted my clients as dangerous, murderous terrorists. I wished that all those who had
feared and hated these men could have heard the requests
now addressed to me. Although they had all been quite
abandoned by the white ministry of the churches to which
they belonged, they still longed to join with a priest in prayer.
Despite all that they had experienced they were faithful to
their gospel and wanted to practice it. Again, I promised to do
what I could—in fact, it took me three months to find a
churchman willing to minister to these men.

It was winter, and bitingly cold as there was no heat in the
room, and the men standing before me were shivering. They
wore no shoes or socks and were barefoot on the cold
concrete floor. Their cotton shirts were torn and ragged as

were the short pants worn by two of them. The others wore long pants but these too were thin and torn in places. Warm in my vest, suit, and coat, I was painfully conscious of this shivering consultation. The only warmth I could give my clients was a promise to do my best and to bring them whatever assistance I could. They expressed their gratitude to me for coming to see them and said they looked forward to my next visit and smiled as I left them, saying I would be back the next day. I was let out of the room and having reported to the orderly that the consultation was over, hurried down the long red-granite-floored passages, through the heavy steel doors that had to be unlocked each time someone came by, and signed myself out of the prison.

Getting into my car I suddenly realized that I was alone and that no one at my office or my home would know what had happened that morning or when I had come out of the prison. One never knew when the security police would act, so before returning to Johannesburg I decided to pay a social call on my Pretoria correspondent. We had tea and I telephoned my office to say I was about to leave for Johannesburg and would be there within the hour.

On my way back to Johannesburg I had time to reflect. It was now June 27 and the trial had been set down in a special supreme court in Pretoria where it would be heard on August 3.—in just over five weeks' time. For a trial of this magnitude I would need to weld together a team consisting of a senior counsel and between four and six junior counsel. The July holidays were already upon us and schools had closed. Many of the advocates would be going away with their families. Those who decided to join me would have to make sacrifices—give up holidays, and give up, or try to dispose of, work for which they already had commitments. In South Africa there is an endless stream of political trials. At the same time, there is only a small band of lawyers who are prepared to act in political cases and their numbers have been steadily dropping over the years. Many lawyers have been restricted by house arrest orders; others have been arrested and finally brought to trial for their political beliefs and actions. Even after being acquitted, prolonged detention in prison and forced absence from their offices often proved financially catastrophic as well as being an enormous physical and mental burden. Many lawyers were compelled to leave the country.

The dual structure of the legal system in South Africa created other problems, too. Advocates who alone can appear in the superior courts must be instructed by attorneys who can themselves only appear in the lower courts. Thus, the attorney is the pivotal point in the legal defense for it is he who organizes a defense team. Advocates may only act on the instructions of an attorney and may receive payment only from the attorney and not directly from the client. The attorney is required to pay his advocates within ninety days whether or not he has been funded by the client, or face being blacklisted, barred from instructing any further counsel. The state recognizes that if attorneys stop organizing defense teams for political trials, all effective legal representation will disappear—hence their constant pressure on these men and women.

Not only are there more trials than lawyers to take them, but the state adds to all the difficulties by conducting many political trials in remote villages and towns. Lawyers are forced to leave family and practice for long periods of time, to face the hostility of the local white population in the villages where the trials are run.

Finally, there is always the problem of funds. The almost full-time nature of the political defense work done by the few available lawyers makes it necessary that they charge fees for the trials that they conduct. There are always other heavy costs, too, involved in a major trial—and the majority of political defendants come from the oppressed who have no money.

There has been an international response to this harsh situation and defense funds have been collected all over the world, but problems, some deliberately created by the South African government, often interfere with the smooth flow of such funds.

In the case of the thirty-seven, as the attorney, once I had instructed five or six advocates to form a defense team, I would be personally liable to pay them. The advocates would want an assurance from me that I would have the necessary funds available so that they could complete the whole trial. But I was not really in a position to give that assurance. I had no idea how long the trial would last and in addition to all the other difficulties I faced, I did not know whether the lawyers in London would be able to make sufficient funds available for me in time to enable me to brief counsel.

Over the next few months, I dealt with no less than three London lawyers as one succeeded the other. It appeared to me in Johannesburg, six thousand miles away, that the London lawyers showed little or no understanding or concern with the problems with which I was faced. In the end I decided to take the chance that funds would become available. I gave counsel the assurance they would be paid so I could brief them, and made arrangements with the bank to provide me with overdraft facilities. Regrettably, I found myself bearing heavy financial burdens I could not afford, with only the hope that payment would sometime, somehow be made to me.

I talked to many advocates at the bar in Johannesburg before obtaining an assurance from one and then from another junior advocate that they would act and then I managed to obtain the services of a senior advocate. The rest of the team was welded together almost at the last moment but finally we did get a team of lawyers.

Immediately, however, my major concern was the men in prison. I sent off letters to their relatives though I wondered whether any of them would ever be received. I called a few of my friends to tell them that clothing was urgently required and could be dropped at my house. The next day I returned to the prison for my second visit to my clients in the milk bar. At once, they told me that all the rest of the thirty-seven wished me to act on their behalf. I asked the prison authorities for permission to see them and this was arranged without fuss. They were herded into the milk bar and my original clients introduced me to each of the other thirty-two in turn. I tried to shake the hand of each one but as they were crowded into one small room this proved impossible and all I received from many was a nod of the head as the introduction was made. There was an advantage to their being so tightly packed for huddled together, they kept each other warm. The continual hum of conversation also delighted me for I knew this would confuse the recording apparatus.

Greetings over, the defendants handed me many copies of the indictment. It alleged that the thirty-seven defendants were all guilty of the crime of "terrorism" (under the 1967 act) in that between the years 1962 to 1967, they had all been members of SWAPO, the South West African Peoples Organization, a legal organization, which had planned to use force to overthrow the South African government's administration of the territory of South West Africa. It then divided the thirty-seven up into groups, detailing how they were guilty of different acts of violence. It alleged that thirty of the thirty-seven sought military training both in and outside Namibia. Two of them had attacked a police camp at Oshikango and another four had attacked a police encampment at Oshikati. Six defendants, as leaders of SWAPO, had intimidated government-appointed chiefs and headmen. The state detailed two more attacks on headmen in which *none* of the thirty-seven had participated but it alleged that they were guilty by association as these attacks were made by other SWAPO members.

The state's apparent determination to make these unknown Namibians guilty of the crime of terrorism and to hang them as a strong deterrent against other "liberation fighters" in and outside of South Africa's borders, warned me of the long battle ahead and the importance of this trial. Not one of these black political activists was known in South Africa. All of them had been brought to trial in Pretoria, some two thousand miles from their homes in Ovamboland. The security police had already built up an intense emotional atmosphere of hate against these "foreign terrorists." If they could conduct the trial along their own lines, they would build up sufficient public pressure against these "terrorists" to encourage a judge to pass numerous death sentences.

I was depressed by the grim condition of my clients. Most of them were in a poor state of health. All of them were very badly clad—many were half naked. None of them had heard from their families—they did not know whether their wives and children were alive or whether anyone knew that they were alive. Some of them told me that they had been in prison for nearly two years. It soon became obvious to me that I was going to have to act in a capacity other than the normal one undertaken by an attorney. I would have to try to find clothing for these men if for no other reason than simply because I could not work with them while they stood shivering in the cold. Those in pain would have to receive medical attention and I would have to devote some time to seeing that this aspect of their problems was attended to. Finally, they were insistent that I provide them with the services of a priest and as their only contact with the outside world, I saw this as part of my duty. Their own friends and relatives were thousands of miles away; they were imprisoned in a strange land where a strange language was spoken and where they were complete strangers to everyone but their prison guards and myself. In the weeks that followed I spent many hours a day in the milk bar with my clients.

The first goal I set myself was the restoration of the morale of all the prisoners. Calling for any outside psychiatrist would almost certainly be futile. I would have to rely on time and their will and strength of character. I began by spending as much time as possible talking to the men most disoriented by their long detention. Their positive response was obvious and encouraging. I went shopping and bought tobacco, cigarettes, and the like, to take to prison. I knew from the prisoners that they only received a quarter of what I delivered to the prison officials for them, but rather than complain, I decided that it was wiser to accept this as the price I had to pay in order to allow a constant flow of purchases to my clients. Normally I did not smoke but I made a point of smoking whenever I visited the prison so that I could offer cigarettes around. I always offered cigarettes to the prison guard who stood on duty outside the narrow prison window and if he accepted one, I would give him the rest of the pack. All this ensured that our consultations were conducted in a relatively relaxed atmosphere and made our time together as productive as possible.

The indictment served on the defendants had given me some information about the charges that they would have to face, but did not supply me with any personal details or information as to how each of them came to be involved in the activities set out in the charge sheet. The best way of ascertaining quickly what the involvement, if any, of the defendants was in these activities was to work up a questionnaire which each of the thirty-seven would complete. It would also tell me something of their background, the time of their arrest, how they were treated in detention, and what their response was to the charges brought against them. The questionnaire was drawn up and copies were made for each client, but early in our meetings, I realized that language would be a major barrier separating my clients from me. Out of the thirty-seven defendants, only five spoke English or Afrikaans fluently. I could not communicate directly with most of these men who were on trial for their lives and there was so little I could do to understand them or be understood by them. Only a handful of the defendants could read or write and most of these only in Ovambo. Fortunately, two of the defendants were teachers, Jason Daniel Mutumbulua and Johnny G. Otto, who could speak English and Afrikaans. With their help we went through the questionnaires with each of the defendants and learned something of their life history. In the long consultations, we built close bonds of confidence and trust in each other.

The first man I came to know well was Herman Ja Toivo, the defendant about whom that first note had been written. He was a leader of SWAPO in Ovamboland, and had a long history of opposition to the oppression of his people. In the 1950s, he had worked in Cape Town but had been hounded out of the area when he protested some police action in a letter to the local white newspaper. When he was sent back to South West Africa, officials in Windhoek, the capital, refused to grant him permission to work there and he returned to Ovamboland. There he opened a shop and soon was recognized by the people as their leader.

He had been brutally tortured by the security police after his arrest in 1966, and was still badly shaken when I first saw him. When I gave him the questionnaire, he completed part of it and then tore it up, explaining to me that it was all useless. He said he was certain that he would not escape the fate he saw in his dream every night, and there was nothing that either he, or I, or anyone could do about it. The security police had promised him that he would hang before Christmas, and in his dream, he saw his own death throes as he hung from a rope at the end of a pole.

Herman's recovery was important to the morale of all the other defendants so I spent much time talking to him. I found that he was born in 1924, the son of a Finnish Mission schoolteacher. Educated at an Anglican school in Ovamboland, he finished the eighth grade in 1950 and was then made a teacher at the school.

He was drawn into the protests about the conditions under which his people suffered, and more and more, like so many of his comrades, he turned to the United Nations to provide a solution for the problems of his people by taking over the territory.

South West Africa, a former German colony, had been entrusted to South Africa's administration under a League of Nations mandate in 1920. The terms of that mandate enjoined South Africa to administer the territory in the interests of the indigenous people and guide them to independent self-government. South Africa had totally failed to honor this sacred trust and had applied her most vicious *apartheid* policies to the territory. When the United Nations was established in 1945, it became the legal successor to the League of Nations and attempts were made to persuade South Africa to carry out her obligations in terms of the original mandate.

SWAPO, Herman's organization, believed in peaceful, non-violent change, but as the young men saw the ineffectiveness of this policy, they began to question the leadership and many of them left the country illegally and sought military training to prepare themselves for a confrontation with the South African authorities. Against the wishes of the local SWAPO executive, many of the trained Ovambos returned to their country to fight for their liberty. On their return, the man that they turned to in Ovamboland was Herman Ja Toivo. Herman was torn by conflicting feelings. He did not believe these young men were right but could not bring himself to refuse them all aid and thus expose them to the security police.

When attempts of the United Nations failed, two members of the original League, Liberia and Ethiopia, then applied to the International Court of Justice, asking the court to set aside the South African government's administration and occupation of South West Africa. SWAPO members decided to await the World Court's decision, believing that if the court ruled against South Africa this would greatly strengthen their position.

South Africa, too, was affected by the World Court case. It did not want to charge the thirty-seven defendants with treason, fearing that this might raise an argument about the legality of its own administration and occupation of South West Africa in its own courts. This then was another reason for the passing of the Terrorism Act; it could then charge the thirty-seven defendants with terrorism and not with treason.

Ultimately, in October, 1966, the World Court decided that it did not have jurisdiction to hear the case and dismissed it. South Africa and its allies were jubilant, the African states and the majority of the countries in the world were saddened, and the South West Africans who had trained and returned to their homeland now readied themselves for action. The South African security police were, through their informers, well aware of the activities of these guerrillas and moved swiftly against them, using helicopters and modern weapons. They destroyed the camps, killed some, and arrested many. At the same time, they swooped down on ordinary SWAPO members in the territory and arrested and detained many leaders. In terms of the Terrorism Act all SWAPO members were later held to be jointly responsible for any and all acts of violence committed by any SWAPO member both in the territory of South West Africa and beyond it.

Herman Ja Toivo was one of those arrested. He was flown by a South African army plane to Pretoria and taken to security headquarters, Compol. There, Captain Theunis Jacobus Swanepoel and Captain van Rensburg, and Lieutenants van Rensburg, Ferreira, and others, began the interrogation by calling him a Communist and telling him, *"Kaffir, jy sal kak van aand."* (Kaffir, tonight you will shit yourself.) He was assaulted by Swanepoel, the van Rensburgs, Ferreira, and Lt. Erasmus, and Sergeants Breda and Dippenaar, each of whom hit and kicked him, and when he fell on the floor, the beating continued. He was blindfolded and handcuffed to a hot-water pipe; then wires were attached to various parts of his body and he was given electric shock. Threatening to crush his genitals while he was thus suspended, they mocked him and told him, "Here in Pretoria, we will make a new man of you. You will become young again." They told him that while he might be a big man in Ovamboland, he was nothing in Pretoria and would tell them everything. "Where is your United Nations now?" they jeered at him. "We have one hundred and eighty days for Kaffirs like you and we will do what we want with you."

Herman told me that he had been suspended in that corner for four days and nights continuously except when he was allowed to go to the toilet and when he was eating. While suspended on the hot-water pipe, he could only rest by stretching out his toes. Periodically, van Rensburg would feel his ankles to see how swollen they were. He could no longer stand on his feet and was finally removed from the pipe because his legs had become so swollen. (Later, the security police were to boast to other detainees about how Herman had been suspended for four days and nights and had then told them everything.) Finally, although he was allowed to lie down for a while, his interrogation continued day and night, the police changing shifts and interrogating him two at a time.

In the end he gave way and agreed to make a statement. Swanepoel gave him a pencil and paper and he wrote a long confession, which I later saw, as the police readily made it available to the defense. Herman had been driven to admitting to every conceivable sin about which he had any feeling of guilt, including adultery, usury, and theft. Even this degradation was not enough. The police wanted Herman to sign a further incriminating statement they had drawn up and when he refused, he was immediately hung up and assaulted again until he agreed to whatever answers the security police wanted.

Despite their brutality, the police had not been able to totally crush his spirit. He responded with increasing strength as we worked together to build a defense case. In the end, he stood in court as the spokesman for all the thirty-seven.

As our consultations proceeded, it became clear that almost all the men had been subjected to torture in their interrogations. The methods that were now practiced were slightly different from those used at the time of Looksmart, when prisoners were pinioned and handcuffed in a sitting position. Now they were handcuffed and suspended from a hot-water pipe so that sometimes only their toes touched the ground.

Many of the prisoners gave me affidavits about their experiences that I was able to submit to court in December, 1967, when I unexpectedly received enough information to bring a habeas corpus petition on behalf of Gabriel Mbindi, a sixty-eight-year-old SWAPO member who had been similarly tortured. Somehow, although being held under the Terrorism Act in solitary confinement, Mbindi managed to smuggle notes to his fellow Namibians telling them he was being tortured under interrogation. Bravely, these men passed the notes on to me in court although this, too, was a crime under the act. Immediately I launched an urgent habeas corpus petition asking the court to hear Mbindi and to issue an injunction against the security police, preventing them from torturing him further. In support of Mbindi's allegations, I used affidavits of torture of some of the thirty-seven.

The minister of justice and the attorney general denied that Mbindi had been tortured. The security police denied assaulting Mbindi or anyone at any time. Eleven magistrates responsible for visiting detainees in prison, filed affidavits stating that the detainees had never complained of any of these assaults. A medical specialist filed an affidavit saying he had examined Mbindi after the petition was brought to court and among other things, found two perforations of the ear drum.

Suddenly, a day before the matter was scheduled for hearing by the supreme court, Mbindi was released in Windhoek, more than one thousand miles away from Pretoria. At the trial, the state attorney approached me about a settlement of Mbindi's case. He emphasized that Mbindi had been released and that I had got more than I had asked for in court and that, therefore, I should withdraw the petition. I refused to do this but agreed to postpone the matter in order to seek instructions.

Instructing attorneys in London advised me to accept the settlement, but Mbindi, despite the risk of reprisals, wanted the matter openly heard in court. He stressed that he was an old man and had been brutally tortured and had already suffered enough. There was not much more that could be done to him and he wanted his people, and the court and the world, to know the truth of what happened to him. "They must pay for the damage that they did to me," he said. I explained to him that the Terrorism Act did not permit any payment of damages to him but promised that I would act on his behalf. Fortunately, the Washington-based Lawyers Committee for Civil Rights Under Law instructed me to set the matter down for a full hearing by the court and I proceeded to do this.

Eight days before the court was due to hear it, the state attorney approached my counsel and offered to pay R 2,000 ($3,000) in costs, the only matter then outstanding before the court and to which we were entitled only if the allegations made by Mbindi were true. I refused to accept this and insisted that the court determine the truth. I also insisted on obtaining a payment of damages for Mbindi although I knew the law did not permit this.

The minister's response was to offer to pay me another $1,200 which he insisted was for costs but which I was told I could use as I liked. This indicated to me that I could pay Gabriel the amount as damages if I so wished. Counsel advised that I had no alternative but to accept the state's offer as the court would, in these circumstances, refuse to hear a lengthy trial on an issue which had now become academic, the state having conceded on all the issues raised in the petition brought by Mbindi. By the terms of the settlement, the minister of justice paid $4,200 and gave Gabriel Mbindi a full indemnity against prosecution.

I immediately flew to Windhoek to see Mbindi and to explain the settlement to him. I gave him a check for what, in effect, was damages but advised him that he could not claim this was official damages because the minister had not paid it for that purpose. Mbindi was pleased with the result of the case and with the indemnity. He felt that he had been vindicated. In this way, however, the minister and his security police, the attorney general and the magistrates, managed to avoid having the full truth exposed in court.

One of the results of the Mbindi case was that I was arbitrarily banned from visiting prisons which meant that I could not consult with my clients in prison or see them peronsally because I had "received notes from a detainee". Although I had fully disclosed all my actions to the court and had acted properly and in the interests of justice, this did not help me. The security police were obviously itching to act against me and had this ban imposed on me.

During the course of the trial of the thirty-seven, I received copies of the sworn confessions that each of them had made to the police. No one had been able to withstand police torture. Now I noticed that although the process was slow, even those men who had shown marked disorientation were readjusting gradually to life as prisoners awaiting trial. They were able to talk to me more and more, and many completed the questionnaires. I remember clearly the interview when the first thing the men told me, with great joy, was that they had received letters from their families. These were men of great courage and I grew to respect each of them as I came to know them better.

Eliazar Tahuduleni was the first defendant named in the indictment. He was a thin, wiry man in his fifties, who had actively participated in the guerrilla camp that had been raided by police helicopters. He had managed to escape and had spent the next year avoiding the police net. Finally he was caught and brought to Pretoria for interrogation. When I saw him, he too was convinced that there was nothing he or I could do to avoid the death sentence being imposed on him.

One morning, speaking through one of the teachers, he took me aside to tell me that the guilt of all the defendants was on him. He wanted to take the blame for all of them and he was prepared to be hanged immediately. He asked me to tell this to the security police so that, having hanged him, they would then free the innocent men among the thirty-seven. He insisted that this was the Christian way and that he was prepared to carry his cross. Eliazar would quote at length from the Bible as he talked to me, giving me the numbers of chapters and verses that explained more articulately than he could, his point of view on any matter. He was a simple man, a peasant, who had only completed the fourth grade. His hair, which was turning gray, his wiry, sharp features, and his anxious look made him appear much older than his years. He was always very serious and concerned and the only time I made him smile was when I teased him about taking too much snuff to clear his nose and his brain. The fact that I should know about snuff and what this meant to a man like him amused him.

Among the accused was Simeon Shihungeleni, a striking-looking young man with beautiful, even, delicate features. It took a long while to piece together his story since he could only communicate through an interpreter. He, too, had been at the camp raided by the police and escaped, but only for a moment. The police had seen him in the open veld, and run him down in their jeep, breaking his arm. Even as I interviewed him, more than a year later, I could see where the bones had not knit properly. He told me that the prison doctor in Pretoria had refused to treat him and had told him, "You are a terrorist and you will soon hang—there is no point in treating you. It is a waste of money and a waste of my time." Simeon swore in an affidavit in the Mbindi case, that after his arrest the local police had allowed him to have his arm set. Then the security police from Pretoria had arrived and had handcuffed him to the iron bars of the prison cell. In this position he had been subjected to electric shock.

Another of the young defendants was Joseph Shityuwete —a tall, thin man in his early twenties. He had a low, resonant voice and spoke English and Afrikaans. He had a beautiful sense of humor. He had recovered quickly from the police methods of interrogation and was always quick to smile or laugh with me. Unmarried, Joseph was particularly worried about his mother in Windhoek—he was her only son. (Six years have passed since his arrest and it was not until 1972 that he, still in prison, was able to have his first visit from his mother—and he is luckier than most of the thirty-seven, some of whom have still not seen any of their family since their arrest.)

All the men really required medical attention but Festus Nehale was one of the older men whose health and frame of mind disturbed me particularly. He insisted that he was suffering from leprosy and that the disease was spreading and would infect the others. He, too, had been brutally tortured and was very bitter about his treatment. The prison doctor had also refused to treat him or listen to him and told him that it did not matter what happened to him because he would soon be dead.

Among the thirty-seven men were peasants, teachers, shop-keepers, and city workers. There was also a lay preacher, Emmanuel Gottlieb Nathaniel Machuiriri, a round-faced, be-spectacled man, who would preach to me as easily as he talked; when I teased him about this he would smile broadly. Although he had been on the periphery of the events in the north of the territory, he would not for a moment deny that he had been a leader of his people. As a lay preacher he had protested from the pulpit, had written to the authorities—even to the administrator of the territory himself. He insisted that he had acted only as a good Christian and had tried to show the white man the "error of his ways." He could quote a parable to me for each of the protests he had made. He came from a family steeped in Christianity—was a man of peace, prayer, and protest—but he had been on the executive committee of SWAPO and as a result of this he was held liable for the acts of all the other SWAPO members.

Probably my closest contact was with the two young teachers who had taught at the Lutheran Rhenish mission in Windhoek. They were invaluable to the whole defense team and we relied on them completely as our interpreters. Jason Daniel Mutumbulua was a math teacher—patient, tolerant, and masterly. Quietly, and with great efficiency, he helped me with all the others in completing the questionnaires and the like. He was my main spokesman. Every task given to him was handled in a responsible and reliable way. Unlike the preacher, he was quiet—he spoke in soft tones and used few words. I came to respect the short, stocky man most highly. As an executive member of SWAPO, and the most educated of all those I had met, he had also impressed the police. They tried in vain to make him a state witness and I knew how hard they had tried. At twenty-seven, a married man with children, he had shown sterling qualities as a leader and a man to be relied on in any difficulty. Over the many months I knew him, I developed a strong feeling of friendship toward him.

Jason was arrested at the school in Windhoek and was then taken to Compol, in Pretoria, by Lieutenant Ferreira and two black constables, Johannes and Lidker. He drew a map of the torture room when he was describing his experiences to me and showed me that he was taken to a large room in the southwest corner of Compol. After a brief wait, he was ordered by Lieutenant Ferreira to go to an inner room, where Bantu Constable Johannes started the interrogation by warning him that he had better tell everything because the police knew all about his activities. Furthermore, he told Jason, the police in Pretoria—unlike the police in Windhoek—were not afraid of beating the hell out of people. "They would be beaten until they died and nobody would say anything after that."

Johannes boasted that Herman Ja Toivo had told everything after they had beaten him for four days, and if Jason did not talk he would be given electric shocks and would be shown no mercy.

Jason replied that he was prepared to talk only about matters he knew something about. At this point, Ferreira ordered that Jason be "hanged up" until he told them what they wanted to hear.

Jason described the procedure to me in horrible detail. His jacket was removed, his shirt buttons were opened, and the shirttails were tied behind his back. Handcuffs were put around his wrists, a strong rope was fastened to the metal band and thrown over an iron pole some seven feet above the floor. Then he was pulled up so that he could touch the floor only with the tips of his shoes. There were a great many police spectators; among others, Lieutenant Ferreira, who jeeringly remarked in words Jason clearly recalled, "You think you are

big shots [*groot menere*] when you are on political platforms
in South West Africa. Now you are here in the Transvaal and
we will show you how we treat a Kaffir here. Now you know
[the United Nations] can come here and take you off that
pole."

Then one of the black constables began to pull out Jason's
beard, saying they would first make him young because they
did not talk to people who thought they were big if they had a
beard. Each time Jason moved his head he was hit across the
face and punched in the stomach or the ribs.

Jason related that he was then beaten for three hours, "as I
have never yet experienced in my whole life." The police took
turns in the beating. Jason remembered the names of several
who took part—Captain van Rensburg, Lieutenant Ferreira,
Sergeant Stryver, and Bantu Sergeants George and Simon. He
said, "These faces I shall not forget in all eternity."

He formally stated that the beatings consisted of:

"A) Kicks on my posterior by taking me by the feet and
picking up my legs.

"B) Taking my feet and then pulling my whole body which
was hanging on the rope by the handcuffs, away from
the wall and then pushing it violently back against the
wall.

"C) Pulling out my beard, including my mustache.

"D) Throttling me with the left hand (presumably so as not
to make a noise).

"E) Punching my stomach and ribs with the right fist.

"F) Hitting me across my cheeks and across my face."

At the time of the assault, the windows were closed and
curtains drawn. After several hours of continuous beating, he
was untied and the handcuffs were removed. Then Bantu
Constable Johannes gave him a broomstick and ordered him
to walk up and down with the broomstick raised above his
head, lifting his knees as high as possible. The policemen
made a rough circle around him while he walked up and down
at the command of Lieutenant Erasmus and was hit as he
passed each man. After ten minutes, Jason said he could not
go on and he threw the broomstick on the floor and rested
against the wall.

"Lieutenant Erasmus took off his jacket and said he would

now show me. I was not now on the air trip to Pretoria where I had looked at him with strange eyes. He ordered me to stand straight up against the wall and told the other men to watch how he kicked out [*uitskop*] a kaffir's genitals. The other policemen encouraged him, shouting, 'show him, Lieutenant, he wants to fight.'"

Then Erasmus dragged Jason around the room by his shirt collar, punching him all over his body. When Jason staggered and fell back along the table, Erasmus started to kick him on the shoulders and chest while he lay on the ground.

Somebody then told Erasmus it was enough. A black policeman dragged Jason back to the iron door, handcuffed him, and hung him up again. Most of the white policemen went away and only a few of the blacks remained behind.

Later, Simon came back to Jason and said that the police would treat him in such a way that when they were finished with him he would be sent to a *malkamp* (lunatic asylum).

Jason told me that the whole interrogation took five days. He said, "It was accompanied by the most barbaric swear words that I have ever heard in the whole of my life history."

There were also such threats and insults as:

"A) You had six years to build up your organization; we decided to break it up in 9 months.

"B) If you thought that UNO would help, then you made the greatest mistake. Now we are going to fuck you up here.

"C) The police in SWA treat you like big fish 'menere'; here we shall treat you as ordinary kaffirs or even lower than kaffirs.

"D) Here you are beaten up by officers not by ordinary policemen. You have nowhere to go and complain.

"E) Here we shall work you so that if you don't go to the gallows you will at least go to a lunatic asylum.

"F) You attack the government in your meetings and now we will show you what the government does to people who think they are clever."

Finally, he was forced to make a statement. He was then told by the police and a man who said he was the state prosecutor that if he wanted to save himself from hanging he would have to become a state witness.

He was taken to a smaller police station where he found the cells big, drafty, dirty, and full of lice. The food was half-burned corn meal without salt, and he went on a hunger strike. Lieutenant Ferreira, all "friendliness," came to inquire after his health and said he would improve the treatment and food that Jason was getting, if he agreed to testify against his fellow prisoners. Furthermore, for the first time Jason was given a chance to wash. He was provided with soap, cigarettes, matches, and candy, but Jason refused to sign any statements containing false information. He also refused to sign the blank sheets of paper that were presented to him. Finally he was left alone.

While he was on trial, Jason described his torture to the International Red Cross representatives but they appeared unable to intervene in any way. There is no doubt in my mind that Jason told me the truth. The statements of twenty-seven other accused who were tortured corroborated his story.

The other teacher who worked closely with us was Johnny Otto—a Bible study teacher. He was mercurial, full of energy and passion, and deeply frustrated by the unjust rule applied to his people. He, too, gave me a long statement detailing both the aspirations of his people and the tortures that both he and they had persistently suffered.

Throughout July and the first weeks of August, I concentrated my efforts on what seemed to be the most important needs of my clients. I continued writing to their families again and again, in the hope that some of them would communicate with the defendants in prison. Apart from this and the crucial work involved in obtaining full and detailed statements, I also spent considerable time in trying to persuade the prison authorities to do something about the health of my clients. Although the defendants received little medical attention despite all the complaints made, they were at least aware of my efforts to assist them and this contributed further to the slow buildup of morale. At no stage in the first seven weeks did counsel have an opportunity of consulting with any of the defendants, but two counsel had already begun to work on some of the legal arguments being raised in court.

When I was not attending to the defendants in Pretoria, I was struggling to complete a full team of lawyers to take the matter and argue for a postponement on August 3. When that problem was surmounted we began to build the arguments relating to the international status of the territory which, in my opinion, had to be placed before the court. This was discussed with the lawyers and with a young professor of international law at the University of the Witwatersrand, who was rapidly acquiring a reputation as an outstanding international lawyer.

The status of South West Africa in the international legal field was unique. It had already been before the World Court and in 1966 the United Nations had finally taken the step of canceling South Africa's mandate. The UN adopted the name Namibia for the territory of South West Africa and set up machinery to administer the territory until it could be handed over to the people. Not surprisingly, South Africa refused to accept the UN's actions and continued to occupy and administer South West Africa illegally.

But in these circumstances, the defense team, acting for the Namibians on trial, were prepared to argue that the South African court had no jurisdiction over the former territory of South West Africa and could not, therefore, try these defendants under the Terrorism Act. I wrote to the United Nations in New York and obtained from the secretary-general a document concerning the resolution of the United Nations that terminated the mandate. We were anxious to stress that this case was of the utmost importance, involving international legal obligations and involving men whose status was the subject of international dispute and concern in the highest forums of the world. The court would be forced to act very carefully once it recognized that the spotlight of the world's attention was focused on its deliberations.

On August 3, the thirty-seven Namibians were brought to court for the first time. The security police seized their chance to stage an intimidating show of strength. A convoy of police vehicles, headed by an armored car with men sitting behind machine guns, drew up outside the prison; then came armed police in trucks and cars, followed by the special vehicles with police dogs. A completely enclosed steel truck, painted black, windowless, with headlights on, drove out of the prison gates and took its place in the middle of the column. Police on motorbikes, riding the length of the convoy and leading it, flicked on their sirens, all headlights were lit, and the convoy moved at a cautious speed down the highway from the prison to the court through the center of Pretoria. One could hear the approaching column from a mile away. Outside the old synagogue, now converted into a special court, more heavily armed police waited. Some of them carried sub-machine guns, others rifles, and some held police dogs on heavy metal leashes. The major in charge of the operation walked anxiously around the area, giving instructions over his walkie-talkie. No unauthorized person was allowed into the precincts of the court and there were security police everywhere. An atmosphere of great tension was being built up for the public who had come to see the terrorists and applaud their capture.

Waiting outside the court we heard the noise of the sirens growing louder and louder. Armed policemen rushed to the intersections to stop all traffic and the convoy rounded the corner. The major barked orders and the policemen jumped to attention. The convoy stretched all along the street in front of the court and the boxlike truck was driven into the courtyard and disappeared behind high fences. I heard the comments of the whites around me: "Hang the Kaffirs," "Kill the terrorists," "Jail's too good for them."

As I moved toward the courtroom, my picture was taken by press photographers. Someone in the crowd hissed as he learned who I was. Inside, every door was guarded by two policemen armed with Sten guns. I walked through the courtroom to find my clients and as I got to the back door, I saw an army of police guarding them. I told the major I wanted to see my clients. He shouted orders and the police, some of them controlling dogs, formed two lines opposite each other. As I walked down the steps and through this police gauntlet, over the growls of the dogs I could hear a series of clicks as the safety catches on the Sten guns were thrown. I was determined to show none of the fear I felt and I ignored this deliberate intimidation.

The prisoners had been placed in a corrugated-metal shed. A metal section of the side wall facing the court had a steel barred grille from top to bottom, part of which opened to allow passage in and out. The floor was concrete and there were a few rows of benches. At the back of this shed were two half-drums that served as a latrine.

I joined my clients, greeting each of them and shaking their hands. Through the open grille, the police watched me angrily, resenting my familiarity with these black men. While some of the accused were wearing the clothes that I had delivered to the prison, others were still in rags and barefooted. I was really upset by this since they had expressed the wish to be decently clothed when they appeared in court. They seemed to be tense and apprehensive and I tried to be as cheerful as possible and wished them luck before going back to court.

My team of counsel, fully robed, were already gathered and waiting for the proceedings to commence. Less than a handful of Africans were upstairs in the public gallery reserved for blacks. In the white gallery, crowded with spectators on this first day of the trial, relatives and friends of the security police filled the front benches. For the most part, however, there was little public interest in the legal proceedings that were to follow, although each morning when the defendants arrived, and each afternoon when they left, there were groups of white men hanging around to curse the terrorists.

Court proceedings that day were brief. We asked for a postponement and after some state opposition, the judge granted our application setting the next hearing for a date late in August.

Following this first court appearance, the government press dubbed me "The Terrorist Lawyer" and front pages of their daily newspaper carried security police–inspired smear stories. One paper asked, "Who is paying the defense lawyer for the defense of these terrorists?" Another suggested that whether I knew it or not, I was being paid by red gold from Moscow. More specifically, it was alleged that organizations banned in South Africa as Communist were financing this case under cover names.

The defense team was obliged to take notice of these statements, irresponsible as they might be, for they were serious allegations. If they were not answered they might be followed by serious criminal charges. I wrote to the London solicitor asking him to disclose the source of the funds. His reply revealed the source as a perfectly legitimate one, Lord Campbell of Eskan, a prominent member of the British House of Lords. However, in view of the implied challenge to the legitimacy of my funds, counsel now requested that they be paid on a monthly basis. I had no alternative but to agree to this, so while I awaited the arrival of funds from England, I paid them out of my own pocket, using the overdraft facilities I had set up at my bank. My London solicitor was sending me about one-third of the monthly expenses in small amounts every six or eight weeks and would not set up a more equitable arrangement.

The trial dragged on slowly. Each day the prisoners were brought to court with a repeat performance of the security police show. The long days in court placed a severe strain on them. They were constantly treated with callous inhumanity. Although on trial for their lives in a strange land, where language unfamiliar to most of them was used, no translation of any of the legal arguments submitted to the court by either side was made for them. Only the direct question-and-answer sequences involving witnesses were interpreted for their benefit. The interpreter could only speak Afrikaans and Ovambo, not English, and had been employed earlier by the security police during their interrogation of the accused. He was both incompetent and biased. We managed to demonstrate in court that his translation of documents was so inaccurate that finally even the prosecutor accepted the use of translations made by the two defendants, Jason Mutumbulua and Johnny Otto. But the security police interpreter continued to interpret the evidence given by the Ovambo witnesses in all cross-examination. I was most unhappy with this arrangement and we raised our objection with the judge. The prosecutor insisted that there were no other interpreters available and my counsel decided not to make an issue of it. This was one of the many situations in which they preferred to play down disputes with the state and the court, fearing that any such disputes might aggravate matters for the accused.

The conduct of the whole trial reflected contempt for the

rights of my clients as individuals. They were subjected to constant humiliation. Each man had to wear a piece of cardboard with a large number hung around his neck. Neither the judge, the prosecutor, nor even the defense counsel took the trouble to become familiar with the names of the men on trial. They all referred to each defendant as number so-and-so. Whatever their personal feelings toward the defendants, defense counsel acted within the strictures of the required behavior of "officers of the court" in South Africa. Their primary aim was to save the defendants from extreme punishment and they believed this end would best be served by a conciliatory attitude on their part that would keep the temper of the judge and the court cool.

The security police, on the other hand, were deliberately provocative. Each morning I had to walk a police gauntlet to greet my clients. Each morning the judge, prosecutor, and defense team would know when the prisoners were being brought into court by the growling of the dogs. Many of the defendants told me that walking past the police with their Sten guns and barking dogs was the most frightening of all their experiences. Two armed policemen stood at every door of the court throughout the day and the whole building was surrounded by police. Inside the courtroom, armed police lined the walls and two rows of public benches immediately behind the prisoners were also occupied by armed policemen. They were restless and bored and would often doze in the hot, stuffy atmosphere of the courtroom. They resented their tedious duties and wanted something more active to do.

One day, in the fifth month of the trial, court adjourned early, soon after the morning tea break, to enable us to consult with our clients on some witnesses' evidence. The judge had left the bench and the prosecutor had gone back to his office. The defense team was using the whole of the well of the synagogue to consult with all thirty-seven defendants. Not that we were alone with our clients—the room was crowded with armed police, standing around, sitting everywhere, even in the judge's seat. Two police dogs had been brought in and were lying at the front of the court. The summer heat hung dry and heavy over the whole Pretoria valley. I watched the police becoming increasingly restless. Young policemen outside were throwing stones through the windows, hoping to hit someone. In the courtroom itself they were playing with their guns and quarreling over who should sit on the chairs. This might all have been viewed as boyish pranks, but I knew that there were live bullets in those guns. I decided to break early for lunch because I did not like the atmosphere, but as time with our clients was limited, we began our consultations again about forty minutes later.

For the first half-hour, the atmosphere was calmer but the oppressive tension of the midday heat soon made itself felt again. The police began teasing the police dogs and when the dogs barked, senior counsel—who had been a colonel during World War II—shouted at the warrant officers: "Keep those damned dogs quiet—this is not a bloody circus." The officer ordered his men to behave; the young policemen resented this and looked sullen.

The tension grew as another hour passed. Some of the police were standing, holding their Sten guns hip-high and pointing them toward us. As I was consulting with one of the junior counsel in one corner of the hall, I looked up at the two other junior counsel who were working diagonally opposite me. I froze with horror. I had brought some candy into court for everyone. Absentmindedly, one of the counsel had blown the empty candy-bag taut as a balloon and I saw his fist poised to hit down and burst it. For an instant I was immobilized with fear, anticipating the effect of that exploding bag. Then as his hand moved down to smash the bag, his colleague's hand shot out to stop the descending arm.

The movement jerked me into action and I rushed over and snarled, "You blithering idiot—do you want to have us all shot?"

He was already apologizing profusely to the rest of us: "I'm sorry boys, I'm sorry." We had all had enough and were glad to end that day's consultations.

The defense team took a long time to hammer out the best tactics to be used in dealing with the question of security police torture of our clients. The prosecutor was anxious to use Herman Ja Toivo's confession because it was a most degrading and all-embracing one. By using it, the state hoped to destroy Herman's reputation and credibility as a leader. Since it seemed clear to me that no sane man would have made such a confession, we told the prosecutor that we would attack any confession submitted and would seek to show the court that it had not been freely and voluntarily given, but had been extracted under security police torture. In the face of this threat, he gave way and decided not to use the confessions at all.

Some of the defense team then argued that it was in the interests of our clients to keep the atmosphere cool and not raise the issue of torture at all. I reluctantly had to bow to the decision of the majority. However, it was agreed that the matter would be raised with the judge and left in his hands. If he showed an interest in it, we would then pursue the matter. If he showed no interest, it would at least be on record.

Accordingly, the next day, the security policeman then in the box, Ferreira (who had given evidence in the Looksmart case), was questioned about police brutality. We told the judge that many of our clients had given us statements saying that they had been seriously assaulted by members of the security police during their interrogation and that this officer, Ferreira, was one of those whose names had been given to us as being actively involved.

The judge turned to Ferreira and asked him, "What do you know about these allegations of assault?"

Ferreira replied, "No, your Lordship, absolutely nothing."

The judge accepted his reply. He was not interested in the allegations of torture and told us to proceed with the rest of the case.

Concerned that the police should not get away with this brutality scot-free, I tried to indicate to my London solicitor that I could provide him with such evidence if he asked for it so that police torture could be exposed overseas. His reply was curt and unimaginative. I was told that copying such documents for him was an unnecessary expense and was uncalled for.

In addition to working with counsel and attending to the mechanics of the legal work, I was trying to take care of the personal requirements of the thirty-seven. Each day, when the court adjourned for lunch, I would take parcels of food, fruit, and cigarettes to the back door of the court. There, the officer on duty alerted the police, who took up their positions. Drawing a deep breath, I would shoulder my packages and walk past the Sten guns pointing at my stomach and back toward the grille of the shed. There the police would carefully inspect each item before handing it through the bars.

I was still receiving constant complaints about the lack of attention from the prison doctor. Ephraim Kaporo, one of the older men, had complained of a perpetual headache since being assaulted by the police. He was finally treated for toothache! His condition deteriorated and he was removed to the prison hospital—which resulted in the trial's being brought to a standstill. Defense counsel, the judge, and the prosecutor all wanted to proceed and looked on the defendant's illness as an inconvenience. They adopted the attitude that since the defendant could not follow the proceedings anyway, his absence was not a good reason for delaying the trial.

One of my counsel and I visited the jail to see if we could communicate with the sick man. We found him in an isolation ward, too far gone to know where he was or what we were talking about. He died the next day. It was then my sad duty to see my clients in the iron shed and tell them of the death of their comrade. Many of them wept, as I myself did, but justice could not be interrupted and they were taken back into court almost immediately so that the trial could proceed.

The death of Kaporo added to the apparent hopelessness of our case cast a deep depression over the defendants and the defense team.

From then on, the defendants, sitting in long rows in the witness box, were more silent than I had ever seen them. They had to listen to the evidence of state witness after state witness, men whom they knew well as their brethren, describing their involvement in acts of "terrorism," and they had to see how helpless the defense was to rebut this evidence. When the court adjourned for us to have consultations, we had to ply them with questions to evoke any response from them. The hostility of the court and the police was oppressive.

Each day when we drove back to Johannesburg, a heavy gloom pervaded the car. We felt we were fighting only to keep the number of hangings as low as possible.

The defense team's impotence in the face of police power was demonstrated the day Swanepoel testified. He was a heavy man, broad across his shoulders, and the most outstanding thing about him was his ugliness. His face was pockmarked, blotchy pink and purple. His nose was flabby with wide, flat nostrils. His ears stood out from his head beneath his close-cropped ginger hair and his head sat on his shoulders as though he had no neck. I watched him as he stood in the witness box in front of me and tried to fathom what made him so fearsome a man. With tremendous arrogance, he dispensed with the formalities, swore himself in, dismissed the role of the judge's registrar, and proceeded with his evidence. He made it clear that he was in control of the proceedings.

After beginning his testimony he suddenly turned to the judge and asked to be permitted to have a private word with the prosecutor. This was highly irregular. "It is a matter of state security," said he half-smiling. The judge consented helplessly although he clearly resented this man who toyed with the court's authority. Swanepoel left the witness box, had a word in the prosecutor's ear, both men smiled, and then he returned to the witness box. State security now being safe, he proceeded with his terrible tale.

His hand rested easily on the box. His fingers, fat and short, moved a little uneasily but he seemed self-possessed. He described how he had found the camp where some of the defendants and others were in training and had planned and led the attack on it. The defendants were taken by surprise as helicopters landed on top of them. Swanepoel related how some had tried to attack the planes with bows and arrows. Factually and coldly, showing no emotion, he told how "this one raised an arm and I shot him dead;" "that one I killed flat"; "another I shot dead where he stood and another." Asked to identify some of the defendants, he turned his face and stared through me at the defendants immediately behind me. I saw the essence of the man in his eyes; they were cold, oily, and frightening. I had seen the evil of the man's soul and it made me shudder.

A bitter rage took hold of me. We had twenty-nine statements detailing this man's brutality. We knew that he was, in fact, the leader of a gang of torturers, yet the judge treated him as a man of honor, accepting all his evidence, and because of my counsel's tactical decisions about the conduct of the case, we could not challenge his story in cross-examination or expose the viciousness of his actions.

Only one incident brought the thirty-seven some cheer. I had never succeeded in finding the minister they had repeatedly asked for and had almost despaired of their ever having a church service when one day they told me there was an Afrikaner Ovambo-speaking priest in the Pretoria area. I never learned how they found this out. Ignoring the protests of my counsel, who told me my duties lay in court and not in searching for priests, I set out to find the Dorothea Church Mission, a traveling mission supposed to be somewhere north of Pretoria. I spent the whole of one morning in a vain search and the next day I continued my hunt. Toward noon, hot and tired from driving on dusty roads, I began to give up hope and was about to turn back when I suddenly saw the bright colors of a huge tent far off the road. I found the path that led to it through the open veld and came upon a cluster of small brick houses, some as yet unfinished.

As I got out of my car, a big man dressed in a white safari suit addressed me in Afrikaans: *"Kan ek jou help?"* (Can I help you?) Although he looked tough I noticed he was being very gentle with the two young blond children he had with him. Even before I told him the name of the Afrikaner priest I was seeking, I had a hunch that this was the right place. As soon as he heard my Afrikaans he spoke to me in English and told me I would find the preacher I sought in the tent.

Under a high canvas roof I found a minister conducting a service. The congregants were both black and white, standing together, intermingled, praying and singing hymns. I had never seen this anywhere in South Africa. I felt I was in another country and I watched this unlikely congregation with growing amazement, enjoying the service.

When the service ended I inquired after Dominie du Plessis and found him with his junior ministers. I said to him, "My name is Joel Carlson. I am the attorney acting for the thirty-seven Ovambo men who are now on trial in Pretoria. I have been sent by them to ask—"

He interrupted me, his face alight with joy, and exclaimed, "This is truly a miracle, you are a messenger from God. We have been praying and praying for them and we have begged the good Lord for guidance."

I listened in amazement as he said, "We know them, you see, we knew them in Ovamboland, and others in Windhoek and in Walvis. Guilty as they may be, they are still men, entitled to God's mercy and his guidance. What can we do for them?"

I told him joyfully, "They wish you to come and pray with them."

Eagerly he agreed to hold a service if it could be arranged with the prison authorities. I was not sure how this could be managed but I asked him to come to court wearing his clerical garb early the next morning. I would speak to the major in charge and arrange everything. He assured me he would be there with two Ovambo evangelical brothers. As I left he blessed me once again and driving back to Pretoria I felt happy for the first time in many weeks.

Back in court, I sought out the major, and told him that a dominie would be coming down the next morning to conduct a prayer service. I did not ask his permission but was deliberately casual in my approach. Equally casually, he said, "That's fine." I hurried out to the shed to tell my clients the good news.

True to his word, the dominie arrived before eight the next morning with his two assistants. The major refused to permit the black churchmen in but he did allow the dominie to enter the shed and see the prisoners. As he entered the iron shed, my clients showed great pleasure at seeing him and welcomed him with deep feeling. After exchanging greetings with the many men he knew and to whom he spoke in Ovambo, he gathered them around him and began to pray in Afrikaans. Outside the shed, still carrying their Sten guns, the policemen clustered in curiosity. The dominie's voice rose in strong but clear tones and the police recognized the prayers. One by one, they removed their hats and standing at ease, their guns in front of them, their hats on the butts of the guns, they bowed their heads as they listened to the dominie's fervent words.

The prayers ended and as they sang a hymn, all thirty-seven voices reverberated through the courtyard. Their voices, deep and melodious, seemed to echo on and on. Even the policemen were visibly moved; the language spoken was their own, the prayers were familiar. Suddenly, for a moment, they saw the prisoners in the iron shed as Christians, and fellow men. Then Johnny Otto, our Bible study teacher, thanked the dominie, telling him they had waited a long time to have such a church service and they were very grateful that he had come to them.

The dominie left after arranging with the major to return again on a regular basis. Some mornings later, the major told me with great pride that he had brought his tape recorder and had recorded the prayers and the hymns because they were so impressive. Then, suddenly, by orders of the security police, the church services were stopped and there was no way we could get this order rescinded.

Within the defense team, tensions and disagreements were increasing, caused by the frustration and helplessness we all felt in the face of the mounting evidence against the defendants and ever-present fear of the death sentences. I decided that whatever we might be able to do within the confines of the Terrorism Act, it was essential to seek other means to save the lives of my clients. This was a political trial and political pressures had to be brought to bear upon the government so that they would realize the "unwisdom" of hanging any of the thirty-seven defendants. It was no use waiting until sentence had been passed because then the government would not be swayed. The time to bring pressure was now before any judgment had been given. I was sure that once those in authority had decided that death sentences were impolitic, the message would be passed to the right persons on the golf course or over a drink, to ensure that there were no hangings.

My job was to see that the initial decision was made—the rest of the process would take care of itself. Thinking of ways to achieve this end, I decided that the United Nations and the United States would provide the most powerful focus and although I had absolutely no idea how this could be done in practice nor whom to see, I was sure that somehow answers would be found after I arrived in New York. Hurriedly, I made plans to go to America.

XI
THE TRIP AND
THE AFTERMATH

In 1965, hoping to spend a December holiday weekend outside South Africa, I had applied for a passport. The holiday did not materialize but I kept the passport. Now, armed with this precious document, I went to the Jan Smuts International Airport to fly to New York. I was not sure I would be permitted to board the plane. The security police could find much to question me about and my attempt to leave might provide them with a good opportunity to do this.

Jeanette took me to the airport and after going through the normal procedures without incident, I sat down in a seat in the departure lounge, which was visible from the restaurant upstairs. We had arranged that if things went smoothly I would go straight to that seat where she could see me. If I did not appear she would know that I was being questioned or otherwise delayed. The next fifteen to twenty minutes seemed like as many hours. At last the call came to board. Only after an hour in the air did I begin to relax and accept the fact that I was really on my way.

We left Dakar, our last African stop, at midnight and flew

on into an endless night across the Atlantic. When we arrived at Kennedy airport at about 5 A.M., I was relieved to leave the plane. Friends, Mike and Jenny Davis, fellow South Africans who had been forced to leave the country, were going to meet me. Mike had been an advocate at the Johannesburg bar and Jenny was an economist. I searched in vain for a familiar face, then found my way to the main exit of the building. There the whole Davis family came running through the doors and I was given a warm and affectionate welcome.

I had given myself a fortnight to do whatever needed to be done in America so during the ride into the city through the icy winter morning I immediately began planning with Mike and Jenny whom I should see and who was likely to be the most helpful. At their apartment, over a good strong cup of tea, we talked endlessly about my problems and what was happening in the case. It all came spilling out; this was, in fact, the first time that I had been able to talk openly and without restraint, without wondering whether the security police were listening in. We called a halt for breakfast, then they had to go off to work and I was left to bathe and relax for a few hours.

I suddenly realized that I was in New York and I noticed for the first time the long, monotonous rows of tall apartment buildings, and became aware of the never-ending noise of traffic. Fortunately, the apartment overlooked the Hudson River. It was a cold, gray day and the river was black; barges and tugboats moved slowly and deliberately through the calm, deep waters of this wide river. Far to my right were the graceful lines of the George Washington Bridge. The city seemed singularly unattractive and unwelcoming—it was too vast to care about any one person, but the room I was in was full of African mats and lovely green plants. Some of the furniture I recognized since I had helped to pack it in Johannesburg. It was really a home away from home.

Jenny arrived back at noon and gave me some lunch. She also told me about my first appointment. We took a cab and drove through the maze of streets between overpowering buildings toward the United Nations. I felt completely lost and had no sense of direction whatsoever. On the way, Jenny told me who I was going to see and what his function was in the United Nations' organizational structure. She also explained what I might reasonably expect from this official.

The United Nations, a huge glass building, occupied by diplomats and secretaries from the far corners of the earth, was beautiful to look at, but inside it was full of paper and words. It is the heart of world bureaucracy. Its advantage, of course, is that gathered in this one building are representatives of most countries, which makes it easy to communicate with governments throughout the world.

Once in the office of the man I had come to see, I roughly brushed aside his diplomatic and formal words of welcome in order to stress the urgency of my visit. Tremendously overwrought, I was intolerant of courtesies and insistent on getting things done. Very briefly, I described the trial to him and emphasized the real threat of a mass hanging of the defendants. I talked of the hopelessness of all our efforts in the face of the "act of terror" under which my clients were being tried.

By the man's occasional interruptions, I realized that he was familiar with the background and sympathetic to my cause. I also recognized, however, that his acceptance was primarily an intellectual one; it was difficult for a stranger, however dedicated, to grasp what all this meant in human terms. I was forty floors up—far below on the ground people seemed insignificant, but I talked to him of real people and what was happening to them. I told him that we needed immediate action to save my clients from further tragedy. I asked him what he saw himself able to do to help them. I was not so much interested in general condemnation of laws and policies. I wanted action taken toward a very specific objective. Hanging, I said, was irrevocable and must be prevented. He said he would set up meetings with the ambassadors of the Western powers, and promised to call me back within the next forty-eight hours.

That evening my friends had arranged a meeting with five or six New York lawyers. I had corresponded with one of them—Charles Mandelstam—from Johannesburg, and I had formed a picture of him as a groovy-type lawyer with bright suits and wide, loud ties—a man who would smoke endless cigars. In fact, he, like the others there that evening, was a modest, quiet, very bright and alert man. He came with Peter Weiss, who, I was to learn subsequently, was the president of the American Committee on Africa and a strong supportor of the African's struggle for freedom.

They listened intently and interrupted only with pertinent questions. I was struck by their vigor and determination and was satisfied that they had quickly acquired a full grasp of the situation. Drained as I was by the end of the evening, it was tremendously exhilarating to be with these men. I began to feel confident that something would be achieved by my visit.

The following day was a Saturday and we rose late. As the sun shone weakly through a watery sky we drove up to the Cloisters and walked through the wild grass and the old buildings and for a while, I sat and watched the river. In front of me I could reach out and hold strands of grass but the city of New York was too big to comprehend.

On Monday morning I met Wayne Fredericks, who had just taken a senior post at one of America's largest foundations, after having resigned as Assistant Secretary of State for African Affairs. He had an extensive knowledge of South African affairs and like most of the Americans I met on my trip, was deeply opposed to racial discrimination. While I was talking to him, a colleague and friend of his, Burke Marshall, who had served as Assistant Attorney General in the Kennedy Administration, called on him and stayed to listen. They speculated for a few moments as to what action could be taken. Then having rapidly reached a decision, they called a number of people including several in the State Department, Congress, and the Senate. Further, they offered to do whatever they could in their own spheres to help me.

Throughout my stay in America I was impressed with the quick grasp of the men and women I spoke to and the perceptive questions I was asked. These were extremely busy people holding key positions, yet it was only a question of hours or days before they found time to see me and then made time to take action. There was no formality or pomp about the way they conducted their affairs.

The next morning I set off for Washington, D.C. I flagged a

cab in the cold early light and asked the cabbie to take me to the airport.

"*Oy vey!*" he said, "at this time in the morning you vant I should go to LaGuardia—I'll go, I have to."

I told him that I thought it would be a good thing for him to have such a long trip.

"You should only know the traffic, mister, you'll see, I'll show you," he replied.

I did see. On the way to the airport we passed astonishing expressways and bridges and for as long as we traveled there were three to six lanes of unending bumper-to-bumper traffic.

"You see vot I mean," he kept on saying, "through this you make me drive back." My guilt was adding up to a fat tip for him.

Some of his other comments were also illuminating. "Vere you come from, mister?" he asked soon after I got in the cab.

"South Africa."

"South Africa! They got vite men down there, I thought there was bushmen there. That's sure a long way away."

His ignorance of Africa seemed astonishing but then he asked, "Ever been here before?" I told him "No." He drew my attention to the Ruppert Brewery. There was a millionaire back home with a similar name and for a moment I wondered whether my South African millionaire had extended his interests to New York.

"Whose brewery?" I asked.

"Ruppert Brewery," he exclaimed indignantly. "You don't mean to tell me you never heard of Jacob Ruppert, the great Ruppert—the philanthropist—you never heard of him?"

All our ignorances, I realized, were relative.

He dropped me at the entrance to the Eastern Airlines shuttle flight. The casual procedure there surprised me. Every previous air journey I had made, particularly in South Africa, had necessitated a reserved seat and a ticket. This was like catching a bus! Once in the aircraft I found even more to amaze me. Plane after plane sped down the runway to take off in front of us. No one but me seemed perturbed at what was happening. I took to timing the intervals between each takeoff and found that the average time was fifty seconds. To my relief we were airborne at last and had not collided with anything either on the ground or in the air!

Forty-five minutes later we were circling above Washington and I could see the Potomac River, which I knew only from my history books. Around and around we flew for as long a time as it had taken us to fly from New York. Out of the window I could see other planes flying above and below us. With a rush of homesickness I remembered the last time I had watched a lion kill in a wild game park. High above, the sky had been filled with vultures circling round and round. Slowly, they narrowed their spiral flight and dropped down to land near the kill. Suddenly I was interrupted by the hostess reminding me to fasten my seat belt and I was once more aware that I was now in the land of technology.

I was met by a man who was a stranger to me but in response to his quiet, unassuming manner, coupled with a warm friendliness, I felt an instant liking for him and looked forward to getting to know him. He took me to an old Volkswagen and we drove to the State Department buildings. After a quick cup of tea a group gathered to hear what I had to say. I spoke at length, reporting on the Terrorism Act and the trial. The meeting lasted three to four hours, and never before had I talked for so long or been questioned with such depth and thoroughness on the subject of South Africa. All my views, all my actions, over the past twenty years were discussed and reviewed. I felt as though I was being mentally x-rayed. I did not hesitate to speak openly to these men but at the end of the period I was exhausted.

Almost immediately, however, after a quick lunch we were off again to meet a group of congressmen. I had about ten minutes to spare and walked leisurely along the wide corridors reading the plates on the doors, until now only names in newspapers. Congressman Donald Fraser's secretary took me into a beautifully paneled room and asked me to wait. I sat down on a well-worn leather couch. After the congressmen had assembled one of them jocularly told me I was sitting in the Vice-President's seat. He recounted how years before the Speaker of the House had sought Vice-President Truman to tell him of the death of President Roosevelt and had found him in this very room, sitting on this very couch.

I was introduced by Congressman Jonathan Bingham to Congressmen Fraser, Benjamin Rosenthal, and Bradford Morse and I again explained the purpose of my mission. They were horrified by the provisions of the Terrorism Act. Congressman Bingham said, "I have never seen a retroactive clause before; read it to me, I want to see how it's worded." I was also asked to comment on United States policy toward South Africa, and questioned on sanctions and boycotts. I said that I was a lawyer, not a politician, but that I felt much more pressure could be applied by America on South Africa. At the end of the meeting I again felt that progress had been made and I was satisfied.

During the meeting, Senator Edward Kennedy, who had been unable to keep an earlier appointment with me, phoned and asked me to return later to his office. When I got there, he came out to greet me and apologized for his previous absence. He walked with some difficulty, using a cane. He lowered his tall body into an armchair opposite me and I began my story yet again. Its effect on him was the same as on all the others I'd talked to—horror—and he volunteered to assist in whatever way he could. He also insisted I talk to his brother Robert.

Next morning my friend from the State Department picked me up and took me to his office. I met a number of lawyers and heads of departments and was also taken to an immigration section where I was given very helpful advice should I decide one day to immigrate to the United States.

Then I hurried back to the Senate building to see Senator Robert Kennedy. He listened intently as I spoke and I was aware of his electric personality and his dynamism. When the quorum bell rang he apologized and asked me if I would walk with him to the Senate while he cast a vote. I told him that it would be a pleasure to walk with him but I didn't want to have any pictures taken with him. I did not want to risk the attendant publicity. With some amusement he told me it was the first time that anyone had objected to having a photograph

taken with him. As we walked across the lawn, two sightseers
hurried up to take pictures and I ducked behind my newspaper. Once we reached the Senate building, Senator Kennedy ran up the steps, three at a time, and I waited for him to
return. He was back within five minutes and we strolled back
to his office.

The senator had himself recently been to South Africa and
was well briefed about my country. He was, nevertheless,
shocked by what I told him and when we got back, he picked
up the telephone and asked me to see a number of other
people, among them the under secretary of state, Nicholas
Katzenbach. He assured me he would use his influence in
whatever way would be most effective.

The office of the under secretary of state was plush,
blue-carpeted, and very large. It was the most sumptuous
office I had yet visited. Secretary Katzenbach himself was in
shirtsleeves and as he dropped into a large chair and stretched
out, I noticed a tear in the left sleeve. Once again I was struck
by the total absence of ceremony and the easy informality
that characterized even the most prominent Americans.

Speaking slowly, he told me he had heard much about me
and wanted to know what I thought he could do in the matter.
Again I explained that I thought pressure could be brought to
bear on the South African government in order to stop any of
my clients from being hanged. I told him that I thought it
should be possible to apply such pressure firmly, but quietly
and privately, without any publicity.

He commented wryly, "I wish I had the ear of your
ambassador and I wish he would listen to me. I do not have
the key to the safe." He indicated, however, that he would
take some action.

We discussed a number of other matters relevant to American policy in South Africa and I suggested that the American
government could show its concern for justice by sending
observers to this and other such trials and by having its allies
join them in this activity. Then he asked me what he said was
the sixty-four-dollar question—What did I think of sanctions
being imposed on South Africa by the U.S.?

My answer was simple. "Anything that supports, condones,

or which is seen to condone racial discrimination in South Africa, is support for *apartheid*. No action should be taken to support *apartheid* in South Africa—every action should be taken to oppose and end *apartheid* policies."

Finally, I raised with him the possibility of my being pulled in for interrogation on my return to South Africa. I advised him that if I was forced to disclose my conversations here I would be frank and honest. However, it was possible that the security police would force my signature on a document that might be embarrassing to the United States government. While I would try to avoid doing this, it should be understood in advance that under conditions of interrogation by the security police I might not be responsible for my actions. He said he understood the position and hoped it would not occur. I left his office considerably heartened by the interview.

Next day I began visiting ambassadors at the UN, including Arthur Goldberg, the U.S. ambassador. He received me with cordiality and great warmth and took quick command of our conversation by asking me questions rather than listening to me talk. Having accepted the justice of my cause and the need for action, he hesitated only on the question of timing. I reminded him that the South African government was proud of its granite inflexibility in the face of the world. Once the sentence of death was passed, the government would be determined not to show weakness in response to pressures. I convinced him that the time to act was now. He congratulated me on undertaking a mission which was, in his opinion, in keeping with the highest ideals of our profession.

"Should you be arrested on your return," he said, "I assure you that I will be the head of the defense team appearing on your behalf. It would be a privilege to act for you." I was moved by the humanity of this man and felt sure that my visit to him would bear fruit.

That evening, I talked to a meeting of lawyers from the New York City bar, and much of the rest of the week was spent in talking to other groups, particularly to church leaders. I felt strange talking to these Christians for in my experience such men were mostly privileged whites, enjoying high standards of living and totally absorbed into the South African way of life. Black Christians in South Africa were good Christians only if they recognized their place in society as servants to the white masters. Even Christian churches beyond South Africa's borders had scarcely raised their voice against the intolerable opposition of blacks. I was not a Christian nor did I hold any religious beliefs and I did not wish to sound impertinent but I was deeply aware of the wrongs perpetrated in South Africa in the name of Christianity.

I met American church leaders of all denominations and was impressed by their real concern for change in South Africa. They sought my views both in the nature of the assistance they could render in regard to the trial of the thirty-seven, and in the aid the church could give in South Africa to all oppressed groups. I had many criticisms to voice arising out of the trial. Thirty-two of the thirty-seven were practicing Christians and I told them about Eliazar Tahudaleni, Johnny Otto, and Emmanuel Machuiriri. Many of the defendants were third-generation Christians and some were descendants of priests. They had given me the names and addresses of the ministers at the churches where they and their families worshiped, and I wrote them but none answered. They wanted nothing to do with these "terrorists." Eventually I did receive a reply from an Anglican priest who provided some assistance to some of the families and who offered to help me further if his bishop consented. Subsequently, Bishop Robert Mize, an Episcopalian from the United States serving in Namibia, wrote advising me that the church disapproved of violence and could not support the views or actions of my clients. The bishop refused to allow his priest to give me further assistance but added that the church, in its wisdom and mercy, was praying for my clients. At this stage, not even the judge had convicted the prisoners and some of them were, in fact, to be acquitted.

(In 1972, I met Bishop Leonard Aulua, a black Lutheran from Namibia. He told me how he had traveled the two thousand miles from Ovamboland to Pretoria in an attempt to see the defendants in prison but was frustrated by white officials and sent back to Ovamboland.)

These American church leaders were dismayed by the

revelations I gave them. They said they had not known how their black brothers had been rejected by the white church in South Africa. Some of them offered financial assistance, and before I left America, I was given a large check that helped to cover the costs of the trial. They also asked me to visit the World Council of Churches in Geneva and arrangements were made for me to address that body on my way home.

I always made clear at these meetings that I was not a Christian nor religious in any way, and I was touched when, on one occasion, a bishop put his hands on my shoulders and said, "My son—may I call you my son? May I say God bless you and watch over you."

There remained now only a few last interviews with some UN ambassadors before I could leave America for home. I saw a number of African and Asian representatives and was pleased to learn that a motion on the trial was being prepared for admission to the General Assembly. I found the black representatives distrustful of Britain and France. The Swedish ambassador, Sverker Astrom, was particularly sympathetic and made it quite clear that this was his government's concern as well as his own. He could not have been more helpful to me.

When I saw Lord Caradon, the British ambassador to the United Nations, I had no doubt where his personal sympathies lay, but in true diplomatic style, he made no specific commitments. He did, however, indicate that Britain would support a resolution in the General Assembly and might have its representatives in South Africa attend the trial as observers, and although nothing specific was said, I gained the impression that some other form of representation might well be made.

There remained now the question of finding some lawyers who might be able to attend the trial in Pretoria as official observers. I talked to a number of people, including Professor Richard Falk, of Princeton University, who eventually did come to South Africa in 1968 as an observer for the International Commission of Jurists.

After ten hectic days, I began to feel certain that my trip had been worthwhile. While it was true that I had few firm commitments of any kind from anyone, I was satisfied that action would be taken. In fact, the less I knew about the particular kind of action, the better.

Reluctantly, I caught a plane to London, the first step on my journey home. I left in New York my friends the Davises, two exiled South Africans dedicated to bringing about change in their homeland. Understanding my problems, they had given me ready assistance throughout my trip. I knew that both would maintain their ties with me as my liaison in the United States, and they were well placed to build new ones.

Soon after my departure from America, one of the lawyers I had spoken to, Morris Abram, had among other things raised the question among his colleagues of my being instructed in South Africa by the Lawyers Committee for Civil Rights under Law. This proposal was supported by many other men I had seen. The Lawyers Committee was an organization formed by President John F. Kennedy in the early 1960s and consisted of many of the most prominent American lawyers, including such men as Arthur H. Dean, an adviser to President Dwight D. Eisenhower and past president of the American Bar Association; Whitney North Seymour, a prominent American lawyer and president of the American Bar Association; Robert Kennedy, William P. Rogers, Eugene Rostow, Theodore Sorensen, Burke Marshall, Erwin N. Griswold, and Nicholas Katzenbach, all of whom had served in the Kennedy and Johnson administrations; and Louis F. Oberdorfer, who had acted as Robert Kennedy's personal attorney.

Not long after I returned to Johannesburg, the Lawyers Committee sent me a letter of instruction backed by funds, to assist me in the work of the Namibian case and subsequently, I received further instructions from them. All of this was of great importance in that it provided a channel of communication along which a full exchange of information flowed. It was a link with professional colleagues dedicated to upholding civil rights in America, who fully understood what was necessary for lawyers working in a police state. Of the many worthwhile results coming from my trip, this was of inestimable value.

I knew there were others, too, some of whom had long been

deeply concerned about the black struggle in South Africa, who would go on building pressure—men like Peter Weiss and George Houser, of the American Committee on Africa, and Charles Mandelstam, who had agreed to continue acting as my New York attorney. In all, I was extremely pleased with the informal organization that had been built. It was an important achievement that would last.

In London I first went to the offices of my English attorneys. In contrast to the helpful attitude of people in America, I had great difficulty in making an appointment at any time within the next two weeks. Only my really angry insistence eventually led to a meeting at 8:30 that evening. Immediately, the solicitor made it clear that he knew nothing about the proceedings concerning the trial and relied on part-time advisers. It became clear why there was so much delay and inefficiency in dealing with the case. I made some constructive suggestions in the rather faint hope that matters would improve but I also insisted on seeing my client, Lord Campbell, personally. I wanted to ensure his personal involvement in the trial. As I could only see him later that week, I decided to fill in time in Geneva where I wanted to visit several international organizations.

In South Africa I had represented the International Commission of Jurists, had acted as observer for them in political trials, and had reported to them on various matters. I had happy memories of my visit to Geneva in 1960, when the commission had produced an excellent book on South Africa and the rule of law. At Geneva airport, I was astonished by the lack of formality in getting through customs. It seemed that a bowler hat, umbrella, and the title of jurist was sufficient to permit my entry into this country. I was met by two members of the commission who took me to the office of Sean MacBride, the secretary-general, where I spent some very pleasant hours talking with colleagues and making plans, not only for the present case but for the commission's continued intervention in South Africa.

With MacBride's assistance, I made an appointment to see Mr. Claude Pilloud, the secretary of the International Committee of the Red Cross. To him, I stressed the importance of

long-term prisoners like the Namibians being visited by
members of the Red Cross while they were in detention. He
agreed that the whole subject was an issue that might benefit
from new procedures and was one requiring thorough investigation.

While in Geneva a meeting was also arranged for me with
the World Council of Churches and I restated what I had told
American church leaders about the church's lack of concern
for black Christians in South Africa. Next morning I at last
received a call from London advising me that if I flew back
Lord Campbell would give me fifteen minutes of his time. I
hurried to the airport and caught the first plane to London.

At the stroke of 12 noon I was outside his lordship's door.
His offices were located on a square and from the outside,
there was nothing to distinguish one entrance from another.
Announcing myself at the front door, I was directed to an
elevator just big enough for two people, went up to the top
floor and stepped out into a small dark passage that led to the
door of the apartment I sought. The carpeting deadened all
sound. I was shown into the apartment by a very English
secretary who was most charming.

Lord Campbell came out to greet me and was warm and
friendly. Shaking my hand in a firm grasp, he took me through
to his study. It was immediately obvious that he was quick
and sharp. I outlined to him the allegations that had been
made in South Africa that I was getting money illegally from
Defense and Aid, an organization that gives aid to South
African political prisoners and is illegal in South Africa
because it is deemed, by law, to be "Communist." Since such
allegations could lead to criminal prosecution, I felt it particularly important to have his personal assurance that he was
indeed not merely a legal fiction, but truly my instructing
client.

Swiftly he assured me that this was so, and went on to
say—in response to my obvious concern—that if the South
African police tried to challenge this by bringing a prosecution
against me under the Suppression of Communism Act, he
would support me fully and would be proud to testify in court
that he was funding the Namibian defense.

Having dealt with our formal relationship, we turned to a discussion of the case itself. My fifteen minutes stretched into an hour and by the time I had left him I was deeply impressed by his commitment to the principles of justice and I was gratified by his too generous congratulations on the work I was doing.

My mission overseas was complete. We would now have to wait and see what success it had achieved. It had been a relief to escape for a while the constant surveillance of the security police. But as soon as I stepped onto South African soil it started up again. As I went through customs and immigration, I was taken off to a separate section and I and my luggage were methodically searched. Despite my protests, papers relating to the defense were removed from my briefcase and taken off to be copied. Meanwhile, my wife had been told that I was not on the plane. After making exhaustive inquiries and waiting over an hour for the next flight to arrive, she left the airport and went home, tremendously disturbed.

When I was eventually released and made my way into the terminal building, I found no one to meet me. It occurred to me that if the security police wished me to disappear, this could now be easily arranged. No one even knew I was back in the country. I hurried to a telephone and called my office, telling my staff exactly where I was and asking them to telephone my wife on the other phone while I stayed on the line. I dictated cables to my American friends, advising them I had arrived, that I had received a "warm" reception, and that I was safe and well. I continued talking to the office until I saw Jeanette come in. My trip was over.

The day after my return, I was back in Pretoria seeing my clients. In the milk-bar, with the aid of pen and notepaper, I explained to them what I had been doing and told them about some of the people I had seen. They welcomed me back with great excitement. I was pleased to see they were now reasonably dressed; it was obvious that the arrangements to supply each of them with clothing, which I had made before my departure, had been carried out.

I visited counsel, received a report from them on the progress of the trial, and discussed future developments. I, in turn, reported to them on some of the matters that I had attended to on my trip overseas.

About a week later, a lieutenant colonel of the prisons department phoned to arrange for me to see the special representative of the International Committee of the Red Cross. I wanted to meet him where there would be no bugging devices so we met at the main airline terminal office in Johannesburg. The colonel introduced me to Mr. G. C. Senn, and a younger man, Dr. Burkhardt, and left us to talk in private.

These two were deeply concerned about the thirty-seven. Mr. Senn had been working as a Red Cross representative for more than twoscore years and his dedication to his work was obvious. While we were talking I suddenly recalled having seen him before. I had been on a visit to Robben Island to see Nelson Mandela. The sea that day was particularly rough and I had been struggling to keep my footing on the small police ferry taking us across from Cape Town. I had noticed this elderly and striking-looking man dressed in a khaki safari suit, quite unconcerned at the boat's lurchings.

I gave him as many details as I could recall from memory about the complaints of my clients. I told him of the man with a broken arm and of the tuberculosis sufferers, and of the man who believed he had leprosy. I told him of the attitude of the prison doctor. I offered to give him full details of all the complaints but suggested that an examination of each of the men by Dr. Burkhardt would establish the true position more accurately. I also advised him of the nature of the tortures my clients had suffered. He interrupted me and told me he had already received statements from Jason Mutumbulua and some of the others. He assured me that the doctor would examine the men and would strongly recommend treatment for those who required it.

Subsequently, my clients told me that they had seen Dr. Burkhardt and they said they were receiving much better treatment and that in addition, the prison doctor had been removed. They were heartened and encouraged by the progress that was being made. If nothing else resulted from my trip, this alone would have made it worthwhile. However, all of us began to see the other results of my visit overseas.

On December 16, the General Assembly of the United
Nations approved by a vote of 110 to 2 (Portugal and South
Africa) a demand that South Africa stop the trial of the
Namibian leaders in Pretoria. The General Assembly termed
the arrest and the trial of the Namibians "a flagrant violation
of their rights." Ambassador Goldberg, speaking in favor of
the resolution, analyzed in some detail "the atrocious Terrorism Act under which 37 South West Africans were charged
and brought to trial, under conditions repugnant to all who
believe in justice under law." There were fifty-eight sponsors
of the resolution; it was supported by the great powers and
all Afro-Asian and Latin American countries. The morale of
the thirty-seven rose as they saw this surge of world interest.

Soon after this, local newspapers carried news of Vice-
President Hubert Humphrey's African tour and the speech he
delivered in Zambia, strongly condemning the trial of the
Namibians in Pretoria. He termed it a farce and called on
the South African government to act in accordance with the
United Nations resolution. He warned of the consequences if
any of the thirty-seven were hanged.

In South Africa, December 16 is celebrated each year as the
"Day of the Covenant." It is enjoyed by the Afrikaners as a
holy day of rededication to the aims of *die volk,* and the prime
minister and his cabinet ministers mount platforms all over
the country to talk to their people. This day is frequently
chosen to make important policy speeches charged with
emotion. That year the prime minister made the theme of his
speech the trial of the thirty-seven. He declared that South
Africa would not allow anything or anybody to interfere with
the trial; he rejected all demands that the trial be stopped. The
deputy prime minister, Ben Schoeman, charged Vice-
President Hubert Humphrey with making "poisonous attacks
on South Africa" and alleged that the terrorists were "nothing
but murderers."

When I read the reports of these speeches I was elated. The
attention given to the trial signified that the government was
concerned at the response of the world to this trial and to the
enforcement of the Terrorism Act. I thought that the prime
minister protested too much. Although still uneasy, I began to

feel that the threat of hanging any of the thirty-seven was now considerably reduced.

When I saw my clients in Pretoria, they smiled at Prime Minister Vorster's loud words. "We are fighting back now," they told me. "He will not dare to hang us." Even the more stern and serious among them began to smile and see some hope.

The pressure on South Africa continued unabated. The Association of the Bar of the City of New York resolved to record "its deep concern and its protest over the actions of the Republic of South Africa, in applying its own law and judicial process extra-territorially, to South West Africans and by prosecuting 37 of them under the Terrorism Act of 1967. . . . This Act offends basic concepts of justice, due process and the rule of law accepted by civilized nations and violates the Declaration of Human Rights."

In response to this resolution, I learned later that the bar association received a letter from the South African ambassador in which he commended South Africa on not summarily executing terrorists on their arrest, but first bringing them to trial!

Protests by congressmen of the United States and British members of Parliament, as well as the press of both countries, continued. The South African press reported much of this pressure and they condemned it as an interference in South Africa's domestic affairs. However, it was nevertheless regarded as significant. The thirty-seven could see the world's concern represented in the flesh by the presence of a number of official observers from foreign governments who sat in the special diplomatic section of the gallery. The police dogs suddenly disappeared, the armed police force attending the trial was halved, and only those security policemen who had been responsible for the interrogation of each witness sat in court.

In December the prosecutor closed his case. Throughout the trial he had been anxious to stop any revelations about security police torture and he had not introduced any of the statements made by my clients. He was aware that they had made complaints to officials of the Red Cross about their torture, and he knew that the most articulate of them wished to take the stand to give evidence about this and to express the real grievances of the people of Namibia and the brutality of the oppressive white rule. He did not want the platform of the court used for this purpose.

For this reason, it suited the prosecutor's purpose to "do a deal with the defense team." He proposed to withdraw the charges of terrorism against the leaders of SWAPO—the most articulate of the defendants who could convey to the world what their people were suffering—provided they made no address to the court and pleaded guilty to a charge under the Suppression of Communism Act. In these circumstances, the prosecutor, too, would not address the court on sentence. This meant that those defendants who were a party to the deal would serve only short terms of imprisonment and would have the balance of their sentences suspended. Under the Terrorism Act, the minimum sentence was five years with no provision for suspension of any period. Undoubtedly, the proposed deal was in the interest of the few men to whom it was made and we reluctantly agreed to it. Thus, at the end of the state case, the judge acquitted one defendant of all charges, and at the end of the defense case, the plea of not guilty to the Terrorism Act charge was accepted on behalf of Johnny Otto, Jason Mutumbulua, and Nathaniel Machuiriri, leaders of SWAPO, who were then convicted only of the Suppression of Communism Act offenses.

Lord Campbell sent his London solicitor to attend the trial and I introduced him to my clients in the iron shed before the court resumed. He brought them a message of support and encouragement from his lordship. Subsequently, he paid for his attention to the accused and was unable to have his visa renewed for any further visits to South Africa.

As the trial proceeded, the United Nations kept the matter before it and referred it to the Security Council. All representative governments had been asked to report on the actions they had taken concerning the trial. Argentina, Canada, Finland, France, India, Jamaica, Kenya, Kuwait, Somalia, Sweden, the United Kingdom, the United States, Venezuela, Yugoslavia, and many others reported that they had made express representations through their ambassadors or other channels to the South African government. Typical of the reports was that of the United Kingdom, which said "that because of the abhorrence of the legislation under which the prisoners were charged, and because they wished to add their weight on behalf of the prisoners to the strength of the United Nations call to the South African government to stop the trial, the British Ambassador in Pretoria had conveyed to the South African government, concern about the trial and about the legislation under which the prisoners were charged, and had demonstrated that concern by sending an observer to the sessions of the trial."

The day before the judge in Pretoria was to pronounce judgment, the Security Council met and unanimously passed a resolution condemning the continuation of the trial and calling upon the South African government to release the defendants and permit them to go home.

Then the court convened, and speaking in Afrikaans, the judge read out his full judgment. It took five hours. He convicted thirty-one of the accused under the Terrorism Act. Then he went on to belittle the actions of the defendants and to evaluate them as "feeble and without the slightest hope of success." He praised the courage of the security police and commended them for being astute and alert; he said they had acted in a responsible manner and that the security of the state was safe in their hands.

During our address to the court, we had applied to the judge for the acquittal of one man against whom the evidence was particularly weak, and to our surprise, he acquitted the man standing next to him. Had he made a mistake? Had he mixed up the names and the numbers? There was nothing we could do about it. It was obvious that only token acquittals were being given in order to preserve the image of an impartial judiciary.

Having concluded his judgment, the judge then adopted an extraordinary procedure. He read a one-page document, copies of which were immediately handed to the press and especially to the foreign observers. This "press release" said that despite the serious crimes of which the defendants had been convicted, the judge considered that they had been misled by agitators. He deemed it necessary, therefore, to indicate at this stage to the defense team that he had already decided not to impose the death penalty in this case.

I had to be restrained from jumping up with excitement. As the statement was interpreted to my clients, a number of them smiled at me, their faces showing their relief. We had won a significant battle. No one had expected any acquittals under the Terrorism Act and at the very least, everyone was prepared for lengthy prison sentences, but the major fear had been the death sentence and this was now ruled out. Despite the convictions, therefore, we made the journey back to Johannesburg in a happy frame of mind and for the first time in months, the defense team relaxed in lighthearted banter. We now had to wait for sentence to be passed.

The convictions rightly raised a storm of protest throughout the world. The Washington *Post* said, "How many more men will be forced on to the byways of violence before justice marches to Pretoria?" *The New York Times,* in an editorial entitled "Justice, South African style," commented that South Africa's white minority government was about to stage the last act of an atrocious offense against civilized behavior, social and legal justice, and international law.

As the trial was going on, I had found it increasingly difficult to keep a staff and I had a number of staff changes—at least eight secretaries left me, some after working for only a few hours. At last I employed a very reliable woman, Phillipa Levy, the wife of a man who was a political prisoner then serving a sentence in jail. Almost immediately police told her to report to security headquarters. When she called they asked her about a number of her activities and reminded her that her husband was soon to come out of jail and under "normal" procedures would automatically be placed under house arrest. This, they hinted, might be avoided if she cooperated with them. They also offered her a substantial sum of money if she would inform on me.

When Phillipa returned to my office, she told me of the offer made to her by the security police. She was worried about her husband and the possibility of her own detention and reluctantly she decided that in order to avoid any further black-mailing threats she would leave my office, so I gave her notice. We parted on very good terms. Subsequently, when her husband was released from prison he was placed under house arrest and he and Phillipa left the country. Living in South Africa had been made intolerable for them.

After the convictions, there remained the work necessary for presenting an argument to the court on mitigation of sentence and the defense team set about preparing a case. Some members of the team worked with a local professor who had done extensive research on South West Africa and its people. Others prepared some of the defendants who wished to make a statement in court. Herman Ja Toivo had slowly regained his self-respect and was once again accepted by his comrades as their leader. He undertook his role of spokesman with dignity and pride and began writing an address he wanted to deliver to the court.

Some members of the defense team were opposed to his saying anything; they believed that this would aggravate the sentence to be imposed. Indeed, the professor we were going to call did not give evidence for this reason. Herman was torn between his desire to voice the grievances of his people and his anxiety not to have the punishments meted out increased. In his dilemma, he received conflicting advice from members of the defense team. He talked to me for long hours about the alternatives open to him and asked my opinion. It seemed to me that the judge would impose severe sentences in any event. Herman, himself, was likely to be jailed for fifteen to twenty years. I felt that if he spoke up, as he so strongly wanted to do, he would not have accepted his sentence in silence and each night in prison, he would be able to recall that when the time came to speak he found the courage to do so. This would warm him in the cold days and nights ahead. But I told him I recognized that the final decision was his. I was not facing any prison sentence and it was, therefore, easy for me to give advice.

Herman finally reached the decision to act as a spokesman, after the judge, in his judgment, denounced him as a coward. The judge had said that although Herman proclaimed himself a man of peace, when others came to him with guns and ammunition he was afraid to report them to the police.

Next day when we arrived at court Herman expressed his anger at the judgment. "This judge," he said, "saw fit to call me a coward. Yet in the last war I joined the army to fight for this country while this judge was a traitor and belonged to the pro-Nazi underground organization which committed sabotage as I stood on guard at military installations, facing the bullets of his colleagues. Now I am called a coward and he is the judge."

As the final days of the trial drew near, journalists, TV newsmen, and international observers arrived from overseas. From Princeton came Richard Falk, professor of international law, who represented the International Commission of Jurists. From Duke University came professor Arthur Larsen, former adviser to President Eisenhower and representative of the World Lutheran Federation. The whole gallery was packed as Herman Ja Toivo walked to the stand to deliver his address to the court. He spoke in English, in quiet and dignified tones, without emotion or much inflection. His words were telling and his manner convincing. It was a strong and direct statement of the grievances of his people.

Taking the stand and addressing the judge, he said:

My Lord, we find ourselves here in a foreign country, convicted under laws made by people who we have always considered as foreigners. We find ourselves tried by a judge who is not our countryman and who has not shared our background.

We are Namibians and not South Africans. We do not now and will not in the future, recognize your right to govern us, to make laws for us, in which we had no say; to treat our country as if it were your property and us as if you were our masters. We have always regarded South Africa as an intruder in our country. This is how we have always felt and this is how we feel now and it is on this basis that we have faced this trial.

We are far away from our homes. Not a single

member of our families has come to visit us, never mind be present at our trial. The Pretoria jail, the police headquarters where we were interrogated and where statements were extracted from us and this court, is all we have seen of Pretoria. We have been cut off from our people and the world.

The state has not only wanted to convict us but also to justify the policy of the South African government. We will not even try to present the other side of the picture because we know that a court that has not suffered in the same way as we have cannot understand us. This is perhaps why it is said that one should be tried by one's equals—we here are being tried by our masters. Had we been tried by our equals it would not have been necessary to have any discussions about our grievances; they would have been known by those set to judge us. We know that whites do not think of blacks as politicians, only as agitators.

I do not claim that it is easy for men of different races to live at peace with one another. I myself had no experience of this in my youth, and at first it surprised me that men of different races could live together and in peace. But now I know it to be true and to be something for which we must strive. The South African government creates hostility by separating people and emphasizing their differences. We believe that by living together people will learn to lose their fear of each other. We also believe that this fear which some of the whites have of Africans, is based on their desire to be superior and privileged and that when whites see themselves as part of South West Africa, sharing with us all its hopes and troubles, then that fear will disappear. Separation is said to be a natural process but why then is it imposed by force and why then is it that whites have the superiority?

We do not expect that independence will end our troubles. We do believe that our people are entitled, as are all peoples, to rule themselves. It is not really a question of whether South Africa treats us well or badly, but that South West Africa is our country and we wish to be our own masters.

I am a loyal Namibian and I could not betray my people to their enemies. I admit that I decided to assist those who had taken up arms; I know that the struggle will be long and bitter. I also know that my people will wage that struggle whatever the cost.

Only when we are granted our independence will the struggle stop. Only when our human dignity is restored to us as equals of the whites will there be peace between us.

We believe that South Africa has a choice— either to live at peace with us or to subdue us by force. If you choose to crush us and impose your will on us, then you not only betray your trust but you will live in security for only so long as your power is greater than ours. No South African will live at peace in South West Africa for each will know that his security is based on force and that without force he will face rejection by the people.

My co-accused and I have suffered—we are not looking forward to our imprisonment. We do not, however, feel that our efforts and sacrifice have been wasted. We believe that human suffering has its effect even on those who impose it. We hope that what happened will persuade the whites of South Africa that we and the world may be right and they may be wrong. Only when white South Africans realize this and act on it, will it be possible for us to stop our struggle for freedom and justice in the land of our birth.

Many in the court were visibly moved. The judge adjourned and shortly thereafter returned to pass sentence. Twenty of the defendants were sentenced to life imprisonment for the rest of their natural lives. Nine others were sentenced to imprisonment for twenty years at hard labor, among these

Herman Ja Toivo. One was sentenced to five years, and the three convicted under the Suppression of Communism Act were sentenced to one year imprisonment—nine months suspended.

The court adjourned for the last time. I shook hands with all my clients and each said good-bye in turn. It was a sad and moving farewell. On leaving the court, each of the defendants handed me his file of papers. My eyes filled with tears as I packed the papers into the suitcases I had brought for this purpose.

We lodged an appeal and as it was a matter concerning a fundamental interpretation of the constitution, all eleven judges heard the appeal. None of the defendants was present but full teams of lawyers attended the appeal court as did many foreign observers. The appeal did not alter the judgment and conviction of the lower court. The struggle to free the Namibians would have to be concluded in other ways.

XII
THE LENKOE CASE

Late in 1968, the government reclassified as white land the ancestral home of the Bakwena tribe, an area some one hundred fifty miles west of Johannesburg. The tribe had lived there for well over a century and refused to move. The government then employed a favorite device. It appointed a puppet chief who would comply with the order to move. Even though the majority of the tribesmen did not recognize this man as chief, if they refused to follow his orders they were victimized and persecuted, and a number of the tribal leaders were arrested and detained as terrorists under the Terrorism Act.

Eventually the state brought some of these men to trial and having been instructed by the relatives, I acted for the defendants. I heard the inevitable complaints of brutal assaults. The day before the trial began one of the defendants died in prison. Captain Swanepoel, who was in charge of the investigation, was anxious to avoid criticism of his men's treatment of this defendant and the other witnesses in the case. He also realized that there would be strong criticism of the application of the Terrorism Act to these people who were clearly not terrorists. So he offered me a deal: If three of the defendants would plead guilty to a common-law crime, they would go to jail for only a few months and the rest of my clients would be acquitted.

Three of my clients agreed to make the sacrifice and I informed Swanepoel. The prosecutor and the attorney general were somewhat reluctant to accept the arrangement but Swanepoel persuaded them and the deal was struck. As chief investigation officer, he then gave evidence for the defendants and persuaded the judge that this was nothing more than a tribal dispute. As he stepped out of the witness box, I shook his hand to show the judge that defense and prosecution were not opposing each other. The next day, as Swanepoel had promised, three of my clients were sentenced to a few months in jail and all the rest were acquitted. This handshaking incident was a grave error on my part. It might have impressed the judge but Swanepoel was to use it against me later to impress detainees and others that I was working with him.

In the midst of these events, three men came to see me in my office. The story they told me of the death of their brother sounded much like the many cases of injustices I was now almost accustomed to hearing. Indeed, because these had become so common, generally they were only of significance to the immediate circle of sufferers. Only once in a while would a case break out of the circle and assume national and international significance.

Of the men in front of me the eldest was in his sixties but the youngest, Johannes Lenkoe, did the talking. According to his account, James Lenkoe—a national of Lesotho (formerly Basutoland, a British protectorate), had come to South Africa over twenty years before and had married a native-born South African. The couple had two children and had acquired a house in Soweto, the major black ghetto and labor reservoir for Johannesburg, some twelve miles southwest of the white city. For the last eighteen years, James Lenkoe had worked for the South African Railways, the government-owned railway service, and had attained one of the highest positions to which a black man could rise. As a barrier attendant, he collected tickets from black railway passengers on the "black trains." He had never been arrested for any offense of any kind whatsoever—not even an offense under the pass laws. This was a rare record for any black man in South Africa.

Early one morning, at about 2 A.M., the wife of James Lenkoe said that the whole house had been "bumped up" and white and black men had come in, beaten her husband, and taken him away. About a week later she received a message that her husband was dead and she could call and collect the body.

Johannes Lenkoe asked me to act for the widow, and I was sympathetic when I learned that she was too shaken and upset to come in and see me herself. Johannes said James had been a healthy, able-bodied man and that he and his wife were very happy together. He was very handy about the house and spent most of his weekends improving his home. All this could be confirmed by the neighbors who knew him. Johannes insisted that I investigate how James Lenkoe had been killed, maintaining that he must have been murdered by the people who took him away. There was no doubt in my mind that he was right but I could not express this to him in my bugged office. The three men promised to talk to the wife and explain how important it was that she speak to me.

The following day Mrs. Lenkoe accompanied her relatives to my office. She was dressed in heavy mourning and only her eyes were visible. With great difficulty, and obviously under severe strain, she briefly confirmed her brother-in-law's story. Remembering the lengths to which the security police had gone in their attempts to prevent me from acting in the Looksmart case, I took a power of attorney from Mrs. Lenkoe immediately, but she was too upset to do anything more that day.

She returned the next day to tell me about herself, her husband, and her children. It was clear that they had been a close and devoted couple; both had held good jobs and had lived quiet lives. On the night of March 5, she told me, the family was asleep, the house was in darkness. Just after midnight there was hammering on the windows, the doors, and the walls all around the house. "I caught fright," she said.

When her husband jumped out of bed to go to the door she whispered to him, "No, do not open; first see who is outside." She peeped through the curtains and pulled her head back in shock; a white man was staring in the window. She shouted, "Who are you?" and he called back, "It's the police." She told me she would recognize that face anywhere.

Her husband went to the kitchen door at the back of the house and she followed him. He opened the door and a voice outside said, *"Is jy Mofokeng?"* (Mofokeng was the name of her husband's clan but not his own name.) James did not have time to respond before she saw two white hands and arms appear from behind the door and pull her husband violently outside. She screamed.

At this point in her story she began to cry but after a while she was able to continue. A black policeman appeared, she said, and told her to shut up and not make so much noise.

"You come here, you pull my husband out like that and then you tell me to be quiet," she said to him.

The policeman told her to get dressed and they brought her husband back inside the house. Then she saw the man whose face she had seen outside the window. He was short and heavily built and as she described him, I knew it was Swanepoel.

She told me how, as she watched from the bedroom, this man hit her husband on top of his head and kept saying in a threatening manner, "You will tell me the truth."

She came out of the bedroom to protest and he turned to her, "Get back to bed, sleep." But she remained where she was until another white policeman pushed her back into the bedroom. She left the door half-open and could see that again and again her husband was hit on the head. Two policemen then came into her bedroom and ordered her out of their way. She was afraid to move and sat still on the bed. They opened every door and every cupboard, and while they did not find whatever they were looking for, they taunted her with questions—"Where did you steal these blankets?" "Where did you steal these dresses?" She had not stolen anything and wanted to show them the receipts but they were really not interested.

Because she was afraid, she asked if she could call her

next-door neighbor so that another woman could be present. They forbade her to do this. All they said was, "Where are your husband's shoes? We're taking him away."

She again asked for permission to call her neighbor and told them, "You say you are police and come here and hit my husband and take him away. I want my neighbor to see you and see my husband with you."

"You can tell your neighbors when we are gone," was their reply.

Her husband came into the bedroom to dress. He put on his trousers, the ones he wore for work which she had altered so that he didn't have to wear a belt, his work shoes without socks, a black shirt, and he took an extra shirt with him. His pass book was on the dressing table but they did not ask for it, nor did they take it.

Mrs. Lenkoe said she had the book with her and she gave it to me. It showed that his full name was James Lenkoe, that he was born in Lesotho, and had official permission to work and reside in Johannesburg. There was no mention of the clan name Mofokeng.

Before her husband was taken away she asked him why he was being arrested and he replied, "I do not know but I am afraid. They say that when I get to the police station they will kill me." He was put into a car with a Pretoria license plate that was parked outside their house. She called to her neighbor and they watched as this car and another and a van drove off.

Mrs. Lenkoe sat up until sunrise. Then she went to see her brother-in-law, Johannes, who accompanied her to the jail in Pretoria. She was told that her husband was there but she could not see him for one hundred eighty days. If she came on Sunday, however, she could bring him some food and some clean clothes. On Sunday she went with her packages and was told that her husband was not there. No one listened to her entreaties and she was ordered to leave.

Two days later, while Mrs. Lenkoe was sitting with her sister-in-law and friends in her kitchen, two white and one black policemen walked into the house. They did not knock; they simply walked in the door and demanded her husband's pass. She pretended to look all over for it and told them she could not find it—she had decided she would not give it to them until she knew more about why they were keeping her husband. She must continue looking for it, they said, and they would be back the next day. She watched them leave her house and get into their car. They sat there, talking for some time, and she decided to walk past the car. She saw a man sitting between the two policemen in the back seat. Recognizing him as a neighbor and seeing how swollen his face was, she hurried to call his wife.

Suddenly, Mrs. Lenkoe said she felt a sharp stab of fear; questions hammered in her head. "Why did they bring my neighbor's husband but not my own? Why did they not take my husband's pass when they arrested him? Why do they come now? Something has happened to my husband; I think he is dead."

The police did not come for the pass on Wednesday as they said they would. On Thursday she went to the Moroka police station. She thought she might be able to get some news of her husband there because she had recognized some of the black policemen who came on the raid as policemen from that station. But the Moroka police gave her no news. She heard nothing more until the following Tuesday when three policemen came to her home. They said they had come to get her husband's belt. She was suspicious of this strange request and her fears for her husband returned. She broke into tears and did not look for the belt, and the police went away.

The following Thursday when she came home, her neighbor, Agnes, came to see her and said, "The police, they came. When they did not find you they said I must tell you, your husband is dead." Mrs. Lenkoe collapsed. Her neighbors put her to bed and called for relatives who went to the Moroka police station and were told, "It is so. James Lenkoe is dead. He hanged himself by his belt in the prison cell."

Hardened as I was to the ruthless methods of the police, I was shocked by the callousness of their behavior, and the way they had tormented Mrs. Lenkoe. She now handed me the belt that the police had been asking for and said, "This is my husband's belt. He only had one and he didn't take it when he was arrested. How can he have hanged himself with this belt? I do not believe them; he never hanged himself. Why should he do such a thing? They have killed him. You must find out how it happened."

Her brothers had made arrangements to fetch James Lenkoe's body from the prison so that the burial could be held that weekend. I asked them to postpone the funeral but they said that all the arrangements had been made and that messages had already been sent to faraway relatives. As sympathetically as possible, I explained that if they wanted me to find out how James Lenkoe had met his death it was essential that a pathologist, independent of the government, examine the body. I would need a court order for such an examination and this would take some time. Meanwhile, the body would have to remain in the mortuary and the burial would have to be postponed. It was a difficult decision for them to make but they wanted to know the truth so they agreed and asked me to act immediately.

Thus, the next morning, armed with powers of attorney and affidavits, I went to Pretoria to apply to court for an order permitting a second postmortem examination. Unknown to me, the inquest court there only sat on Friday mornings and by pure chance, I had chosen the right morning.

The judge, Mr. G. J. Strijdom, was elderly, fat, and bald as a coot. I realized that the reason he was still sitting in this junior court was that he had not managed to pass even those few law examinations that would have helped him get a promotion. I decided to be exceedingly polite to him, to talk slowly and simply, to spell everything out.

When court convened, and the judge acknowledged my presence, I told him that my client was the widow of a man who had died in detention, and I mentioned the circumstances of his arrest and disappearance.

The judge became impatient, interrupting me by demanding, "Where is your power of attorney to act?"

I was not surprised at this ploy, first used against me in the Looksmart case five years before, for it had now become the standard challenge to attorneys appearing for detainees. Attorneys are officers of the court, and normally, when they say in court that they are instructed by clients, their statements are not challenged. The security police were changing this.

I handed Judge Strijdom the power of attorney. He said, "Wait," and carefully read the whole document to see if it was in order. This was a further insult and I stood with my hand on my hip, waiting for him to discover that the document was valid. He knew from my attitude that I had realized his reluctance to hear me. The very mention of the word detainee had indicated to him that this was a political matter.

I ignored his insults, determined to give him no opportunity to refuse to hear me. When he accepted the power of attorney, I began reciting the facts of the affidavits I wanted him to officially accept. There were representatives of the press in court. Perhaps because he did not want them to hear the contents of the affidavits he said, "It is not necessary for you to read all that out, I can read," and he held out his hand for the documents. That was just what I wanted. The documents were now officially before him and he would have to deal with my application. Now the press could quote the documents in full. We all waited while he slowly read the affidavits. He then looked up at me and said, "What are you asking for?"

"Your Worship will see that we seek an order for a second postmortem examination by a doctor of our own choice, together with a doctor nominated by the state, if the state considers his presence desirable. We also seek an order giving the doctor appointed by my clients access to the available medical-legal evidence relating to the cause of death of my client's late husband, James Lenkoe."

The judge looked at me sternly and for a moment there was complete silence in the court. Then, without any warning, he stood up. As he started walking to the door, he turned around to me and lifting an admonishing finger, said, "You stay right there." He left the courtroom, taking the papers with him. At this late stage, the court orderly, caught unawares, jumped to his feet and shouted in the two official languages, "Silence in court—*Stilte in die hof.*"

The young inquest prosecutor asked me, "What's all this about?"

"I'm only applying for a second postmortem examination," I replied, "I can't understand what all the drama is about. The state surely has nothing to hide and is not worried about such applications."

My clients understood more than the prosecutor. They may not have understood the language or even heard all the words, but the judge's face could be clearly read. "He doesn't like it; what are you going to do?" they asked me.

I had no idea what I was going to do nor did I know what would happen next.

When Judge Strijdom returned, we were in the passage outside court. The senior public prosecutor, Jacobus de Jaager, approached me and asked, "You are Mr. Carlson?"

"Yes," I said.

He had my affidavits and held them out to me. "Here are your papers," he said.

"Oh no," I replied, "those papers are in court. I cannot take them from you."

"I am the senior public prosecutor and I am handing these papers back to you," he said, rather threateningly.

As casually as I could, I replied, "Well I'm not accepting them from you. Where, may I ask, did you get them? I gave them to Judge Strijdom. I suggest you give them back to him."

He turned on his heel angrily and went back into court.

When court resumed I kept a poker face as de Jaager, replacing the inquest prosecutor, now rose and addressed the court. "These papers are Your Worship's papers," he said, and once more they were handed to the court. Their little ploy had failed.

Judge Strijdom called on me again and I began my argument once more. De Jaager, who had already suffered one defeat and was smarting under the embarrassment of it, could not counter my arguments and made no real objection to the order being granted. Thus, the judge had no choice. He asked de Jaager which medical officer would represent the state and for the first time, I heard the name of the state pathologist, a name I was to remember—Hieronymus van Praag-Koch.

We had been more successful than I had expected; at least there was a chance of examining the body of a detainee and of determining the real cause of death. On my return to Johannesburg, I began to look for a pathologist who could conduct the postmortem. Immediately I encountered difficulties. One pathologist after another refused. Finally, a professor at the medical school recommended a young man, Dr. Sonny Abrahams, a member of a large firm of pathologists, and he agreed to conduct the examination. My counsel, David Soggot, and I consulted with him in the presence of the firm's senior partner, Dr. Jonathan Gluckman, and in fact, the latter soon took control of the investigation.

Dr. Gluckman asked me, "What do you expect to find? What in particular are we looking for?"

"I want you to tell me what caused his death. One thing you might find," I said, "are electrical burn marks and these may be on the ears, fingers, genitals, or toes."

"What do they look like? I have never seen an electrical burn mark," Dr. Gluckman said.

I described what I had seen on the fingers of many of the detainees I interviewed during the Looksmart case.

The postmortem was held and the state pathologist attended; I declined the invitation to do so. I called our pathologists immediately afterwards and was told to be patient as tests still had to be made.

Meanwhile, I had been making repeated attempts to get hold of Koch's report on the first postmortem. I was given the usual runaround, going from prosecutor to inquest clerk to judge without success. Finally I asked David Soggot to speak to the senior public prosecutor and a copy of the report was sent us.

David immersed himself in the forensic-medical aspects and spent long hours reading the authorities on electrothermal injuries. We decided to divide up the work. I would ferret around for information, see clients and officials, and complete the groundwork for cross-examination while David would concentrate on presenting our evidence to court.

When we next saw Dr. Gluckman, David quietly demonstrated to him his knowledge of the subject. This put the pathologist on his mettle. He told us then that he and his colleague could not determine the cause of a curious mark on the second toe of the deceased's right foot, and they were doing further research on it. They had photographed the mark and described it as "a transverse linear mark on the superior surface, broken up into two positions; a medial one measuring a quarter of an inch, and a lateral one, measuring an eighth to a sixteenth of an inch in thickness."

The pathologists raised another question. According to the police the deceased had hanged himself with his belt. If the fracture of the neck was made while Lenkoe was still alive, then there would have been a hemorrhage at the fracture site. Their examination had revealed no trace of blood there—it was quite clean. This led them to ask whether the hanging could have taken place after death.

The evidence that I had about James Lenkoe's belt had already made me suspicious of the circumstances surrounding the hanging. I knew it was normal procedure for the police and prison guards to remove shoelaces and belts from prisoners. The deceased only possessed one belt and that had remained in his wife's possession at home at the time of his arrest. In addition, there was the visit from the police seeking his belt before they advised Mrs. Lenkoe of his death and after his death had already occurred. From my experience in the Looksmart inquest, however, I knew that this was not sufficient to show that the deceased had not hanged himself. We had to establish how he had met his death. This was my first priority. The case was challenging and the pathologists responded enthusiastically. They made telephone calls to London, Paris, and all over South Africa. I felt that fortune had guided me to just the right team of experts.

In terms of the instructions that I had previously received from the Lawyers Committee for Civil Rights under Law, I reported the progress of events to them. They now formally instructed me to act for Mrs. Lenkoe and indicated their readiness to give me whatever assistance they could.

Dr. Gluckman had found that photographic slides of the cross section of the toe injury showed a classic resemblance to a series of similar slides published in 1947 in the *Journal of American Pathology* by a famous American pathologist, Professor Alan R. Moritz, a recognized world authority in his field. He had been the chief consultant pathologist to the United States armed forces and was, in addition, one of the pathologists who had performed the autopsy on President Kennedy and had been an adviser to the Warren Commission. With the help of the Lawyers Committee we managed to establish the whereabouts of Professor Moritz and a telephone conversation between him in Ohio and Dr. Gluckman in Johannesburg was arranged. Over the phone Dr. Moritz suggested that an atomic spectographic test be made to determine conclusively, and within an error of one in a million, whether the injury was of an electrothermal nature. He also promised to comment on slides and photographic material sent to him and I arranged for this to be done.

Dr. Gluckman had taken a section of the deceased's neck, and using this as a control, a section of the toe injury and sections of skin cauterized after surgery from two different people were taken, and all four specimens sent to the South African Government Bureau of Standards. The bureau was requested to carry out an atomic spectographic examination of all these sections. The results showed that the deceased's toe injury and the two cauterized pieces of skin had been subjected to electrothermal treatment and the skin showed copper content. The section of the deceased's neck gave a negative result.

A closer examination of the slides showing the cross section of the toe injury was now made and compared with those in Dr. Moritz' 1947 article. The slides of Lenkoe's toe showed cysts or balloons just beneath the skin, the beginning of a blister formation that had developed but had not been completed, as death had intervened. This enabled us to fix the time of death as somewhere within a period of two minutes and twelve hours after Lenkoe had received the injury.

Dr. Moritz, responding to our queries as to the so-called hanging, said he felt the lack of any hemorrhage at the fracture site supported the possibility that the hanging had been simulated. Further, chemical tests showed that James Lenkoe had sustained an electrothermal injury, which additionally corroborated the evidence we had from the slides and the atomic spectographic test. But we still had to determine where the deceased was during the last twelve hours of his life and who was with him during that period. If he was undergoing interrogation, where was it being conducted and who was interrogating him? Only with this information could we pinpoint responsibility for the injuries he sustained.

The day of the inquest hearings arrived. In the courtroom, the black side of the public gallery was filled with friends of the Lenkoes and with police informers. The white gallery was filled with security policemen. The well of the court, particularly around the prosecutor's table, was crowded with more senior security policemen. A special political prosecutor, Mr. C. G. Jordaan, had been appointed to conduct the inquest and the regular inquest judge, Strijdom, had also been replaced. Van Praag-Koch, the state pathologist, a short man with curly hair and a huge handlebar moustache, appeared confident and obviously enjoyed being at the center of this investigation.

The atmosphere was tense; the security police and the prosecutor made their hostility apparent. We were refused permission to see any of the inquest evidence or photographs taken of the deceased after he was found hanging in the prison cell. The façade of fairness practiced in the days of the Looksmart inquest had now disappeared.

Judge J. J. H. Tukker was a short, square man; his sleek dark hair was plastered down on his head and he boasted a Hitler moustache. He looked very businesslike and important, and gave the impression of being determined to get on with the job. Speaking in Afrikaans, he introduced and swore in his assessor, a specialist in the field of pathology, who was to assist the judge in these matters. This assessor, Dr. J. de Villiers, was a member of the state's district surgeon's office in which Dr. van Praag-Koch served.

Jordaan was told to proceed and he handed the inquest court file to the judge. This file contained affidavits taken from witnesses who were working at the prison on the night of James Lenkoe's death. We at last learned the time of death, which was given as 10:30 P.M. Jordaan stated that the deceased was found hanging by a belt around his neck which was fastened to the bars of the cell window. A handkerchief was tied across his mouth and knotted at the back of the neck.

There was a picture in the file showing the position of the body at the time it was found. It was given to us to look at, but when we asked for copies, our request was refused. We were reduced to making a quick tracing on copy paper. The picture had been taken from behind and showed the whole body suspended, but failed to show the prison window bars or how the belt was attached to them. The deceased's right arm extended above his head, but the way the photograph was taken, it did not show the hand or fingers of that arm, so we could not determine why it was in that position. His left arm was bent at the elbow and his left wrist was level with his left shoulder; his toes were just above the floor. He was dressed in a workman's coverall which did not require any kind of belt.

Dr. van Praag-Koch was called to the witness stand. The brief evidence he gave was in support of the postmortem report that he had filed, namely that his findings were consistent with death due to hanging. He was then subjected to detailed and lengthy cross-examination by David Soggot, and finally conceded that the features described were as consistent with hanging before death as after death. With regard to the toe mark, he described it as an abrasion rather than a burn, but he further conceded that he could not exclude the possibility that it was caused by an electrical burn. He agreed that tests could establish this—that if any metal was used in causing the burn, minute particles would have been discharged into the skin at the site, and the presence of these metal particles could be detected. Pressed further, he conceded this would establish beyond doubt that the mark was an electrothermal injury.

Dr. van Praag-Koch was then told that an atomic spectographic test had been carried out by the government's Bureau of Standards, which had indicated the presence of copper in the skin surrounding the toe injury. This evidence took him by surprise. He stated he would have to know more about how the tests had been conducted. But at the same time, he also conceded that electrocution—even fatal electrocution—could take place without any visible sign being left on the body. Very high voltage, he said, could enter the body through a very small area, and leave no detectable sign of its exit. If a contact point of entry and exit were firmly and carefully made, no marks would be left. He concluded that the findings in his postmortem report were consistent with electrocution provided it could be established that the mark on the toe was an electrothermal injury.

At the end of Dr. van Praag-Koch's evidence, the assessor, Dr. de Villiers, put one question to him relating to the picture of the deceased hanging and the position of his arms. He asked, if death was by suicidal hanging, how was it possible that Lenkoe's arms had not fallen to his sides once he became unconscious.

Because the deceased had had an instantaneous cadaveric spasm causing instant rigor mortis, Dr. Koch replied.

Such a spasm was an extremely rare occurrence, so rare that three of the four pathologists I consulted knew nothing about it. Dr. Moritz, when asked to comment on it wrote that it was "a common practice in some of the concentration camps, early in the Hitler period, to conceal homicide by suspending the body of the murdered prisoner so that death could be officially reported as due to suicidal hanging." He went on to say, "the contracted arm does not fit with the theory of death due to hanging and makes it necessary to search for alternative explanations for the cause of death."

The question put by Dr. de Villers was to be the last one he asked at that inquest. When we arrived at court on the next occasion, Judge Tukker, without any notice or explanation, swore in a new assessor.

I was extremely pleased at the way in which David Soggot had shaken Dr. van Praag-Koch's confidence and gained these reluctant concessions from him. I was also astonished at the depth and extent of the latter's knowledge of electrothermal injuries. I had, over the past few weeks, been working with four senior pathologists, all experts in their field, and one a world authority on electrothermal injury. Dr. van Praag-Koch showed that he had the combined experience and learning of all these experts. How did he acquire such expert and extensive knowledge of the use of electricity on the human body?

The next witness was a handsome young security police-

man named Lieutenant Karel Richter. He told how he had
been called to the prison at 11 P.M. to find the detainee hanging
from the bars of his window. He couldn't understand it, he
said. That afternoon, when he had taken Lenkoe back to the
prison, after his interrogation at Compol, he was healthy and
happy. In a separate affidavit, filed later, the lieutenant had
stated that he had forgotten to report previously that Lenkoe
was wearing a belt.

Under cross-examination Richter said that he had taken
Lenkoe to Compol that morning:

Q. So you questioned Lenkoe at Compol?
A. No. I only took him there and took him back.
Q. Well, who questioned him then?
A. Major Swanepoel.

Richter was then asked a number of simple questions about
what Lenkoe was wearing that day. He had great difficulty in
answering them and appealed to the judge as to their relevance even though the prosecutor made no objection. Clearly
he felt that he did not know what difficulties he might be
creating for his colleagues by replying truthfully to these
questions. He could not remember whether Lenkoe was
wearing shoes but when pressed for an answer, he first said he
thought so and finally stated that yes, he was. Asked whether
Lenkoe had taken his shoes off, Richter said no, that he had
no reason whatsoever to do this. Although he had a specific
recollection of the belt, he could not explain why he had taken
such notice of it. Richter testified that the weather in Pretoria
was warm that day and that no electric heaters were used, nor
would Lenkoe have had any access to an electric stove. He
was never left alone—a security officer was always with him.
Lenkoe had made no complaints to him about any assaults
committed on him. His statement to the security police had
been made quite freely and voluntarily.

Richter's testimony ended the first day's proceedings. I felt
we had made good progress. Now the major difficulty facing
us was how to get the court to call Major Swanepoel to the
witness box. I decided to plan our strategy for cross-
examining him and not worry for the moment about when we
would get the opportunity to do so.

A search of all the court records for cases in which Swanepoel had been a state witness and had been cross-examined, revealed he had given evidence in innumerable political trials. Time and again, allegations of brutal assaults had been made against him. The record showed that besides breaking the limbs of several detainees, he had threatened to rip open the penis of one man with a nail hammered through a plank, and had used a variety of cruel methods to break prisoners physically and mentally. He was directly connected with the deaths of several detainees. One man jumped from the seventh-floor window of a security office where Swanepoel was interrogating him. Others had hanged themselves after sessions with him. Swanepoel always denied these assaults, and each time the court had helped him to evade a full inquiry into his methods of interrogation.

I found a dozen cases concerned with electric-shock treatment in which Swanepoel was involved. Because of the nature of Lenkoe's injury, I limited my investigation to these cases. I knew that the judge would rule that any other kind of torture was irrelevant.

There was so much evidence against Swanepoel and there had been so many deaths in detention, that I decided to ask a reporter to do a separate investigation of these matters, providing him with my research material. Eventually, an excellent article entitled "Deaths in Detention," which fully documented all the known deaths and available facts, was published in the *Rand Daily Mail.*

The government was obviously becoming concerned about the publicity the inquest was receiving. General Gideon Joubert, the commissioner of police, issued a statement to the press regarding the deaths in detention of three Africans, one of whom was James Lenkoe. He stressed that there was no evidence of foul play in the death of any of these persons.

Meanwhile, in Washington, D.C., the Lawyers Committee was endeavoring to obtain the services of Dr. Moritz. I was anxious to have him attend the trial as the authority of his evidence would weigh heavily with the court.

As the inquest proceeded, we had no prior knowledge of who would be giving evidence or what their evidence would be on any particular day. This was one of Jordaan's many techniques for making any preparation for cross-examination of witnesses extremely difficult. However, young David Soggot could not have shown more courage or tenacity in adversity.

One morning, as soon as the court had convened, Jordaan stood up and announced without warning, "I call Major Swanepoel."

It was a move designed to take us unawares and complete the major's testimony in a matter of moments.

As soon as the major walked toward the witness box, I leaned over to take my Swanepoel file out of my briefcase. Before I had even extracted the file, I heard his answer to Jordaan's first question confirming that he had made the arrest and conducted the interrogation of James Lenkoe. I opened the file and was putting my papers in order when he answered the second question, saying that Lenkoe had not been ill-treated in any way. Then Jordaan sat down. Major Swanepoel's testimony had been completed.

As the judge turned to David, I leaned over and said, "I've got all the information with me—good luck." We had turned the tables on the state; we had caught them unawares and the sensation was definitely a thrill.

David started very quietly and Swanepoel turned full face, fixing his glare on him. His skin was more splotchy and red than I had ever seen it before. His hands were formed into fists of fat fingers with the knuckles facing us.

Swanepoel described how as the chief interrogation officer of the security police, he had conducted investigations throughout Rhodesia, South West Africa, and South Africa. He said that Lenkoe had been arrested because he was a dangerous terrorist—a hired assassin—and the leader of a terrorist organization, but it was not in the interest of state security to disclose any more information about this. The court upheld him on this point. Then, while looking toward the judge, Swanepoel described how well detainees were treated. There was no truth, he said, in any allegations of maltreatment. David put to him that a number of detainees had said under oath that they had been tortured and the torture had included electric-shock methods.

Since they had named Swanepoel as having administered

the electric-shock torture, this question was relevant. The blood rushed to his face and he clenched his fists even tighter. Furiously he swung around to face us: "I want to know the names of these people who said this about me," he demanded. He ignored the judge, making it clear that the battle was between himself and us.

David kept cool and said incisively, "Certainly, Major, you are entitled to these names, although you know all of them already. Let me give each one to you and tell you what they said about you."

His words bounced off Swanepoel, who in his rage didn't realize that the initiative remained with us. I handed David the affidavits and addressing the judge, not Swanepoel, he read the names of some twenty witnesses whom we could call and whose affidavits had already been filed in a previous Supreme Court case. He outlined briefly what each would say and placed it on record that each one of them would be prepared to face cross-examination. When he had completed reading these horrifying allegations, even Judge Tukker was stunned by the weight of the evidence we had amassed. David told the judge that considerable further evidence of the same kind could be produced. He then turned to Major Swanepoel for his comments.

Swanepoel had been taken by surprise but before he could make any answer, Jordaan rose to object with the familiar complaint that I had heard so often: "Your Worship, this is not relevant to these proceedings." However, Jordaan was unprepared to argue this fully and had no answers to David's contention that Swanepoel had asked for specific details and that we had simply given the court these details. The allegations were serious, he said, and were made in every case against the very officer, who on his own testimony, had interrogated the deceased, James Lenkoe. If the allegations were true they would show that this officer was guilty of systematic brutality. The court must be aware of this and such behavior must be rooted out. If the allegations were false, then this officer would be exonerated. David also told the court that we had evidence that would show beyond doubt that James Lenkoe had sustained an electrical burn.

At this point the court adjourned, giving Swanepoel time to

compose himself and to prepare his answers. But when we resumed, Swanepoel could only answer these precise allegations with irrelevant rantings. Angrily he shouted that he had heard such allegations many times—they were all part of an international Communist plot to discredit South Africa and the security police, who were attacked because they were most vulnerable. David persisted with his probing but Swanepoel denied all knowledge of the use of electric-shock methods and insisted that no unlawful methods were used on detainees during interrogation.

He was both angry and embarrassed. Many of the spectators were members of the security police, who, having heard that their chief was undergoing cross-examination, had come streaming into the courtroom. It was an affront to his vanity to be subjected to the kind of questions we were putting to him. David got him to admit that no record of any kind was kept anywhere of detainees' movements in and out of jails. Security police, he said, had complete freedom to control their movements during interrogation and he argued that this was necessary and in the interests of the security of the state. Swanepoel further admitted that even the regular prison procedures of booking prisoners in and out of jail had been suspended so the security police could question detainees at any time, day or night. This, too, was a security measure.

When asked about an Indian detainee who during his interrogation some years back, had jumped from a seventh-floor window of the interrogation room, he was saved from answering by Jordaan's objecting to the question and by Judge Tukker's summarily sustaining the objection. When asked about his part in the death of two detainees some months before that of Lenkoe, he was again saved by the prosecutor's objection and the judge's sustainment. When asked why Lenkoe had taken his life, Swanepoel expressed great surprise. He said Lenkoe's statement would have given him no cause to take his life but of course, he could not produce the statement, again in the interests of state security.

The hearing was adjourned for another week and Swanepoel did not wait long to take revenge. That night my telephone rang time and again. At first the voice at the other end said, "You will die by morning, you bastard." On other occasions there was just heavy breathing—no one spoke. Other callers swore at me and called me "Communist." I had been threatened with death before and had reported the matter to the police; now there were too many calls to report each one. I had to continue answering the phone as it might have been from someone in need of help. My wife and I decided all we could do was try to ignore these calls, but we were both uneasy. I worried about the harm that might befall my family. Were all the threats just empty ones?

The next morning there was a telephone call of another nature, puzzling and rather ominous. A voice said, "Are you J. Carlson?"

"Yes," I said.

"Do you hold passport J 146298?"

"I hold a passport, yes, but I have no idea what the number is."

The caller then identified himself as an immigration officer at the passport office. He continued: "It seems that some clerical error has been made about this passport. Would you please bring it in so that it can be rectified?"

"That's very strange," I said, "I've never noticed any error. What is it?"

"Well, just you bring the passport down and we will go into it here," he said.

I declined the invitation and promised to check my passport for errors.

The voice grew more urgent. "Would you kindly bring it down right away? This must be attended to."

"I certainly will not; it's not urgent and I am extremely busy." That was the end of the conversation.

It did not take too much intuition to see what was coming. The next morning I went to the office of the American consul and applied for an extension of my United States visa. I told the clerk I was in no hurry for it and asked if my passport was safe in her office. She assured me it was. I knew that this was only a holding operation for once the authorities decided to take my passport I could do nothing to stop them. This would at least give me some time in which to move, but the net was being drawn more tightly around me.

When the inquest proceedings reopened, the tension was

even more pronounced and it mounted with every session. The room was filled to capacity with security policemen who did nothing but stare at us as if this would make us disappear. When I left the courtroom, I was careful to put all my books and papers in my briefcase and take everything with me. I always parked my car right outside the building and made sure it was completely locked. I didn't try to conceal my open distrust of the security police.

We now called to the witness stand Dr. Hillel Shapiro, a professor who had once been a government pathologist and was accepted as one of the senior men in the field. An elderly man with a shock of white hair and a deep, resonant voice, he had a most impressive personality, and the arrogance and rudeness of Jordaan could not ruffle his dignity or shake his confidence as a witness. He told the court of the abnormal traces of copper found at the site of the burn mark, which could have been driven there by an electrode attached to the toe. He agreed with Dr. van Praag-Koch, the state pathologist, that the findings he had made were consistent with death by hanging or by electrocution, and he reiterated that the cross section of the toe injury showed that only several hours could have elapsed from the time of injury to the time of death. Jordaan sought only to embarrass and discredit his character, but did not attack the substance of his testimony. At the end of the day the hearing was again postponed to the following Friday, the regular inquest day.

Early on Saturday I was elated to receive word from America that Dr. Moritz would arrive in Johannesburg that day. That was welcome news indeed even though he could only stay for a few days. Now my immediate problem was whether the inquest court would agree to reconvene during the adjournment to hear his testimony. Accompanied by David Soggot and Dr. Gluckman, I met Dr. Moritz at the airport. He had been en route for thirty hours, having flown from Cleveland to New York, from New York to London, and finally from London to South Africa. He was understandably exhausted. We booked him in at a hotel, briefly acquainted him with the evidence, and allowed him a good night's rest. Early the next morning we plunged into the case, working all day and into the night. We went over the evidence piece by piece, and Dr. Moritz agreed that what we had amassed was overwhelming. He supported our conclusions on the electrothermal injury and its particular relationship to the cause of James Lenkoe's death.

After the pathologists took him back to the hotel Sunday night, David and I worked on a petition that I would present to the inquest court early Monday morning, asking the judge to reconvene especially in order to hear Dr. Moritz' testimony. We summarized what evidence he would give. I clearly remember that it took less time to do this than to write up a statement of his qualifications. I do not think I have ever had a witness who was so well qualified.

Next morning I sought out Jordaan in Pretoria and introduced Dr. Moritz to him. He refused to accept a copy of my petition, saying he was not interested in what I had to say. He would give me no assistance whatsoever and would not even accompany me to see the judge. When Judge Tukker arrived in chambers he refused to hear me unless Jordaan was present, and also refused to call Jordaan himself. I returned to Jordaan's office but he told me he had already given his decision. We had reached an impasse.

My next step was to take the matter to the chief judicial officer who presided over all those courts. I asked him to intervene or to appoint another judge to hear my application. He contacted Judge Tukker and then advised me to go back to the judge's office. This time Judge Tukker left his chambers and went to see the prosecutor. When he returned he told me he would hear the matter in his chambers. As soon as Jordaan arrived, I made the application and submitted that Dr. Moritz could give invaluable evidence to assist the court to determine the issues before it. After listening to me and to Jordaan, the judge dismissed my application—the court would not reconvene.

There was nothing to do but return to Johannesburg, where I consulted with David. We decided to make an urgent Supreme Court application, stressing the need for Dr. Moritz' evidence to be heard. Working at top speed, we completed all the papers and the next morning I was back in Pretoria at 8

A.M. to serve them on the chief judicial officer, the inquest judge, and the prosecutor.

We proceeded before the Supreme Court that same morning. The presiding judge, Simon Bekker, on reading the papers commented that whether or not he made an order that day, he could not see why the inquest judge should not want to receive such evidence as Dr. Moritz could give and suggested that we should try to settle the matter.

A compromise was then struck. Judge Tukker said that if Dr. Gluckman, the local pathologist, testified the following day, he would then decide whether Dr. Moritz' evidence was necessary. It was a face-saving gesture and I was prepared to cooperate, for Dr. Moritz had now indicated that he could remain in Johannesburg until Friday if necessary. At this stage, the hostility of the judge and the prosecutor had become so apparent that it was clear to me they would reject whatever evidence we could produce. I was, nevertheless, determined to produce the evidence in order to have it on record. The fact that it would be rejected would further demonstrate how unjust the system really was.

That night we consulted with Dr. Gluckman and Dr. Moritz and prepared all the paraphernalia we would use in court—photographic equipment, slides, projectors, and screens; microscopes, instruments, bottles of specimens, and masses of books. I was convinced that we would prove beyond doubt that James Lenkoe had sustained an electrothermal injury to the second toe of his right foot sometime within a period of two minutes to twelve hours before his death.

For once I had my own cheering section in court—Dr. Gluckman's wife and family, my wife, and a number of students. Even so, we were outnumbered by the security police. Jordaan now had two of his colleagues assisting. The state pathologist, Dr. van Praag-Koch, sat next to him, and Swanepoel and his gang formed a semicircle behind Jordaan's table. The courtroom crowd of police overflowed into the passage; the air was heavy with tension. With all this drama, the widow was almost forgotten. Dressed in black, her head and face covered, she sat quietly through each day's proceedings, dignified and lost. Each day I explained to her and her relatives what had happened and what would happen. I had also confided to her how pessimistic I was about the findings of the court and she had replied, "We see you are doing your best."

On Wednesday morning, David rose to call Dr. Gluckman as per arrangement. Judge Tukker suddenly turned to Jordaan: "Will you present the evidence of Dr. Gluckman?" he asked. His maneuver was obvious. Although Dr. Gluckman was our witness, the state was intent on capturing him as theirs, hoping thereby to prevent some of the evidence he could give from being presented in court.

When David began to address the judge, he turned angrily on him and said sharply, "Sit down—kindly do not interrupt me."

David, however, remained standing and said, "I am entitled to address Your Worship. I object to the prosecutor, Mr. Jordaan, usurping the function of counsel for the widow. It is irregular and unreal for the state to present evidence which is of a highly technical and detailed nature and for which we have prepared. We have the impression that the state will move heaven and earth to prevent us presenting this medical evidence. The court has asked the prosecutor to lead Dr. Gluckman and if this is the order you make, we ask for an adjournment to consider our position."

Without hesitation or argument, Judge Tukker adjourned court. This was the first time no objection had been raised to our request for an adjournment. The reason was only too obvious. Judge Tukker did not want to hear Dr. Moritz and knowing that he would soon have to leave the country, any delays were welcome.

We were presented with a serious dilemma. If we sought any kind of relief from another court, it would inevitably lead to long delays and besides, none of us was optimistic that another court would restore our right to present our own evidence. In any event, the Supreme Court would not look favorably on further urgent applications. We could not have foreseen that the state would go to such lengths and we had now no alternative but to accept the judge's ruling.

We returned to court and Dr. Gluckman was asked to take

the witness stand. In the box he was courteous and polite and Jordaan had to hold his hostility in check as he sought the cooperation of his new witness. Dr. Gluckman was masterly in his handling of the situation. He spoke as a scientist but without condescension. While he endeavored to explain simply to the laymen before him the nature of his evidence, he was acutely conscious of the fact that among his listeners were scientific colleagues who would be very critical of the worth of his evidence. Using the equipment he had there, he explained all the methods of testing that had been used, how each was conducted, and the result achieved. It was technical but logical, and flowed in an easy sequence. He gave Dr. Moritz credit for the conclusions that had been reached, making it clear that Dr. Moritz was accepted as a world authority.

Any further questioning appeared to us superfluous and we declined to cross-examine. In fact, Jordaan was now faced with a problem. Even he was unable to bend the court rules to seek a reason to challenge in cross-examination such a lucid witness. He asked no further questions.

The judge now turned to the assessor but he too could find no reason to question any of Dr. Gluckman's testimony. It stood unchallenged.

Dr. Moritz was then called to the witness stand. Jordaan immediately rose and read into the record a statement that the state disclaimed all liability in bringing Dr. Moritz to Pretoria. We agreed that the cost of bringing Dr. Moritz had been borne by the defense. Judge Tukker now repeated his maneuver and called on Jordaan to present the doctor's evidence. Our objections were, of course, overruled. However, the way in which Dr. Gluckman had testified left me in little doubt that the state's techniques in attempting to hide the truth would fail.

Jordaan tried to limit the evidence that Dr. Moritz could give by confining his questions to restricted sections of the available evidence, but Dr. Moritz expanded the reasons for the conclusions he reached, and in that way covered the ground completely. He explained clearly how it was possible to determine Lenkoe had died within two minutes to twelve

The Carlson home in Johannesburg.

Jeanette Carlson with Jeremy and Meredith.

A Black Sash demonstration in Johannesburg against the pass laws. Jeanette Carlson holds the poster with a Biblical saying that her husband quoted regularly to pass officials, asking them to obey the Bible, not the government.

Students listen to Mrs. Helen Suzman speak at the protest meeting held at Witwatersrand University in Johannesburg on the first anniversary of the detention of the twenty-two.

The author examining bullet holes in the window of his office. As the office was on the fifth floor, the gun must have been fired from the government building opposite.

A bomb concealed in a copy of *Selected Works of Mao Tse-tung*, which was mailed to the author at his office.

Major Theunis Johannes Swane-poel of the security police. He gave the English press this studio photograph when he wrote an article for them in justification of his interrogation methods.

The author persuading the defendants in the trial of the twenty-two and their relatives to go to his house after their acquittal to avoid a police charge of holding an illegal gathering. From left, the author, Douglas Mvemve, and the father of Samson Ndou.

Some of the defendants in the trial of the twenty-two pose with the author on the lawn of his house after their acquittal.

Four of the women prisoners after their acquittal. From right, Martha Dlamini; Winnie Mandela, holding Adam Carlson; Rita Ndzanga; and Joyce Sikakane.

Scenes of a historic party, celebrating the acquittal of the defendants in the trial of the twenty-two. These people will never again be allowed to gather together as long as the present regime is in power. Such a gathering now would be considered a threat to state security. (Top) Lawrence Ndzanga and his wife, Rita, talking to Winnie Mandela (center); (middle) from left, George Mokwebo, Peter Magubane, Joyce Sikakane, Joseph Zikalala, and David Tsotetsi; (bottom) Violet Mvemve, wife of the oldest defendant, Douglas Mvemve.

The author congratulates Winnie Mandela on the appeal court's decision upholding her acquittal.

Joyce Sikakane and the author on the same occasion.

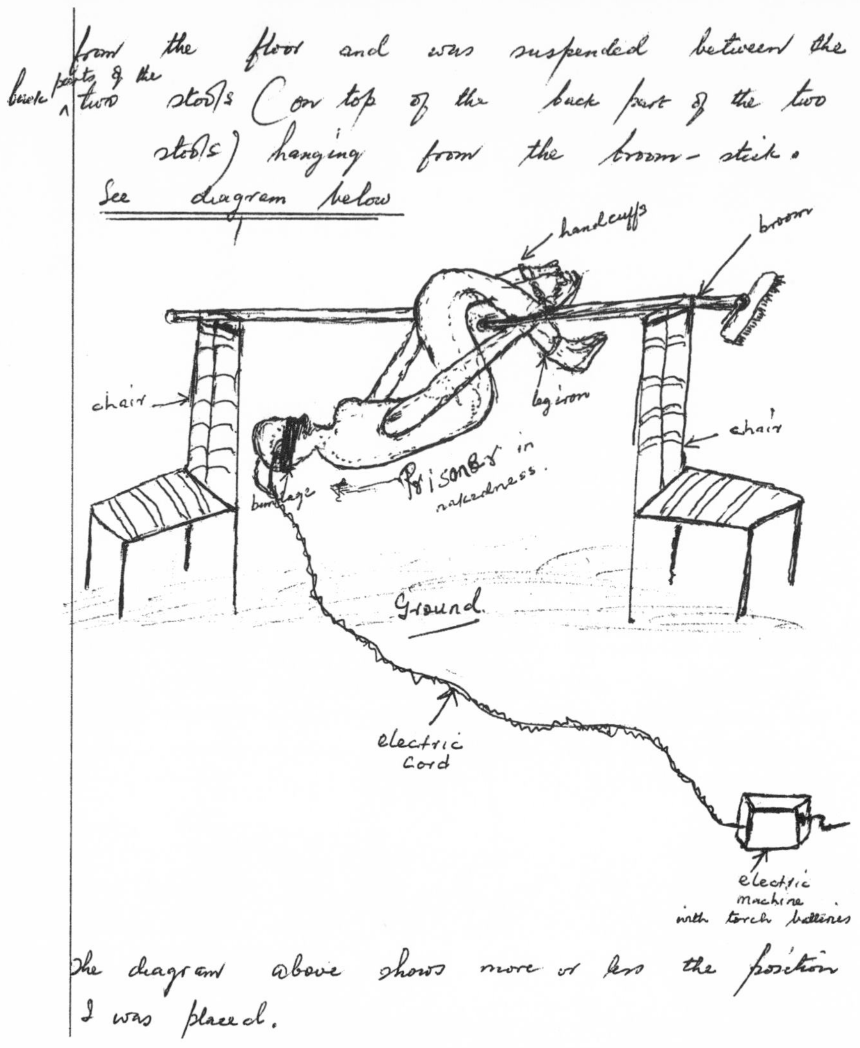
from the floor and was suspended between the back parts of the two stools (on top of the back part of the two stools) hanging from the broom-stick.
See diagram below

handcuffs
broom
chair
leg iron
chair
Prisoner in nakedness.
bandage
Ground
electric cord
electric machine with torch batteries

The diagram above shows more or less the position I was placed.

A page from the statement Benjamin Ramotse gave to the author concerning his imprisonment, describing the way he was tortured.

The author and Winnie Mandela waiting for the ferry in Cape Town harbor to take them to Robben Island where Nelson Mandela is serving a life sentence.

hours of receiving the injury to his toe. On all the evidence available, he said, the only reasonable conclusion he could come to was that the toe injury was an electrical burn.

Before the lunch adjournment, Jordaan asked the judge to prohibit David and me from talking to Dr. Moritz outside the court. Without hearing any argument, Judge Tukker summarily gave the order and the court adjourned. Dr. Gluckman's wife and Jeanette joined Dr. Moritz to accompany him to the luncheon we had previously arranged, since we lawyers were now banned from the gathering. As I walked out of court, I found Dr. Moritz in the center of a heated controversy. Lieutenant Richter, of the security police, was using all his charm to persuade Dr. Moritz to accompany him to a luncheon arranged by the state. Having made Dr. Moritz a state witness against his will, they now wished to convert him to their cause and make him a more friendly witness. The doctor was reluctant to go with Lieutenant Richter but was too courteous to be rude and refuse outright.

My wife solved the problem by saying to Mrs. Gluckman, "I'm hungry and I'm not interested in all this nonsense. Dr. Moritz was invited to come with us. He must make up his mind as I wish to go and eat."

Dr. Moritz grasped at this opportunity. "I cannot be discourteous to the ladies," he told the lieutenant as he left. I saw Lieutenant Richter grit his teeth and as he noticed me watching, I thought he was going to spit at me. Jordaan, who had been looking on, was white with rage.

We lunched separately and were told later by the owner of the restaurant that the security police checked on whether there was any communication between us and Dr. Moritz. We went back to court in separate cars and Dr. Moritz entered the building first. Jeanette, Mrs. Gluckman, and I followed close behind. As he walked up the stairs, Lieutenant Richter, who had been waiting, appeared and took him by the arm. I could not hear what they were saying but I did not trust the security police and I called up to Richter, "Look here, Lieutenant, I was ordered not to speak to Dr. Moritz or interfere with him and no doubt the order applies to you."

He swung around as though about to strike me, his face

distorted with rage and hatred. "You go to hell," he snarled, "I'm taking the doctor to the toilet."

Only when Dr. Moritz was about to leave South Africa did he tell me that Lieutenant Richter had actually asked him to tone down his evidence. Mrs. Gluckman told me later that if she had not witnessed the transformation of the handsome, charming lieutenant as he spun around toward me, she would never have believed my description of it.

When Dr. Moritz returned to the stand, Jordaan, aided throughout by Dr. van Praag-Koch, questioned him on the tests of a German pathologist, Dr. Ekkehardt Böhms. Dr. Moritz said as far as he was aware this pathologist had not concluded his work. We were to learn more about this later. Then Jordaan tried to explain away the existence of copper particles in the toe of the deceased. Didn't Dr. Moritz agree, he suggested, that people working continuously with certain metals would frequently retain traces of the metal on their skin? Dr. Moritz readily agreed that this was possible.

"Then persons working with copper as a metal would have traces of copper in their skin, would they not?" asked the prosecutor.

Again Dr. Moritz agreed.

"Ah," said Jordaan, "then you will agree that if the deceased had constantly come into contact with copper by reason of his work, his skin would contain more copper?"

"Yes," said Dr. Moritz quietly, without a flicker of a smile, "but can you tell me what work the deceased did involving the second toe of his right foot?"

Jordaan resumed his seat and David began his cross-examination. He had Dr. Moritz describe in detail all the reasons leading him to the conclusion that the deceased had sustained an electrothermal injury to his toe. This took all afternoon until the court adjourned, to enable Jordaan to prepare for any reexamination.

Dr. Moritz spent that evening and the following morning in Dr. Gluckman's laboratory following up a new idea. The state had referred to the work of Dr. Böhms, who experimented with the flow of electricity from a metallic conductor through the skin. He had determined that the electrical flow left its burn marks in an exceedingly nonuniform and distinctive manner, while nonelectric but hot metallic objects would also contaminate the skin but leave a burn with a distinctive and uniform pattern. Dr. Moritz studied Dr. Böhms's experiments in light of the examination and tests already concluded on Lenkoe's toe. Microscopic changes there showed a nonuniform burn pattern. This meant that Dr. Moritz had established, quite apart from any findings of copper in the skin, that microscopic changes alone were sufficient to identify with reasonable certainty that the lesion was electrothermal. The other pathologists who made their own examinations concurred with these findings.

On being reexamined by Jordaan, Dr. Moritz placed this new evidence before the court. All the tests now led to the same conclusion: that beyond any reasonable doubt, the deceased had sustained an electrothermal injury within twelve hours of his death.

The state tried to nullify the force of our evidence by calling Professor Bernard Meyer, a biochemist from a local university. His testimony was of a highly technical nature but the gist of it was that there was copper all around us, in the air, in the human body, everywhere. Thus it was impossible to determine how much copper content would normally be in Lenkoe's body. He disregarded all the tests that we had made and the conclusions we had reached. The court then adjourned.

The following day I took Dr. Moritz to the airport. He told me he had expected simply to give evidence at an inquest but he felt as if he had gone through the mill of adversary proceedings. He'd never had such a hectic, hard-working week. He warned me about living too dangerously and urged me to be careful. Then he was gone—back to America.

Later that morning I was busy in my office when my secretary announced that two men were there to see me and she gave me a long, meaningful look. She opened the door so I could see them and I knew that I was in for some kind of trouble. I wondered whether they were just on a search mission or whether they had come to deliver a banning order or possibly even detain me. I invited them in to my office and asked them to sit down, knowing that if they accepted they were only polite visitors. They did sit down and I heaved an inward sigh of relief.

"Well, gentlemen, what can I do for you?" I asked.

They introduced themselves as security police officers and stated, "You are the holder of South African passport J 146298. We have orders from the minister to call upon you to surrender this passport to us."

They handed me a letter from the minister of interior, who was responsible for issuing and withholding passports. The letter was headed "Notice of Withdrawal of South African Passport" and said, "I am directed to inform you that the Minister of the Interior has in terms of paragraph 1 of the Conditions of Issue of South African passports, decided to withdraw with immediate effect, South African passport J 146298, which was issued in your favor. The passport has, therefore, ceased to be a valid document for the purpose of the Departure from the Republic, Regulation Act #34 of 1955. You are called upon to surrender the aforementioned document immediately to the officer serving this notice on you."

Just then I saw another man, whom I again knew intuitively was a policeman, enter my office. I began to wonder whether the removal of my passport was just the first step—and then what? I decided to play for time and let as many people as possible know what was happening. I searched my office, my safe, and my private filing cabinet. I called my secretary and my bookkeeper and my clerk. I told them what was happening and asked each of them whether they had seen my passport. I told the security police that my wife might know where the document was, but she was not at home so I called various friends trying to reach her, using the opportunity to alert them, too, to the security police action.

Finally, I telephoned the American consulate and spoke to the clerk responsible for passports and visas. I was normally very friendly and informal when I spoke to her. I now addressed her by her last name and inquired in a most formal manner whether she had my passport.

She got the point immediately and replied that she did not know and would have to make inquiries. "Is it urgent?" she asked.

"Yes, it is, two security police are in my office now and wish me to hand over my passport to them immediately."

Right away she said, "I will have to ask the passport officer. Will you hold on a minute?" She returned to the telephone and said, "The passport officer is out at the moment. I think we do have your passport. If you'll call here when he gets back at two-thirty, I'll tell him that you need your passport."

I asked her to hold on, and speaking so she could hear, I said, "Sergeant, I think my passport is with the American consul. Could I go up there and fetch it this afternoon?"

He said they would meet me outside the consulate office at 2:30 and I so informed the lady on the telephone. That was the end of my conversation with the two security police and they then left.

But who was the other policeman in my office? He was now shown in.

"Are you Mr. J. Carlson?" he asked, in that special police monotone.

"I am," I replied.

"Well, I have to serve this traffic summons on you. Sign here please."

I smiled as I signed; for once I was more than happy to receive a traffic summons.

There was no court action I could take to keep my passport. In South Africa a passport is a privilege. It is a document issued and held entirely at the discretion of the minister. I alerted the press as to what was happening and told them I would have to hand over my passport to the police as soon as I retrieved it from the American consul that afternoon.

Promptly at 2:30 I fetched my passport from the consul's office but the security police did not appear. The reporters did, however, and asked me whether I knew why my passport was being withdrawn. I told them that no reason had been given to me and there was no reason that justified such action. I waited for thirty minutes but as the police had still not arrived I decided to leave and took the elevator downstairs. As I stepped out of the elevator the police moved in. A few reporters were still around and as some press photographers began taking pictures the police threatened to smash their cameras if they continued.

The sergeant who had been in my office came up to me and said, "The passport—give me the passport."

As I took it out of my pocket he grabbed it out of my hand and left. In the confusion I did not see the American consul general, who had observed the whole incident. As I walked to my car he passed me on the sidewalk and so made his presence known. I was warmed and gratified by this gesture of support.

For the next few days, the story of my passport withdrawal was headline news. Editorials were written in the South African press and in papers in other countries, and the International Commission of Jurists cabled the minister of justice, asking his intervention to secure the release of the seized passport.

I asked to appear before my own law society to solicit their support, arguing that either I was fit to be a colleague or not and that if I had done anything wrong I should be charged; otherwise I should be protected. They said they would do what they could. I also made representations to my member of Parliament, Helen Suzman, and asked her to try to arrange an interview for me with the minister of justice.

Dr. Moritz released a statement in America saying the police action did not surprise him because I had been crusading for human rights and was regarded by the government as a public enemy. He said I was fully aware of the risks I was taking. *The New York Times,* in an editorial headed "South African Justice," referred to the disclosures I had made in the Lenkoe case as well as to the evidence of Dr. Moritz: "However the court case turns out this much is clear. Mr. Carlson has lost his passport because he was too skilled, even when up against monstrous laws and the apartheid system, in protecting the rights of Africans and exposing police barbarism." I received cables and messages of support from the Lawyers Committee in Washington and, in particular, from Arthur H. Dean and Louis F. Oberdorfer, the co-chairmen of that committee, who gave me encouragement, support, and warm praise for my handling of the Lenkoe case. I also received word from the consul that there was sympathy and support for me at the highest levels of government in the

United States, including Burke Marshall, who said: "It appears that Carlson is having official action taken against him solely because he represents people who oppose the South African government."

Meanwhile, the inquest proceedings continued with Mrs. Lenkoe going into the witness box. She spoke in gentle tones and calmly answered several abrupt questions from Judge Tukker, who was obliged to comply with the formality of hearing the widow but was determined to cut her short. She told what had happened the night her husband disappeared into the custody of the police and never returned. The police had come to arrest a man called Mofokeng but had taken her husband, James Lenkoe. Her testimony struck fear in all those who realized that it was their doors that might be banged on next.

When Jordaan began to cross-examine her, he was rude and abrupt. David rose to appeal to the court to bear in mind that she was the widow and had suffered greatly. He asked Jordaan to moderate his tone.

Judge Tukker turned on him: "I have had enough of your objections. Sit down," and he told Jordaan to continue.

We had had difficulty in finding a biochemist to interpret for us what the state's witness, Professor Meyer, had really said. We learned from one expert that Meyer had said nothing new and had added little to disturb the conclusions of the tests our pathologists had already made. However, neither this man nor any other biochemist we contacted was willing to appear. We needed further time to have this part of the state's evidence translated and challenged. Therefore, William Oshry, Q.C., a senior counsel, was briefed to request a postponement of a few days. Alternatively, he was instructed to cross-examine Professor Meyer during the court's next session, which had been fixed for 2:15 that Friday afternoon, despite the fact that David had indicated that he was not going to be available.

When Oshry and I arrived in court that afternoon, it was filled with security police and students from Pretoria University, an Afrikaans-speaking, pro-*apartheid* institution. There were so many whites present that they ignored their own segregation rules and spilled over into the black public gallery.

The tension was electric and it was difficult to function in such an atmosphere. Oshry, who was more used to the courtesies of civil proceedings, was stunned by the intimidating methods of the security police. But he was not deterred by them and when Judge Tukker convened the court, he made his application for a postponement.

The judge interrupted him and stated abruptly, "I will not allow any further hearings of this matter. Even if this court has to sit until nine or ten P.M. tonight, or longer, this matter will end today." He did not have to say he had received his orders—this was obvious. The case was becoming too embarrassing to the security police.

Oshry then asked Judge Tukker for an adjournment, as in these circumstances, he wished to take further instructions.

The judge replied: "The court will adjourn for two minutes."

It was impossible to talk in the courtroom and we went for a walk in the parking lot outside. It was quite clear to us that it was useless trying to persuade the judge with any reason or law. If we were not to be given the facilities normally afforded, it was preferable for us to take no further part in the proceedings. Let the proceedings stand for what they were, and let them speak for themselves.

The one difficulty was that David had made certain applications that were still pending before the court. He was due at the inquest at 3 P.M. We decided to tell the judge that we would not cross-examine further but asked that the inquest stand down for Soggot to deal with the matters pending. We were only asking for an indulgence of some twenty minutes.

As we walked into court, it convened. Oshry rose and Judge Tukker demanded, "Do you want to question Professor Meyer?"

Oshry told him that he did not, but he wished to make his position clear. Besides Professor Meyer, he said, there were other matters pending before the court, matters with which he was unfamiliar and on which he had no instructions. He asked that the matter stand over until 3 P.M. when David Soggot would arrive. Rudely, Judge Tukker interrupted and said his request was being refused and the matter would proceed forthwith.

Oshry was still on his feet when Jordaan announced he had closed his case. It seemed that the inquest was at an end. There was no longer even the semblance of a courtroom—it was a circus. Oshry asked that the matter stand down until 3 P.M. to permit Soggot to make an application.

The judge shouted, "I have heard enough applications."

Oshry replied that it appeared that the judge was bulldozing these proceedings.

Judge Tukker lifted an admonishing finger and in a threatening tone, warned him to be careful: "Count your words; there is no bulldozing here."

Oshry repeated that an application was to be made for the court to hear further witnesses, and again the judge said, "I will allow no further witnesses to be called. The evidence before this court is very clear."

At that moment David arrived and I quickly informed him of what had happened. He rose and drew the judge's attention to the fact that the court was in such a hurry to end these proceedings that the prosecutor had closed its case and the court had refused to hear further evidence, yet a witness was still in the box. He reminded the judge that the widow had stood down so that the state could call Professor Meyer; she had not completed her evidence.

Quickly realizing the serious mistake he had made, Judge Tukker thereupon reopened the case and called Mrs. Lenkoe to the witness box. Jordaan said he had no further questions. Mrs. Lenkoe left the box and David applied to call witnesses to show that systematic brutality had been practiced by Major Swanepoel and his team. Jordaan rose to object and called David "an infamous liar." David replied that he was not prepared to sink to the prosecutor's level and once more tried to address the court, but it was in vain.

The judge's last words were, "I have had enough—this case is closed. The court will adjourn," and he left the bench. A few minutes later he returned and announced that the court, having taken time to consider its verdict (there were no less than four hundred fifty pages of evidence) had reached the decision that James Lenkoe had died as a result of suicidal hanging.

The outcome was not surprising. It was the judgment the

security police had wanted. Nevertheless, they had been burned in the process and I knew that the state would now change the law and the procedures of inquest to prevent a recurrence of the exposure to which they had been subjected.

It was clear that the security police had arrested Lenkoe by mistake. The arrest of the wrong man had resulted in his death, and his innocence had been particularly embarrassing to them but the security police had to shield themselves from any exposure of their errors. This was of supreme importance to them. They needed to pursue their image as an infallible, all-powerful authority.

As he had done in 1967 with the passing of the Terrorism Act, the minister of justice introduced new legislation in the last days of the parliamentary session of 1969. He did this by amending existing security laws and establishing a new security police force, the Bureau of State Security. The minister failed to apprise even members of Parliament of the act's full implications or of his intentions when he introduced the bill. Beforehand, to inhibit possible opposition, the security police embarked on nationwide mass arrests of "dangerous terrorists." A new "Communist" plot to overthrow the state by force was "nipped in the bud" by the ever-efficient security police. As these raids were made in the middle of the Lenkoe inquest hearings, hearings that somewhat tarnished the security police image, this show of efficiency came at an opportune time.

Once again these mass arrests produced the desired results. In Parliament there was no debate and no opposition to the Boss Law, aptly so-called as it is short for Bureau of State Security. It was unpatriotic to refuse to give the security police all the powers the minister said they needed. And no opposition member saw how far the law went. With it the security police could determine what evidence a court could or could not receive. Even a defendant could be prevented from giving evidence in his own defense. The new security bureau was answerable to no authority except Prime Minister Vorster, the man who as minister of justice and police, originally built up the security police.

For me the Lenkoe inquest proceedings demonstrated

beyond any doubt that the courts could and would be manipulated by the security police, and laws would be constantly changed to serve their purposes. Judges, expert assessors, prosecutors, witnesses, and the evidence itself were all controlled. The conduct of the inquest hearings could be considered farcical but for the fact that they were so horrifying. I was nearing the end of the tightrope. The security police had firmly and openly pointed a finger at me. I could begin to count my days. I could no longer travel overseas, I could no longer leave the country. While determined to continue the fight, I wondered how long my luck would last, how long I could depend on the protection of overseas opinion. What little aid and hope I could give was being rapidly whittled away while the system was constantly reinforcing itself. Whites were determined to maintain their power and privileges. I had seen too much and felt too much to have any illusions left about the possibilities of change within the system.

Yet I could see no realistic alternative course of action. I had to continue working inside the system if I remained in South Africa. And I knew the security police were watching me closely and waiting for me to make that one false move.

XIII
HARASSMENT AND
INTIMIDATION

At dawn on May 12, 1969, when I was still deeply involved in the Lenkoe case, I received a call from Soweto telling me that Nelson Mandela's wife had been arrested at 2:00 that morning. She had sent word with her brother-in-law, who was present when she was arrested, that she wanted me to represent her. Like her husband, Winnie Mandela was a symbol of black opposition to the government. She had been a leading member of her husband's organization, the ANC, which was now outlawed. Nelson Mandela was serving a life sentence on Robben Island and Mrs. Mandela had been under a banning order for the last five years.

The morning newspapers revealed the latest mass raids of the security police throughout the country and the arrest of hundreds of people. I immediately made inquiries at the Orlando police station in Soweto, the station nearest Mrs. Mandela's home. I was given the usual runaround and only toward midday was I able to have the security police confirm that Winnie Mandela had been arrested and detained under the Terrorism Act.

Mrs. Mandela's sister and her other relatives came in to see me that day. The family, naturally anxious about her, wanted me to take action to have her freed on bail or at least allowed visits. I had to explain to them that the wide powers of the Terrorism Act did not permit this and that only the security police could alter the terms of her detention. I promised to approach them.

Many people called about Mrs. Mandela, all of them claiming her friendship and plying me with questions about her. While some of them may well have been her friends, I suspected that others were security police informers. I had no way of judging friend from informer and decided to confide only in Mrs. Mandela's family. This decision was resented by some of Winnie's friends. They joined with those who for other reasons were eager to prevent my acting for her, and wanted to appoint another attorney.

I was too busy to pay much attention to all the rumors I heard about this opposition faction. I wrote to the security police asking under what law Mrs. Mandela was held and whether her relatives could see her or supply her with food and clothing. Prior to her arrest Mrs. Mandela was under a doctor's supervision and particular inquiries were made about her state of health. My letters were completely ignored but the security police called on Mrs. Mandela's sisters and asked them to provide clothing for her. I invited the relatives to come to my office or house whenever they wished and to report anything that happened between themselves and the police.

In the meantime, the families of many others of those arrested in this most recent sweep were also coming to me for help and I saw each of them and gave them whatever guidance I could. They were particularly anxious about the prisoners in view of the disclosures in the Lenkoe inquest and feared that their loved ones, too, would be subjected to electric-shock torture. The recent statements about the number of deaths in detention also increased their anxiety. The only reassurance I could give was that the blaze of publicity might act as some sort of brake on the security police. I, of course, did ask the security police whether the detainees were in good health but

HARASSMENT AND INTIMIDATION

I hardly expected them to answer truthfully, if at all. Nevertheless, it was useful to have their reply on record.

I kept on writing regularly, asking what progress had been made in each case and insisting on being told the time and place of any trial involving any of my clients. It was important that the security police realize that the prisoners, though held in total isolation, had not been forgotten. The extent of the assistance which they gave to each family enabled me to guess how far they had gone in breaking the detainee under interrogation. If a wife or mother was allowed to see a prisoner, I could assume that this privilege indicated that the prisoner had become a state witness. If the family was allowed to take the prisoner food, then some deal was being made and the police were using this privilege to convince the prisoner that they were playing square with him. If no information or help was forthcoming, I could assume that those detainees were proving difficult to break.

It did not matter to me that the security police contacted the various families and warned them against seeing me. I knew I always had my clients' confidence, and my clients, in turn, knew that whether a detainee proved to be a state witness or a defendant, he had my support. I had learned not to make any moral judgment about the reaction of people in prison. I had known over a hundred detainees and not one of them had managed to hold out completely. All of them had eventually made statements to the security police. My belief is that no one is able to resist security police methods. Even without physical torture, their assault on the mind eventually breaks all resistance. No one can withstand being kept awake for days and nights on end. Though some are able to hold out longer than others, everyone gives way in the end.

My clients distrusted the security police and placed their faith in me. In turn, I had to warn them and protect them from making any report to me in my bugged office. As they came in to see me, I would say "Hello" without mentioning any name and would point to my telephone to remind them of the bug. They smiled and we understood each other. They would motion with their index fingers, indicating that they wanted to talk outside. Then we would walk up and down the passages, or stairways, or ride the elevator. In this way we learned to live with the police state and developed ways of communicating despite the bugs.

News was circulated but some of it was planted by the security police. It was difficult to tell an innocent man from an informer. I adopted the maxim: "If in doubt, don't trust." It was a hard judgment but a necessary one. Yet I also had to remain flexible and be ready to change my opinions.

A number of my clients began reporting to me that they had been visited by a white woman, a stranger to them, who called herself Mrs. Kay. She paraded her friendship with Mrs. Mandela, showing them a picture in a newspaper of her presenting flowers to Mrs. Mandela when she came out of jail at the end of a previous term of imprisonment. She spoke of her sympathies with the ANC and the aspirations of the Africans. Because she knew it was against the law of the land, she mentioned to some that her husband, Musa Dinath, was Indian and had been a member of the outlawed Indian Congress. She offered them financial aid and said she was arranging for the defense of their relatives. I also heard that Mrs. Kay had visited members of the Mandela family, had gone to Winnie Mandela's home, and had invited Winnie's children to her home.

Mrs. Mandela had herself worked for Mrs. Kay and Musa Dinath. Although Mrs. Mandela was a qualified social worker, after her banning she was unable to find a job. The security police visited each prospective employer and warned them against hiring her. I had given her work in my office but when the Namibian case started, I felt I had no alternative but to ask her to leave. Her presence in my office at that time would endanger my handling of the case and might be used by the security police as an excuse to raid my office. The trial itself was difficult enough without further complications. As soon as Mrs. Mandela left my office, she was invited by Mrs. Kay and Musa Dinath to work for them. Her employment there was accepted by the security police.

According to my clients, Mrs. Kay had no hesitation in condemning me as a rogue and a thief, and said that I was about to be detained or placed under house arrest and would thus be prevented from acting for them. It became clear that Mrs. Kay had converted a number of Mrs. Mandela's close friends and even one member of the family. This was not surprising; in a police-state atmosphere it is easy to sow dissent and mistrust—everyone is suspicious of the next person.

Mrs. Kay continued to keep in contact with the relatives of the prisoners and she persuaded them to accompany her to the office of an attorney named Mendel Levin where some were induced to sign powers of attorney. Then I heard that she had gone to London. There she advised people that she and Mendel Levin represented Mrs. Mandela and the other prisoners, who had dismissed me because I was untrustworthy and they preferred Levin. On her return, she boasted to the relatives about the people she had seen and about her visit to the London-based Defense and Aid office. She also named many ex-South Africans working actively in London to overthrow the South African government and said she had spoken to them and gained their support. She flourished a letter from another London organization that supported her and claimed that she and Mendel Levin had been accepted as legitimate representatives of Mrs. Mandela and the other prisoners.

I could not dismiss these rumors any more. Clients were apprehensive—who did Mrs. Mandela really trust, they wondered. Through the local newspaper, Mendel Levin then announced that he had been formally instructed by Mrs. Mandela and that he had arranged for a physician to see her in prison.

I knew that I was unpopular with many people in London because of my highly critical attitude of the way in which they supported political prisoners in South Africa. I had firsthand experience of their inefficiency and had complained about it in the past. I was nevertheless astonished at their naïveté and could not believe that they had fallen for Mrs. Kay's story. It was imperative that they learn the truth about these people and their links with the security police.

I took time off to do some research and established that Musa Dinath had over two hundred and fifty convictions for crimes of fraud and theft alone. Despite the fact that he had been sentenced to many years' imprisonment, after serving one month, Minister of Justice Vorster had personally intervened on his behalf and Dinath was released from prison. Although once an Indian Congress executive member, he had changed his allegiance when the Nationalist party came to power and had even sought financial support for this party from his own community. Subsequently, the security police used him and he spent time with Indian prisoners in jail in an effort to induce them to give evidence for the state. (I later discovered that in July, 1969, the security police arranged for Dinath to see Nelson Mandela on Robben Island to persuade him to let Mendel Levin represent his wife. Nelson rejected Musa's entreaties and instructed him to convey to me that I was to continue acting as his and his wife's attorney. Musa never gave me this message and I had to get it from other sources.)

Mendel Levin, the attorney, had been prosecuted for committing a number of crimes, the last of which involved fraud and theft of a million dollars. He avoided imprisonment by turning state's evidence. He had never shown any concern for the ANC and, in fact, was known for his dedication to the Nationalist party. Despite its avowed anti-Semitism, he had become its first Jewish member and had stood as a party candidate.

Mrs. Kay, with her sister, had run some shady organizations that they claimed had police support. Most remarkable was the fact that although the authorities strictly enforced the prohibition on people of different races living together and although Musa Dinath and Mrs. Kay were well known to the police, they managed to live together in white areas in contravention of the law. Other people had been convicted and sent to jail or hounded out of the country for similar actions. Mrs. Kay and Dinath pursued their lives unhampered by the police.

Once I had collected documentary proof in support of these facts, including statements from a number of people who had been visited by Mrs. Kay and spoken to Mendel Levin, I sent everything to a man I could trust in London. I asked him to acquaint those involved with the facts.

The prisoners and their relatives would have been severely

prejudiced had Mrs. Kay and Mendel Levin represented them, and this arrangement would only have been beneficial to the security police. The people in prison were unaware of these dangers and could not be informed of them. The least I could do was inform the relatives of the detainees and the London people. I was extremely bitter that the latter had given any support to Mrs. Kay and Levin. I was heavily involved in conducting the Lenkoe inquest proceedings and attending to the relatives of new detainees and I deeply resented the time I had to spend in preparing the fact sheets for London. However, I knew that my efforts had been successful when some weeks later I received a letter from Amnesty International, a group dedicated to obtaining the release of all political prisoners everywhere, which formally advised me of the approaches made by Mrs. Kay and Mendel Levin and of the derogatory remarks made about me. The letter informed me that their organization did not support Mendel Levin or Mrs. Kay in any way and said that they hoped that I would represent the prisoners.

As this letter arrived via the regular mail, I was certain that the security police would know that the Kay-Levin plan had failed insofar as London was concerned. Nevertheless, both Mrs. Kay and Levin continued seeing the relatives and were still given access to the prisoners. Mendel Levin then visited London where he tried to repair the damage and he later made representations to certain American sources, but I was only to learn of his inability to build credibility much later.

The Mendel Levin incident was only a part of the harassment and intimidation my family and I were subjected to during that period. Not only was open action taken against me in the removal of my passport, but poison-pen letters were widely distributed among my friends and colleagues and some friends began to speculate about the truth of their contents. Journalists from hitherto friendly newspapers told me that they had been instructed by their editors to interview me to probe the veracity of the letters. The allegations made were horrible and farfetched and I was angry and upset when it seemed that some people were willing to believe them. There were other horrors, too. The late-night telephone calls became

more frequent; there were more death threats, more obsceni-
ties, and more heavy breathing.

The harassment aimed at me encompassed other people
too. Friends who visited my house told me that their license
plate numbers had been taken and they had been "visited" by
the security police and questioned about their association
with my wife and myself. As a result, some reluctantly
decided to break off their friendship with us. At my office,
staff members suddenly gave notice and left. A new employee
would start work one day and fail to return the next day
without a word of explanation. This happened continuously
over a period of some eight weeks and I was almost at my
wit's end. My family and I managed to adjust to the other
forms of harassment but this hit at the most crucial part of my
life. I was unable to perform clients' work.

Then the security police mounted another campaign which
was perhaps the most distressing of all. They called on the
secretary of a nonpolitical organization of which I was an
active member. She was an elderly lady in poor health and
lived alone. They first made friendly overtures to persuade
her to inform on me and tried to buy her aid. She rejected
their suggestions. She was then threatened with detention.
Still she resisted and she was taken in for long and irregular
periods of interrogation by teams of security policemen. She
was never imprisoned; that was not the idea. Although the
security police knew that she had no damaging information
about me, they insisted that she sign a false statement
incriminating me.

I did everything I could to help and protect her but all my
efforts failed. The more involved I got, the more the security
police applied the pressure.

I managed to alert my friends overseas to this new danger
but I was unable to help this innocent woman. Finally, after
many consultations with advisers, I concluded that in her own
interests and in mine, too, I should sever all links between us,
hoping that this unhappy end to our association would bring
an end to her torment.

My helplessness and frustration in this matter, added to all
the other pressures, was almost the breaking point. I had

visions of clients taking court action against me for my failure to attend to their work. Innocent people were made to suffer because of me. I felt like a leper. At night I waited for the 2 A.M. knock on the door. In a way it would have been a relief for I would then be beyond the cause of my anxieties. At least in detention I could settle down to facing and fighting my persecutors. I waited and waited but "they" never came, while each day brought a new concern.

At last I told a lawyer friend, "They have won! I cannot go on. It is impossible to work and anyone who comes to me may be terrorized. I am nervous and irritable and I want to give up. I'm closing my practice."

"Calm down, Joel," said my friend. "I know things are bad but take a deep breath. Go away for a week and relax. Forget about your office, forget about this woman, forget about everything. You must not let them hear you talk like this. I'll see you in a week's time."

I took his advice and with the whole family, left for a five-day vacation at the coast. The children were ecstatic at the prospect of staying in a hotel, which they had never done before, and to this day they talk about the wonderful time they had. It was a remarkable achievement of my wife that the children were largely unaware of the tensions and anxieties that beset us throughout our last years in South Africa.

As I entered the hotel to register, the receptionist gave me a message. Edward Lyons, a British barrister and a member of Parliament, was in South Africa as a representative of the International Commission of Jurists. He had come to make representations to the minister about the return of my passport and to express concern at its confiscation at a time when I was acting in matters concerning the arbitrary detention of opponents of the government. I also heard that George Lindsay, a member of the New York City bar and chairman of the Lawyers Committee for Civil Rights under Law, was on his way to South Africa for the same purpose. Both men came down to Durban to see me and I outlined the pressures being placed on me.

By the time of their visit, the implications of the Boss Bill had at last been fully appreciated by politicians and lawyers in

South Africa. Two judges had led off by criticizing the bill and then various groups of lawyers, churchmen, students, and others followed, protesting the overriding provisions of this new piece of security legislation and calling on the minister to withdraw it. On the surface, all this protest was encouraging but the security police and the security laws were now well rooted in the society. They would easily survive this small storm.

Lindsay and Lyons saw the minister and other government officials and leading members of the bar, but when they asked for reasons for the withdrawal of my passport, they were told it was a matter of state security. They issued a statement to the press in which they said that their visit "reflects the deep concern widely felt by lawyers in America, Europe, and elsewhere, at what is regarded outside South Africa as the removal of essential legal safeguards." Revealing what they called their separate missions with a common purpose, they listed the enactment of the Terrorism Act, the so-called Boss Legislation, and "the removal of the passport of Mr. Joel Carlson, a Johannesburg lawyer who has figured prominently in the defense of political prisoners." They described the action against me as being one "taken without any explanation and considered to endanger the right of lawyers to represent clients without fear."

Lindsay further said that "the American Lawyers Committee intended to continue to instruct and support Mr. Carlson in carrying out his professional responsibilities. The Committee hopes that he will not be interfered with and that his freedom to travel, particularly while engaged in counseling clients, will not be infringed." He also drew attention to the fact that many prominent American lawyers were members of the committee.

The International Commission of Jurists in Geneva issued a statement saying, "it was distressed that such action was taken against Mr. Carlson at a time when he was appointed the observer for the Commission at political trials in South Africa. The Commission fears also that other South African lawyers might draw the conclusion that it is safer not to defend too vigorously, certain cases."

The visit by these two eminent lawyers and the resultant publicity their statements aroused, brought floods of mail and editorials in local and foreign papers, all supporting my activities and decrying the removal of my passport. This demonstrated to the South African authorities the extent of the support I enjoyed in the international legal community and the concern not only at the arbitrary and illegal action taken against me, but at the erosion of the rule of law in South Africa. It also gave clear notice that a storm of international protest would follow if I was arrested and detained. There is no doubt that all of this acted as a brake on the authorities in taking any further action against me at that time. I had been given a reprieve.

XIV
THE TRIAL OF THE
TWENTY-TWO BEGINS

Despite numerous protests, the security police took their time about charging any of the people arrested that May. The summer passed without any indication that they would be brought to trial. Late one afternoon, toward the end of October, I received a telephone call from Lieutenant Karel Dirker, of the security police. He told me that five of the people for whom I said I was acting would be appearing at the Pretoria court where the Lenkoe proceedings had taken place, the following morning at 9 A.M. He did not include Mrs. Mandela's name on the list.

Driving down to Pretoria, I abandoned my usual one-hundred-mile-an-hour dash and kept to a sedate sixty miles per hour. I used the extra time to think of ways in which I could handle the matter in court that morning. I didn't know exactly what to expect but I was certain that my right to appear for the defendants would be challenged and I had no powers of attorney from any of them. I knew from the statements that Mendel Levin had given to the press that he had a power of attorney for Peter Magubane and Winnie

Mandela and possibly others. As I had no access to Mrs. Mandela or any of the detainees, I could not ascertain whether they had, in fact, given a power of attorney to Levin. Levin also claimed in the newspaper that he had succeeded in having Mrs. Mandela examined by a private doctor. If this was true, he had obviously been looking after her and was determined to represent her.

It seemed clear that the security police had been cooperating with him in allowing him access to the detainees and encouraging them to abandon me and select him as their attorney. I was only to learn later of the lengths to which Levin and the police had gone in trying to discredit me. I wondered whether Levin had been able to convince the prisoners. They had, after all, been in solitary confinement almost six months and I well knew what their state of mind would be by this time.

The strength of my position lay with the prisoners' relatives. I had powers of attorney from each of them, instructing me to represent the defendants, and I had managed to send them all word that the defendants would be appearing in Pretoria that morning. Other than to make my position clear to the court, I would just have to wait to see how things developed. I was certainly not going to enter into any kind of competition with Mendel Levin.

On my arrival at the courthouse, I took up a position at the back door, the "proper" door for blacks to use, and there I waited for the prisoners' families. Pretoria Magistrates Court is one of the many exceptions to the rule that everyone has equal access to the courts. In the supreme courts and in the courts in big urban centers, all the population has access through the same doors. This back door to justice simplified my task for I would not have to search all over the buildings for relatives who might go astray.

Transportation was always a problem and several families had crowded together in the same car to make the trip to Pretoria. Although they were all united through a common anxiety now, and we were all friends, I knew that before long tensions would divide us. None of us knew which prisoners would be charged or who would be used as state witnesses against them. I showed everyone where to go, wished them luck, and warned them to be careful of what they said to one another or to any strangers who might draw them into conversation. Then I put on my gown and went into court.

The scene was a very familiar one, the same security policemen, the same searching stares. In addition to the faces I knew so well, there were a number of new young security men. Soon, three prosecutors from the attorney general's office arrived. They were senior men and I had opposed them in court before in political trials. Senior security policemen came in next—Majors Cotzee, Ferreira, van Rensburg, Botha, and Swanepoel, and they took up their position behind the three prosecutors. It would not be long now before the defendants appeared. Since there were no sirens, no convoys, no armored vehicles, I realized that the defendants had been brought to court secretly to avoid demonstrations of support and had been quickly hustled into the cells below.

Mendel Levin arrived with his son and partners and sat down at the court table next to me. He picked his nails nervously and spoke to the prosecutors ingratiatingly in Afrikaans. I saw Mrs. Kay come in, smile at me, and sit down in the public gallery. The court was packed with reporters and the public galleries were full. Feeling unbearably tense, I stood up for a moment and looked out over the heads of the security police at the purple jacaranda trees in full bloom across the street. They made a splash of color against a white wall, which reflected the bright sunlight of this midmorning.

Suddenly my attention was brought back to the courtroom. Uniformed police hustled in and took up positions at every door, their Sten guns ready. The performance was about to begin. Three or four policemen marched up the stairs leading from the cells below, and behind them the black defendants moved in a line into court. As Winnie Mandela appeared she saw me, half-smiled, and nodded. Mendel Levin rushed over to shake her hand and she seemed embarrassed by this gesture.

I took a step back to whisper to her, "Winnie, your sisters are in court." She swung around and when she saw her relatives, her face lit up. She waved frantically to them, smiling and blowing kisses.

Elliot Shabangu, whom I had known for a long time, appeared stunned to see me. His eyes were full of astonishment but he greeted me with great satisfaction.

Joyce Sikakane was embarrassed and somewhat hesitant in her greeting and I whispered to her, "Your mother is in court."

I moved along the line, exchanging greetings with the defendants. There were twenty-two in all. Although surrounded by police, they were excitedly blowing kisses and waving to their relatives at the back of the court.

The court orderly, the interpreter, and the police captain bustled about getting the defendants in the right order, roughly calling, *"Kom, kom, kom,"* and Mendel Levin again moved over to talk to Mrs. Mandela, interrupting her waving and smiling to her friends. The orderly shouted, *"Stilte staan stil,"* and called the court to order.

Everyone rose as the fat, bald, elderly magistrate, Strijdom—the one I had first dealt with in the Lenkoe case—took the bench. He nodded to the prosecutor's table and the youngest of them, Willem Van Zyl, stood up for the state. In Afrikaans, he announced that he called the case of the State versus Samson Ndou and others. I was tempted to rise and object to his speaking Afrikaans since I knew that the black clients I represented did not understand the language, but was I representing anyone, I wondered. I stayed seated. After handing the charge sheet to the judge, the prosecutor gave him a certificate issued by the attorney general. This stated that in the interests of state security, none of the defendants should be granted bail. That settled that question. The judge could not grant any bail. The prosecutor then asked for a postponement of the case to December 1 when a summary trial would, he said, begin in the Supreme Court in Pretoria, before a specially convened court.

Immediately after he sat down I was on my feet to address the court. "As Your Worship pleases, I appear, sir. But when I say I appear, the true position is that all these defendants have been detained under Section 6 of the Terrorism Act for five to six months. I have not had an opportunity of seeing any one of them as they have been held in solitary confinement and incommunicado. No lawyer has had any access to them. I, therefore, have not been instructed by any of them personally."

The judge tried to snatch the initiative from me: "What is your name?" he asked me. "Whom do you represent?" He was in turn interrupted by the court stenographer as he had forgotten to switch on his microphone and was not being heard by the recording machines. I seized the initiative back and proceeded in my address to him. I quickly placed my name on record and went on to explain that I had no personal instructions from any of the defendants.

He interrupted again: "Yes, Mr. Carlson, but whom do you represent?"

Again I explained that I had been instructed by the relatives who were present in court and not by any of the defendants who had been unable to instruct me personally.

"But which clients do you claim to represent?" he again asked.

When I began to give him the names he interrupted me further. "No, no, I'm not interested in the names," he said, "just give me the numbers, the numbers in the right order."

I replied, "Sir, I do not have the numbers as I have not received a copy of the charge sheet," and I casually stretched out my hand toward the prosecutor's table for a copy of the indictment. One of the prosecutors handed it to me.

"Ah, now I have been given one," I said, and proceeded to read out the numbers corresponding to my clients.

I went on: "In regard to these people, sir, I ask the court's indulgence. I wish to indicate to the defendants that while their relatives have instructed me, it is for the defendants to adopt those instructions or reject them. I ask the court's permission to clarify the position as I have been unable to see them since their detention in May. The defendants themselves must choose whether or not to confirm my instructions. One further request, sir. The families present in court have also not seen any of the defendants for a considerable time and they wish to have the opportunity to speak to them. They are worried about the effect, if any, of detention and I make a humane request to Your Worship, to allow them to get together. Perhaps the court could adjourn for a short while."

I had finished and Levin stood up. After giving his particulars to Judge Strijdom he told the court, "I have been approached by relatives of the defendants and hold powers of attorney from them. I also hold the personal power of attorney of Mrs. Mandela and Mr. Magubane."

The judge interrupted him. "No, no—I want numbers, not names." As soon as Levin gave him the numbers, he said with some enthusiasm, "Ah, then there is clash between you."

Levin answered, "I want to come to that in a moment, sir. The position is this, Your Worship. Mrs. Mandela, with whom I have been in correspondence over the months and for whom I have acted and whose written power of attorney I hold, confirmed to me in court a moment ago that I am acting for her. I take the strongest exception to Mr. Carlson stating that he is acting for her. Through her own authority, and the lady is in court, I wish to make it perfectly clear that I am acting for her and will continue acting for her."

The judge intervened: "Ah, there is a conflict as far as Mrs. Mandela is concerned."

"No, sir," said Levin, "there is no conflict; she is here, she can confirm that I hold a written power of attorney and have had her confirmation this morning."

I rose to reply, "Your Worship, in regard to Mrs. Mandela, I have no power of attorney from her, nor have I seen her, but her husband, who is on Robben Island, has told members of his family that he wishes me to act for her and the family are present in court. Perhaps if Your Worship adjourns, this matter could be sorted out. I do not wish to compete for instructions. I have made my position to the defendants clear. I assure Your Worship, I will not speak to any of them before they have instructed me."

Judge Strijdom ruled that he would postpone the matter until after the tea break. He instructed the interpreter to tell the defendants that they must settle their arrangements for representation and that if they required it, the state would provide lawyers to act for them and such lawyers, although paid for by the state, would not act in the service of the state but for the defendants. With that he adjourned the court and the defendants were taken down to the cells.

I rounded up the relatives and showed them the way to the cells. When we got there Mendel Levin, members of his staff, and Mrs. Kay were already inside the cell block. Levin was arguing with the police captain, insisting that he should have the first opportunity of seeing the defendants.

Determined to ensure that the relatives were given some time to see the defendants and that Levin did not stop them from doing so, I got the police to admit me to the cell block. At that point Levin made the mistake of trying to demonstrate to the police captain what an important person he was. He had to see the defendants first, he said, because he was a busy man, had to catch a plane within the hour, and could not be delayed. He insisted that the captain allow him to see the defendants immediately.

The police captain was an ordinary uniformed policeman who was no party to Levin's private negotiations with Major Swanepoel and the security police. Levin dared not call on Swanepoel for aid in my presence. I kept silent, watching him misplay his hand and antagonize the officer.

Irritated, the captain finally turned to me. I seized my chance. "Captain, I'm sure you'll do what you think is necessary. It does not matter who sees the defendants first as long as you tell me that the relatives will be permitted to see them as the judge ordered. There is not much time and it shouldn't be wasted. I will accept whatever decision you make."

"Rest assured," the captain said, "all the relatives will be given a chance."

I thanked him and asked his permission to leave the cells. As the policemen let me out I heard the captain order Levin to stand aside and call for the first defendant's relatives. I walked upstairs and out to tea.

At 11:00 I strolled back to court through the back entrance and met some of the relatives outside the courtroom. Their smiles confirmed that all was well. They told me that Mendel Levin was still downstairs and they laughed at his discomfiture.

Major Swanepoel approached me to inquire what had

happened in the cells. I told him I had no idea—I thought he would know more about it than I. No, he said, he had not heard. At that moment Mendel Levin appeared and stood next to us.

"Major," I said, "I do not think you know Mr. Levin. Mr. Levin, this is Major Swanepoel."

Levin flushed at the introduction but completed the formalities of strangers being introduced and shook hands.

Rather pleased with myself, I went into court and the proceedings began. The prosecutor, now speaking in English, told the court that the consultations had been completed and a decision had been reached.

I rose to object. "Your Worship, may I place on record the fact that I have had no consultations whatever and I have not seen the defendants at all."

Judge Strijdom was a little perturbed. "Weren't you allowed in?" he asked.

"No, Your Worship, it was my own choice. The defendants themselves must decide and I have not seen them."

Levin then stood up. He was flushed and he moved both his hands while he talked: "Your Worship, at all relevant times I held the power of attorney held by Mrs. Mandela. This morning in court she confirmed I was acting for her. She confirmed this in the cells, too. But a few moments ago when I saw her, she informed me she wished to make a statement to the court as to the question of her legal representative. I pressed her for an answer and she told me that I must withdraw. She said her husband, Nelson Mandela, had sent word that no one other than Mr. Carlson should act and, therefore, I must withdraw." He sat down and nervously began assembling his papers.

Judge Strijdom addressed him: "But what about the other people you were acting for, Mr. Levin?"

Levin rose a little more slowly and replied: "Your Worship, I have no powers of attorney for any of the others and I must again ask permission to withdraw."

Before he could sit down, the judge again asked him, "In respect of all the accused?"

"Yes, sir," said Levin, while his fingers tried to straighten his papers on the desk in front of him. There was no further response from the judge. Levin collected his papers and left the court.

Treating what he said with some contempt, I asked the judge, "Never mind what Mr. Levin has said, may we hear from the defendants themselves what the true position is?"

"Yes," said Judge Strijdom, "that is the court's intention." Turning to the interpreter he said, "Will you ask accused number one whether he has arranged for legal representation?"

Samson Ndou was the first defendant. He was a young man and had only been chosen as the first defendant so that the name Mandela, which had so often appeared in court, would not now again appear on the court records.

Samson Ndou replied: "Your Worship, all of us agree that Mrs. Mandela will make a statement in court regarding our legal representation."

Mrs. Mandela stepped forward and began to speak but the judge cut her short. He was obviously not going to permit her to make any statement or recognize her as the spokesman of the other defendants.

"That is your decision," he said. "The court, however, wishes to hear from each of the defendants whether they have nominated Mr. Carlson. Each one must be asked separately." He was making a last effort to find some dissent among the defendants.

Again Mrs. Mandela tried to speak and again the judge interrupted her. He turned to each of the twenty-two defendants and I am not to blame that my name appears in the record twenty-two times as one after the other said, "I wish Mr. Carlson to represent me." The interpreter echoed my name and the words of the defendants. Judge Strijdom finally announced that the defendants, one through twenty-two inclusive, had all informed the court that they wished to be represented by Mr. Carlson. It was a resounding defeat for Swanepoel and his maneuvers with Levin.

Rising to address the court, I said, "Now that I am formally instructed by the defendants I wish to object to the trial being set on December 1. It has taken the state over five months, exercising all their extraordinary powers over the defendants, who were in their custody and under their complete control, to formulate a charge and bring the defendants to court. While I accept the compliment that I can do in five weeks what the state has had over five months to do, I place on record that I am not agreeing to this date of trial. I may not be prepared to proceed on December 1. It may not be possible for me to be ready in that time and I will need the full cooperation of the prison authorities to be able to consult with my clients. They have been cut off from the world for so long, I appeal to the court to call on the prison authorities to allow the defendants to see their relatives on the weekend while they consult with their lawyer throughout the week. The state has seen fit to keep all my clients in custody and proper arrangements must be made so that the defense is able to work with all twenty-two persons on trial. Finally, I wish to place on record my appreciation to the security police for the courtesy of informing me about the trial of the defendants, even if only late yesterday afternoon—a courtesy, indeed, these days."

The prosecutor rose to reply, "After listening to all the speeches, sir, the first of December is the final date as far as the state is concerned. The state is not prepared to change the date."

And so it was ordered. The trial was postponed to December 1 and the court adjourned.

Not only was I surprised at having outwitted Levin and Swanepoel, but I was jubilant with the outcome of the morning's hearings. I had only had time to skim the indictment but was relieved that the defendants faced charges under the Communism Act and not under the Terrorism Act. At a glance, it appeared to me that such details of the charges as "wearing uniforms of the banned African National Congress, singing Congress songs and giving a Congress salute at the graveside of a Congressman" might constitute "terrorism" under the law as much as it constituted "Communism." Strangely, the state had chosen the lesser crime.

The Communism Act carried a maximum sentence of only ten years' imprisonment and a minimum sentence of one year, and the court was permitted to suspend sentences under this act. The Terrorism Act carried a maximum sentence of death and the minimum compulsory sentence of five years which no court could suspend. I wondered why the state, having arrested and detained hundreds of others besides my clients in May and June, now chose to charge the defendants only under the Communism Act. Perhaps the arrests themselves had served the purpose of creating the necessary climate of opinion for the introduction of the Boss Law, and the state was now anxious to dispose of the people it had arrested with the minimum possible trouble.

Outside court, I met my opponents, J. H. Liebenberg, D. W. Rothwell, and van Zyl, the prosecutors. Liebenberg taunted me, saying the state had an open-and-shut case. "You should plead guilty and we will let you off lightly," he said. They seemed anxious to avoid a major political confrontation.

In order to test the air and find out how they really felt about proceedings, I said, jocularly, "Well, without having had more than a glance at your indictment, and without knowing anything at all about the case, I'll do a fifty-fifty deal. You must acquit eleven of the twenty-two. You can convict eleven, and I'll bargain with you on sentences."

To my surprise he took me seriously: "No, no—we will want more convicted than eleven." It was clear that a deal could be negotiated.

"Don't try your luck too hard," I said. "Once I start working on the case I'll probably get twenty-two acquittals, so it's a 'take-it-or-leave-it' offer." I smiled and turned to go.

I asked the prison authorities to allow me to have a brief meeting with my clients. Seeing the male prisoners was easily arranged. It proved a lot more difficult to see the women, who were kept at the women's prison. A senior matron on duty, a large blond woman, badly made up, said, "I have no instructions. You cannot see the women without Brigadier Aucamp's permission."

The brigadier was not long in coming. I remembered how he had tried to prevent me from seeing my Namibian clients years before. Then he was only a lieutenant colonel; promotion had come quickly to him.

"You want to see the women prisoners, Mr. Carlson?" he asked.

"Yes, Brigadier, all of them, please."

"Who are they all?" he asked, but began answering his own question, counting on his fingers: "Shanti Naidoo, Winnie, Joyce—"

Before he could go on I interrupted: "Brigadier, you are giving me state secrets."

"What do you mean?" he asked.

"You have just told me you hold Shanti Naidoo here but she is still a detainee, she is not on trial yet."

"Oh, I'm sorry, yes. Well, who are the five, then?" he asked.

I read their names from the indictment.

"*Ja,* all right, you can see those five," he said.

Teasing him now, I said, "Brigadier, your prison security is very bad."

He stopped and gave me a searching look. "What do you mean?" he asked.

"Well, I know a prisoner in a maximum-security prison who has managed for the last two years, to conspire with subversive people all over the country—in Cape Town, in Durban, in Johannesburg, and all over."

"Who is it?" he said, rather gruffly.

"Brigadier, you haven't read your indictment. You see it says here that while on Robben Island, Nelson Mandela did all these things."

Relieved, he allowed a flicker of a smile to touch his face.

"Agh, that's all right, Mr. Carlson. You just see the women prisoners," and off he went toward the big iron door which swung open as he approached.

The white prison matrons obviously resented the sophistication of the black political prisoners. I tried to win their cooperation but all courtesies ended and they became openly hostile as soon as they saw the friendly relationship I had with the five prisoners. Delighted to see me, each shook my hand warmly, all smiles and laughter, and we began discussing the proceedings at court that morning.

These matrons were startled that a white man should shake the hand of a black woman. They were infuriated that I treated black women as my equals. Their hostility was to grow, and eventually make working conditions impossible, but for the moment I ignored it and went about the mundane task of finding out from the defendants their immediate requirements. I promised to bring them writing material and questionnaries that the defense team needed answered to enable us to begin the long hours of routine work that lay ahead.

As I drove home that evening I had a feeling of real elation with the way the day had gone. But I was also uneasy—there was something behind all this that I did not know and I did not understand, and I wondered who was laying ambushes ahead of me and what action of mine might spring the trap.

XV
THE WOMEN
PRISONERS

Nomzamo Winnie Mandela was a strikingly beautiful woman. She was born in the Transkei, one of the oldest African reserves in the eastern Cape. Both her parents were teachers but her mother died shortly after her birth. Her father, who married again, rose to the position of school principal; but teachers earned only a little more than the farm workers, so although the family was somewhat better off than the Africans around them, they were still poverty-stricken.

There were nine children and as Winnie's father could not afford to send her to school, she remained at home, caring for the younger children and looking after the few cattle her father owned. When, as a little girl, she had visited the white village shops of Bizana during her father's shopping expeditions, she soon realized that although she was well off in her own community, compared to the white children she saw, she had nothing. She also realized that in all matters the whites came first. Blacks had to wait until the white man's needs had been satisfied.

When an older sister had to leave school because of illness,

Winnie was given her chance for an education. As there was always work to be done at home, she was unable to attend school on any regular basis in the next few years, but even so, she soon passed her ninth-grade exams. Her father decided that her education should have precedence over that of her sisters.

In those days, in the Transkei, education for blacks at all levels was not the inferior special "Bantu education" it is now, and their curriculum was the same as it was for whites. In her history classes and from her father, she learned of the resistance of the blacks over the last hundred years to white expansion as the white settlers moved inland from the Cape. Her heroes were the Xhosa chiefs who fought victorious battles against the white colonists. She was proud of her own family and its tradition of serving the people. Her father, dedicated to teaching, had turned down a government offer of chieftainship although this would have meant more money and power for him.

She was sent to the Shawberry High School where she was an enthusiastic and conscientious scholar and was made the head girl of her school. The school was, of course, for blacks only but all her teachers, also all black, were well-trained graduates of Fort Hare University. These teachers introduced Winnie to the Unity Movement, a black organization that advocated noncooperation with the government. The strength of its membership lay among the intellectuals, who were mostly the black teachers in the Cape, and among the farm workers in the rural areas, particularly the Transkei and Pondoland. In this way it was distinct from the older and more well established African National Congress, which was formed at the time of the commencement of the white state of the Union of South Africa in 1910, and was the main African political organization, and from the Indian Congress, its counterpart in the Indian community. The congresses were inspired and led mainly by middle-class professional men and their major strength lay among blacks in the urban areas throughout the country.

In 1953, Winnie left Shawberry and the Transkei. She won a scholarship in social science at the Jan Hofmeyer School in

Johannesburg, run by an American missionary. As part of her studies, she did field work as a junior social worker. She was no stranger to poverty but she had never before seen it on so vast a scale—such starvation, disease, and death—as she found in Johannesburg. It completely depressed her. Often, babies died in her arms from lack of food and proper attention.

In 1956, she qualified with distinction, but decided to give up further study because she realized that only political action could bring an end to the poverty of her people and their lack of rights. She threw herself into the activities of the ANC, but in order to earn a living she took a job as a social welfare officer. It was in that year that many of the leaders of the congress parties were arrested in nationwide security raids and brought to trial in a mass treason trial.

In 1957 she met Nelson Mandela, one of the leaders of the ANC and a practicing lawyer. Nelson obtained a divorce from his wife and a year later, while he was still standing trial for treason, but as with all the defendants, out on bail, quite usual in those days, the authorities waived the restrictions they had placed on him for five days to enable him to go to the Transkei where he married Winnie in the Methodist church in Bizana. Then they set up housekeeping in Soweto, the main African township outside Johannesburg.

Although pregnant with her first child, Winnie went to Pretoria to join a demonstration by the Federation of South African Women against the *apartheid* laws. She was arrested and with thousands of other women went to jail where she nearly had a miscarriage. Fortunately, she was released after several days and her first daughter was born in February, 1959. She was later to give birth to a second daughter.

Following the Sharpeville shootings in 1960, the government declared a state of emergency and detained hundreds of political activists, including Nelson Mandela and the other defendants in the treason trial, for several months. The treason trial itself had become a fiasco, and in March, 1961, it came to an end with the judges finding all the defendants not guilty. Meanwhile, however, the ANC had been outlawed and its new underground form was adopting a policy of increasingly militant action.

Winnie was still working as a social welfare officer but in 1962 she was banned and placed under restriction orders. By now she only saw Nelson in secret and at a few rare clandestine meetings, as he had taken over leadership of the underground guerrilla movement. In July, 1963, he was arrested and was brought to trial with several other leaders and sentenced to life imprisonment. Blacks were sent to the prison colony on Robben Island and those whites convicted for life were kept apart in a special section of the Pretoria prison.

Winnie suffered the harassment of continual police raids and other forms of intimidation. All her movements and contacts with people were placed under severe restrictions. Pressure was put on her employers to dismiss her and any prospective employer was always visited by the security police.

Her political commitment brought her other problems too, some deep within her family. The 1960 state of emergency had been applied with particular force and ruthlessness in the Transkei, where thousands of Africans were arrested and held in custody without trial as violence and bloodshed erupted throughout the territory.

Winnie's father, a moderate man, was regarded by the local people as part of the establishment. His home was burned down, all his stock was killed, and he was shot and left for dead. When he recovered, he condemned the violence and sided with the white government. Later he joined the South African-appointed "government of the Transkei"— Bantustan, a puppet regime whose leader is Chief Mantanzima, and he became a "cabinet minister." The majority of Africans in the Transkei, however, supported the old chief and headmen who remained opposed to the *apartheid* regime.

Winnie, a committed militant, was faced with the political dissension that split the family. There was now not only hatred between black and white, but bitternesses between black and black. Winnie could do little but continue living in her home in Johannesburg and caring for her two daughters, but she served as a symbol of the ANC resistance to the government.

And now, in the last days of 1969, Winnie was back in prison, looked upon as the leader of the twenty-two, and my client.

The women's section of the prison had been a fortress of the Afrikaner Republic in the 1870s and retained the primitive facilities and foreboding look. In this archaic building, Winnie's self-confidence brought out every vestige of hostility and hatred in the white matrons. Day after day I would call at the prison and be kept waiting by the matrons until "they were ready" to permit me to see my clients, unconscious of the fact that while I was waiting I observed the normal prison routine.

I could have been living a hundred years earlier seeing conditions in the prison colonies of Australia. Cabinet ministers and other high government officials sent official cars to the women's prison with requests for every conceivable kind of service. I could easily overhear the women prisoners comment on what they really thought of the ministers in whose houses they served. Often as I stood there, young matrons would chase the prisoners, flailing them wildly with canes. These assaults and their abusive language would stop abruptly when they saw me. Yet I could not report any of the things I saw to any authority for fear of losing the right to see my clients, nor could I make any public disclosure as this would have been a crime in terms of the Prisons Act, and I, and anyone publishing my report, would have been prosecuted.

Because of being particularly cruelly victimized by these matrons, the women political prisoners had suffered even more than the men. As a result, they were more disoriented and I had to spend more time with them, building up their morale. On my first visit we were placed in an office where there were not enough chairs for all of us and I gave up mine to one of my clients. On the next occasion, only I was given a chair and when I asked for chairs for the women, I was told that they must stand. The following time we were refused the facilities altogether and put in a passage outside. It was impossible for the women to write down any of the information I needed but they welcomed being in the passage for it was in the open air and sunshine, and a vast improvement on their cells.

The small solitary-confinement cells where they were kept were five feet wide and ten feet long, with brick walls, cement floors and ceilings, and very small, narrow windows covered with bars and wire mesh. There was one unshaded light bulb in each cell, encircled by wire mesh, which stayed on day and night. The cells were dank and cold, and a coco mat, less than an inch thick and about thirty inches wide by seventy-two inches long, was the prisoner's bed. The blankets stank and were filthy from years of unwashed use. There was no furniture in the cell, only a mug for drinking purposes and a sanitary pail. Every morning the latter was removed and a new bucket brought in.

The women spent twenty-four hours a day, seven days a week, in these small cells, except for brief exercise periods when they would be allowed outside into a high walled yard if their matrons could spare the time to guard them. Some days the exercise was for ten minutes, some days for twenty; often, however, if the matrons were too busy, or on weekends and holidays, when most of the prison staff were off, the prisoners would go for three or four days continuously without being let out of their cells.

When I first saw them they had not been able to have a bath or a shower for nearly two hundred days. They said the food was inedible and could only be eaten when they were driven to it by hunger. When they menstruated they were given only toilet paper and were told to "use your big fat hands." And to spread dissension among them, Joyce Sikakane had been given special privileges by the security police so the others suspected her of being a possible informer. It was a wonder to me that they had managed to remain as sane as they were.

As the pretrial consultations progressed and the women gave me their written statements of what they had been subjected to since their imprisonment, I discovered that the security police had spent a great portion of their time interrogating Winnie and Joyce about their visits to my home and office and about my "activities." It was obvious that not only my office was bugged but my home as well. When the defendants denied police allegations conerning some of our conversations, they were told to listen to the tape. Both Winnie and Joyce had been questioned at length about a visit they made to my house when they met my London solicitor and on another occasion when they met a queen's counsel from the English bar who wished to talk to Winnie. On that occasion I let them use my study. It appeared that this conversation had not been recorded and this led to intensive questioning by her interrogators.

They were trying to obtain any kind of evidence to show that I was the backroom organizer and financial backer of the ANC. They wanted to establish that I had secret money links with London and Geneva and that I was engaged in "terrorist activities." They drew sinister conclusions from my association with the International Commission of Jurists in Geneva, saying that this showed I had a secret source of funds in some Swiss bank. It was ironic—if only it had all been true I could have run the trials with so much less anxiety about where the needed money was going to come from and I could have employed extra lawyers to help with the overwhelming amount of work that fell so heavily on so few of us.

The charge sheet served on the twenty-two, cited two particular funerals as "acts of Communism" engaged in by the defendants, making all guilty under the act whether they had been present at either funeral or not. Inadvertently, I had been personally connected with these funerals and I learned through my interviews with the defendants how the security police tried to turn this to their own advantage.

In my professional capacity, I had made the arrangements for a funeral of a political prisoner who had died on Robben Island. Although I had no prior knowledge of it, the ANC organized a political demonstration at the funeral. Speeches were made, eulogies sung, and those attending wore a kind of uniform that the security police said was the uniform of the ANC. Some of them were also alleged to have given ANC salutes; this was featured as a "serious crime" in the later indictment.

The other instance of my connection with a funeral had

more serious implications for me. I had for many years kept between a hundred and two hundred dollars in cash available at all times. In view of constant requests for financial aid from African political opponents of the government from all walks of life, I wanted to be able to make immediate loans to whoever needed them. Those who were able to pay me back did so; if they could not, the matter would be forgotten. This was a purely personal arrangement and the security police could not, in any way, interpret it as a crime under the Communism Act.

Winnie Mandela had once asked for a loan of two hundred dollars to pay for the funeral of an elderly trade unionist who had been placed under house arrest, had lost his job, and had died in poverty. As I never asked questions about how the money was actually to be used, I did not know that Winnie had organized a big demonstration at the funeral, comparable to the one previously mentioned. One of the things the security police kept hammering away at, when they were questioning Winnie and the others, was who had financed this funeral. When it finally came out that I had, the police had an excuse to detain me.

My relationship with Nelson was another thing Winnie was asked about. Security police officers told her that I was a Communist, a supercapitalist, a thief, a rogue, a terrorist, a Jew, and the brains behind her husband's activities and the financial genius behind the ANC. As I read Winnie's account of her interrogation, I realized that the essential truth was that the security police hated me and had revealed this intense hatred and bitterness to her. Swanepoel protested to her his innocence in the Lenkoe affair—he was particularly upset by the allegations of electric-shock torture. I had painted him as a monster and a torturer and ruined his reputation both in South Africa and abroad, and if it was the last thing he did, he told her, he would get even with me.

The security police, in a fantastic effort to break the morale of the resistance movement, and playing on Winnie's exhaustion and disorientation after her long detention, offered her freedom for herself and the other defendants, and later for her husband, provided she gave evidence against me in court and made a statement over the radio to the black people of South Africa. She was to tell them that there was every hope for improvement for her people within the existing framework of the law and to call on them to abandon all illegal struggles. She was to call for cooperation between whites and blacks.

They promised Winnie that they would immediately move Nelson to the special hut built for the leader of the PAC, Robert Sobukwe, and give him various privileges—reading and writing material, contact with the outside world, and long visits from her. Later, Nelson would be released from prison and placed under restrictions in an isolated area of the country, where she and her children could live with him. In time, these restrictions, too, would be removed and Nelson would be allowed to resume practice as an attorney and take his rightful place as a leader among the community, dedicating himself to improving his people within the law's framework.

Swanepoel spent long hours with Winnie, trying to get her to see the error of her ways and the wisdom of his suggestions. He was confident that now that she was in his power, and was so disoriented, and he had sole prerogative to grant or refuse any favor or privilege, however small, he could work out an agreement between them.

I never fully understood what happened during this time but I later came to learn from people in London that Winnie had not only given Mendel Levin a power of attorney but had written a letter to London, saying that I was not to be trusted and that she accepted Mendel Levin as the "new attorney" for the defendants. Of course Levin had arranged with Swanepoel to receive these documents from Winnie while she was still in detention. When I asked Winnie to explain why she gave Levin a power of attorney, she told me that Levin had managed to obtain medical aid for her. In any event, she was sure she could outwit her enemies. Winnie was always convinced that she would succeed in out-maneuvering all who opposed her. She never revealed to me that she had written the letter in support of Levin. After Levin's failure to obtain support in London, Swanepoel's attitude towards Winnie changed and once more he treated her in his usual cruel manner.

One day she was taken to see him and he asked her

abruptly, "Who is Thembi Mandela?" When she explained this was her eldest stepson, he said, "He's dead. He was killed in a car accident," and walked off.

She lost all control and broke down and wept.

With all this pressure Winnie wavered between sanity and insanity and never quite knew whether she would be able to live through her first period in detention. Four days before she and the others were brought to court, Mendel Levin was again brought to see her in Swanepoel's presence. He told her that "Carlson has succeeded in pulling down a steel door on all funds from England," but promised nevertheless to act for her and said she should not worry about the source of funds. When she pressed him on this, he said he would arrange for the state to pay for their defense. He asked Winnie to persuade the other defendants to agree to his representing all of them.

At this stage, she told me, she had decided that she would have nothing to do with him, but she feared that if he saw the others and showed them her power of attorney, they might go along with him and she might not have a chance to prevent this. She felt she must be there when he saw her comrades. So she agreed to Swanepoel's and Levin's plan and her codefendants were brought in one at a time. In English she told them that they should accept the services of Mendel Levin as their attorney but she made some sign or spoke a word in Xhosa, indicating just the opposite. Accordingly, all of them told Levin and Swanepoel that they would wait until they appeared in court before they chose any attorney. As a result, Levin left with only Winnie's power of attorney.

It was only later that I learned why some of the defendants reacted with such surprise on seeing me that first day in court. Elliot Shabangu, one of the older defendants, told me he had been convinced by the security police that I was a state witness, being kept in detention. A number of the other defendants told me the same thing.

The tactics used by the security police on Winnie were used on several of the other detainees. Joyce Sikakane told me how the security police tried to persuade her to be a state witness by saying that if she would only cooperate with them, they would show their recognition of her intelligence by making

her a senior official in the embassy the South African government was planning to open in Malawi, and pay her a handsome salary. As part of the softening-up process, she was
moved from Pretoria Prison to another prison where her cell
was more like a bedroom and anything she wanted in the way
of toilet articles or clothing was provided. Finally, however,
she turned down their offers and was returned to solitary
confinement in Pretoria Prison. She then had to overcome the
resistance and suspicion of her codefendants.

All the women had been treated most brutally. Rita
Ndzanga had been arrested with her husband, Lawrence, at 2
A.M. on Monday, May 12. They were both active trade
unionists. Their four children, the eldest of whom was eleven,
were left alone at home and had to be looked after by
neighbors. Rita was terribly worried about them and pressed
me to make arrangements for their care as soon as I saw her.
She told me how she had been assaulted during her interrogation by the security police and I was eventually able to file her
statement in court.

She had been taken to Compol where the first police officer
to speak to her was Major Swanepoel. He told her that she
would remain standing on her feet until she made a statement.
She had also been beaten and eventually, exhausted, she
made a statement.

Afterwards, Rita was left alone for some weeks. Then
Lieutenant Visser and a colored security policeman took her
back to Compol. In her statement to me, Rita wrote:

> They left me standing in the entrance office at
> Compol building. Then they came and said to me
> "Kom." When I got to the kitchen a white security
> policeman began to hit me; I fell down; I then began
> to scream; they closed the windows; I continued
> screaming; they dragged me to another room hitting
> me with their open hands all the time. I do not know
> the names of the security policemen who assaulted
> me but I know them and I can identify them.
>
> In the interrogation room the security police asked
> me what makes me not to speak. They produced
> three bricks and told me to take off my shoes and

stand on the bricks. I refused to stand on the bricks. One of the white security police climbed on top of a chair and pulled me up by my hair, dropped me on to the bricks, I fell down and hit a gas pipe. The same man pulled my hair again, jerked me and I again fell on to the metal gas pipe. They threw water on my face. The man who pulled my hair had his hands full of my hair. He washed his hands in the basin. I managed to stand up, and they said, "Onto the bricks." I stood on the bricks and they hit me again while I was on the bricks. I fell, they again poured water on me. I was very tired, I could not stand the assault any longer. I then asked to see Major Swanepoel—Major Swanepoel arrived after some time and asked me why I did not want to speak. I said I cannot understand why I should make a statement before and now again be asked to make another statement. He replied that the first statement was merely notes and that I had to make a proper statement and that he was sorry about the unfortunate incident.

I was astonished at the resilience of Rita for she quickly recovered from the sufferings she had endured, and helped me most efficiently and without any fuss, in many ways during the long trial months.

The other two women, Venus Mngoma and Martha Dlamini, were in their fifties. They had been arrested for their participation in the two ANC funerals. Venus suffered from ill health, particularly during her incarceration. She had lost all her teeth, found prison food inedible, made many demands and the white matrons delighted in her discomfort. It was she who was later to tell the advocates and myself:

"Let's get this damned trial over with, then we can start counting our days."

Despite all the punishment inflicted on the women, they had resisted the efforts of their jailers to break them completely but I knew I had a long road to travel to reestablish their morale and to bring them together in mutual trust.

As I studied the prisoners' statements and the evidence produced by the security police, it became clear that the political actions in which the defendants had taken part were insignificant. Even the security police should have realized that they could not make a major political trail out of such activities. From the beginning, when Winnie decided to form a group, she told how she had chosen a certain young man as her second in command only to find out later that he was a police informer. He had been present at every meeting and knew every member; he was also familiar with every activity that the group engaged in. He gave his information to the security police. The particulars given by the state showed that the police never had to wait more than twenty-four hours before their informer gave them full knowledge of all the group's activities. As a result, no significant political activity could have been carried out by Winnie and her colleagues although they were guilty of planning such activities.

The pattern of the security police strategy began to emerge. They had already used the press to build up a picture of the defendants as a serious threat to state security. Even the liberal Johannesburg morning newspaper had been duped. It ran a page of pictures showing "the dangerous weapons used by the defendants." In fact, these pictures were of exhibits in a previous trial. There were no weapons in the trial of the twenty-two.

Afraid that the actual trial would show that the defendants' activities were no threat to state security, the security police had planned, with the assistance of a cooperative lawyer, to sensationalize these "Communistic activities" and in return, offer the defense attorney a deal whereby a number of the defendants would be acquitted and all those convicted would be given only light sentences. Such a course of action would underscore the efficiency of the security police and the independence of the judiciary, who would show leniency. In addition, Mendel Levin would be established as a successful political attorney for opponents of the regime and could be of inestimable value to the security police in future trials.

On this occasion, all the security police schemes had misfired and it was my job to find and organize a proper defense team.

XVI
THE YEAR ENDS

Another search for a team of defense counsel was on. Once more it began just before the school vacation period when advocates had made other arrangements for the month of December. Fortunately, I was able to obtain David Soggot, but he was only available from December 1. George Bizos was only available later in December. It was agreed that David would carry the burden of the work for the first week in December and then would be joined by George and by Arthur Chaskalson, one of the most brilliant advocates at the bar.

The problem of finding funds also had to be faced. As the trial had received wide publicity overseas, I waited for someone there to promise to provide the necessary funds. A German lawyer telephoned a colleague in Johannesburg and asked him to act for the twenty-two but he quite rightly refused and referred him to me. In the course of time I received a letter from this German, and considering him an honorable man, I accepted his word. Without hesitation, I briefed the advocates we had lined up for the trial.

In order to go ahead without delay, most of our consulting took place in the evenings, since during the day I interviewed the prisoners. In the course of the month, we learned that Judge Simon Bekker had been allocated to conduct our trial. I considered him to be one of the least biased of all the judges in the division and even though we were not ready for the trial to proceed on December 1, I thought it important that we allow it to start before this judge in order that he be permanently assigned to the case. If necessary, once the trial began, we could apply for such postponement as we needed to prepare our defense.

During this time I asked the state for further particulars and saw Liebenberg, the prosecutor. I knew him well; he was a senior prosecutor in Johannesburg and had been selected to take this case. He had an excellent record in prosecuting political prisoners and was as sly as an old fox. He had snow-white hair and did not look the shrewd, efficient, calculating man he really was. He never gave up and fought on endlessly. His great disadvantage in court was that he was inarticulate and monotonous. His junior, Rothwell, was not half so shrewd or competent, but he had been especially groomed for this job and I had no doubt that his sympathies were with the state in these political trials.

I met these officers of the court, not in the chambers that they usually occupied in the Supreme Court, but at security police headquarters on the tenth floor of John Vorster Square in Johannesburg. Meeting them at this place indicated to me that these prosecutors had no hesitation in being recognized as merely the legal arm of the security police.

At this informal meeting, which was held in the presence of several security policemen, Liebenberg indicated that he would be prepared to cooperate with me if he received my cooperation in turn. He told me cryptically, "A certain government who should know better in its behavior over terrorists is making life difficult for me. I am being pressed to dispose of one of my witnesses in the trial."

We both knew he was talking of Philip Golding, the British subject who had been detained some six months before under the Terrorism Act. Golding had a close association with a number of the older men among the twenty-two who were, like him, trade unionists, and he had offered them help in trade union activities. The state alleged that these activities were dangerous and Communistic and Golding was now to be used as a state witness.

The British press had made much of the detention of a British subject and British M.P.s had asked questions about it in the House of Commons. As a result, the British ambassador had sought access to Golding and his consul was granted permission to see him in prison. Later, the consul advised that on each occasion, Swanepoel had been present. The consul said that Golding had raised no objection to this and had made no complaint about any maltreatment during his detention and interrogation.

I arranged with Liebenberg that Golding's evidence would be given first provided he would not oppose a postponement before we continued the trial. It was a long and difficult meeting and I was greatly relieved when it ended. I was pleased with the agreement for then the trial would be part-heard and Judge Bekker would remain the trial judge. I instructed David Soggot to attend court on that day and apply for a postponement after Golding's evidence had been given.

Once again the police parade formed outside the prison. A closed police van, accompanied by two trucks packed with armed policemen, collected the five women prisoners and drove on to the men's section of the jail, where a line of troop carriers also filled with armed policemen was assembled. Seventeen male prisoners were loaded into a police van covered with thick wire mesh, and the long heavy line slowly made its way down the main street of Pretoria, following the familiar route to the old synagogue. The special court that the police had used for the trial of the thirty-seven Namibians was to be used again.

There were scores of armed policemen outside the court. A large crowd had collected, many of them friends and relatives who had traveled as much as fifty miles to Pretoria to see the defendants and give them moral support. There were reporters, photographers, TV cameramen, observers from foreign governments, and a whole pack of security policemen.

The senior security officers were on display inside the courtyard while the junior men mingled with the people outside.

The sirens howled, and at a signal from the captain, police
on foot and in cars fanned out, closing the street to traffic. The
trucks carrying the prisoners appeared; police with Sten guns
jumped out of their cars. And then all the power and trappings
of the police—their vehicles, their guns, their dogs—were
dwarfed and drowned in the sound of the song of resistance.
The prisoners' voices, joined with those of the black spectators, rose through the morning sunshine and flooded across
the road and buildings around. The trucks moved slowly
through the narrow entrance to the back of the court. There,
dozens of armed policemen formed two lines through which
the prisoners had to pass. The men were led into the same iron
cage used by the Namibian prisoners and the women were
taken into a small, tightly guarded office.

I stood for a moment in the bright sunshine, warmed and
heartened by the songs and high morale of the prisoners.
Around me, the relatives and friends were smiling; their
spirits too had been raised by the courage of the twenty-two.
Students, churchmen, and other white sympathizers crowded
around the low wall outside the courthouse, held back from
the door by the security police who were scrutinizing everyone who wished to go in, and asking for identification. This
was highly irregular as the court was supposed to be open to
the public. Attendance at court had been turned into a
confrontation, but there was no arguing with the security
police who proceeded to take pictures of some of those who
dared to face them by coming to court.

The black spectators, however, so used to police surveillance, took this as something of a joke. Ordered to leave their
parcels of food outside, they placed them right at the feet of
the police, asking in jest if they would be safe there, and then
jostled up the narrow stairway to the black public gallery.

David Soggot and I were allowed in without argument. As
soon as I had put our briefcases down in the lawyers' room, I
hurried to the door opposite the iron cage to visit my clients.
Replaying a scene still vivid in my memory, one of the
officers barked an order and the policemen formed two lines

and held their Sten guns at the ready. By now I was well used to the sound of the safety catches being thrown, and smiling broadly, I walked through the lines to the cage. This time at least there were no police dogs growling at me. The captain on duty was new and demanded to know what I wanted. When I told him I wanted to talk to my clients he seemed to consider this an unusual request but I insisted and he finally ordered his men to open the cage door to allow me inside.

I was pleased to see that all were dressed in the clothes they had asked me to get for them; their morale could not be higher. I shook hands all around, told them their relatives were there to give them support, and showed them the scores of telegrams and cables from both black and white sympathizers, wishing us success in the struggle before us. This itself was new in my experience and it increased my own morale enormously. Many white people had turned out to help by providing the families of prisoners with food and clothing and with transportation to the court. This had been done even in the face of strong security police intimidation.

I then went on to see the women prisoners and found them, too, in high spirits. The months of solitary confinement and cruelty were behind them; there was laughter now and an eagerness to face their accusers, and to show their resistance to their rulers.

They, too, were dressed in the clothes that they had specifically asked me for. As always, Winnie Mandela had managed to display on her dress the green, gold, and black of the ANC.

I went back into court. The public had not yet been admitted, but seated in the public gallery were some security policemen and Mrs. Kay. Although she flashed a smile at me and waved a hand, I walked past her without recognition. Then the doors of the court were opened and the white spectators hurried in. Women who did not have their heads covered had been refused admittance and had frantically borrowed scarves or large handkerchiefs. David and I took our places and the prosecuting team moved to its seats. Behind them sat the familiar figures of the security police. There were foreign and local white reporters at the press table but in accordance with the rules of our society, no black reporters. They were relegated to the black public gallery where little or nothing of the proceedings could be heard. As usual, white reporters simply accepted this and in all their vivid descriptions of the court proceedings, never mentioned the exclusion of their colleagues.

At a signal from the captain, all the doors of the court were closed and armed policemen took up their positions guarding all the entrances. Orders were barked outside, the impatient bullying call of *"Kom, kom, kom"* could be heard, and within minutes the line of black prisoners came in—the men first, followed by the women, all under the close supervision of the police.

Immediately after being lined up in the dock, they looked up to their relatives who called down to them, and in a flurry of excitement, there was an exchange of words, gestures, smiles, and kisses. Some of the whites began calling greetings to the prisoners. Stern calls for order were ignored and the police were powerless to stop this electric contact between the prisoners and their friends.

The two big, clumsy lieutenants, Karel Dirker and Tiny van Niekerk, moved among the prisoners, giving them their numbers, which they were instructed to hold in their hands. After Richard Falk, the American law professor who had observed the trial of the Namibians for the International Commission of Jurists, had published his criticism of the practice of hanging numbers around the necks of prisoners, this procedure had been discontinued. Another recognition of the humanity of prisoners had been forced on the security police.

The judge's registrar arrived, followed shortly by the judge, and the court orderly called, *"Stilte in die hof!"* The crowded courtroom rose to its feet as "his lordship" entered, bowed, and took his seat. The trial was about to begin. Advocate Liebenberg, the prosecutor, rose and almost inaudibly said, "I call the case of the State versus Samson Ndou and others." He then proceeded to read the charges in a monotonous undertone which could not be heard by anyone but the judge.

Each accused was then called upon to plead. When Winnie

rose, she said that like her brother-in-arms, Caleb Mayekiso (who had also been detained in the mass arrests in May but had died shortly afterward while still in detention), she had already been found guilty by the police in the trial conducted in their own headquarters and had already been punished by them. As far as this court was concerned she pleaded not guilty to the charges. The judge quickly assured her that she would receive a fair trial.

Once Judge Bekker had taken the defendant's pleas the state could not substitute another judge. We had passed the first hurdle.

I listened with only half an ear to Liebenberg's opening remarks. He was unimaginative, dreary, and long-winded. Straying beyond the indictment, he did his best to depict the prisoners as Communist villains who threatened the very foundation of state security. He praised the security police for their vigilance and courage and painted a glowing picture of their efficiency and reliability, which had finally resulted in the apprehension of these dangerous men and women who had now been brought to trial to be punished according to law.

Mercifully, his monotone came to an end. He put down his papers and said, "I call my first witness, Philip Golding."

A short, slight, and very pale young man was guided to the witness box. He was tense and nervous and his agitation increased as he stood in the center of the crowded court. Opposite him were the prosecuting team. Immediately behind them, staring across at him, sat six security policemen, Captain Botha, the two van Rensburgs, the two van Niekerks, and Dirker. Major Swanepoel sat immediately to his right and further to his right sat the twenty-two prisoners, some of whom he had, until recently, called friends. Spread out behind him was a full gallery of whites, while looking down at him were relatives and friends of those he had come to give evidence against.

As the registrar swore him in, Golding was trembling and seemed on the point of breaking down. He avoided looking toward the defendants but looked at Swanepoel and regained control. Liebenberg began his questioning but we could not hear a word of Golding's reply. David rose to request Judge

Bekker to ask the witness to speak up; Judge Bekker complied. Golding was asked more questions but again we could only guess at his answers and the defendants passed me notes saying they had not heard a word of his evidence. David repeated his request and again Judge Bekker patiently and insistently told the witness the defendants were entitled to hear the evidence he was giving against them and he must speak up. At our next objection, since Golding seemed physically incapable of raising his voice, the judge suggested that the witness box be moved toward the dock so that the prisoners could hear what he had to say. When his voice still failed to carry, the box had to be moved again.

It was painfully clear that Golding was too terrified to speak up loudly and clearly, so his whispers were recorded and when we read the transcript of his evidence later, it amounted to nothing.

The defendants he knew were, like him, in favor of trade unionism. He had known that these defendants had been banned by the South African government and they could no longer serve the trade union movement. He was nevertheless prepared to help them try to reestablish themselves and the trade union movement in South Africa. At the request of these defendants, he said, he agreed to make contact with ANC members in London while he was on vacation there. However, try as he might, he could not establish any contact with these ANC people. They would have nothing to do with him. On his return to South Africa he offered to help some of the defendants reorganize political activity, especially in the trade union movement, and gave them money for this purpose.

The defendants, seeing his weaknesses, pitied him. They also felt that the trivialities of his testimony showed how nonsensical the state's case was. Yet they failed to realize that in the eyes of South African law, even such actions could be construed as most serious crimes of "Communism" or "terrorism."

Once Golding had completed his evidence we applied for a long postponement but were granted only one week. Judge Bekker refused to accept that our cross-examination of the first witness, Golding, would determine the structure of the whole case for the defense. At this stage, we had not seen the documents on which the state would base its case and were in the dark as to the evidence that would be introduced.

Golding's evidence suddenly presented us with a challenge and placed us in a dilemma. The defense team was divided and hotly debated what decision to make.

On the one hand, we saw Golding as a reluctant witness and a man ashamed of his betrayal of his friends. He had not come to terms with himself. Under cross-examination he might divulge what had happened to him in detention. We knew he had been maltreated from statements given to us by some of the defendants who had been next to the torture room while Golding had been undergoing interrogation. The defendants had told me something of the torture that they had endured at the hands of the security police but we required corroboration before we could place the matter before the court.

Golding as a state witness could be invaluable to the defense. The state could not challenge the evidence of their own witness. He was white, educated, sophisticated, and a British subject. He could confirm that the police had used torture. This was important, for in all political trials, the defendants always faced the difficulty of proving that the security police used torture. The police were usually careful to ensure that the defendants had no witnesses to testify that torture had been used during interrogation and they, of course, always denied using any irregular methods. In court, in the absence of corroborative evidence, a white judge would always accept the sworn statements of the white policemen, and disbelieve the black political agitators. There was even a danger in raising the question of torture in such trials. The judge might conclude that the court was being used for political propaganda against the forces of law and order. In this event, he could impose heavier sentences on the defendants.

Would Golding give us the corroboration we required and expose the real terrorists? If he did we could seize the intiative in the trial and place the security police in the dock.

On the other hand, Golding's testimony itself was of little if any significance and in not cross-examining him we could emphasize this. This would embarrass the South African government in its relations with the United Kingdom. Golding's arrest and prolonged detention without trial had led to questions being asked in the British Parliament. The British government had been forced to protest his imprisonment to the South African government. It had been assured, in reply, that Golding was a dangerous man and, in fact, was a terrorist, and it had felt obliged to accept the assurances given. If we now ignored his evidence and treated it with contempt, the truth would hurt—it would be another striking example of the abuse of the wide powers given to the security police.

There is also legal wisdom in not asking questions in cross-examination when one is not certain of the answers. When Golding left court after giving evidence, he was once again under Swanepoel's control. The deal that Golding must have made with Swanepoel to guarantee his own release would be threatened if he made any statements about maltreatment. There was no doubt that Swanepoel would apply great pressure to prevent his making such disclosures. We ran a great risk, therefore, in trying to elicit the truth from Golding, for if we were unsuccessful we would lend credibility to the prosecution.

It was argued that we should leave the torture issue alone and concentrate on minimizing the importance of the "crimes" committed by the defendants. Some of the defendants were anxious to get the trial over with in order to start "counting their days." (The prison sentence is calculated in days from the day of conviction and not from the day of arrest.)

I believed, however, that if we were able to break down Golding's defenses, the advantages gained would outweigh the disadvantages, so I supported my colleague who was in favor of taking the risk, and we decided to go ahead on that basis. Later, David said he was surprised that I had had any doubts about the decision and teased me about it, telling me I was losing my grip and getting too old for the game.

George, Arthur, and I were keyed up and tense when we

arrived at court the following morning and only David was confident. This was as well for he was to undertake the cross-examination. The next two hours would tell whether our decision had been advantageous or damaging to our case. Worried about the morning's proceedings, I did not even notice the crowded court but went straight to the prisoners. They inspired me with their confidence and I returned to court easier in my mind and more relaxed.

The scene on the opening day was replayed. Once again the prisoners ignored the commands of the police to be quiet as they greeted their friends and relatives and virtually took charge. There was an air of excitement and expectancy that stopped only when the court orderly called, "Silence in the court," and Judge Bekker took his seat.

Liebenberg formally called for Golding to enter the witness box for cross-examination. Swanepoel had obviously been working hard. The man he led in was not the weak and trembling man who had whispered his evidence the week before; he stood straight and looked almost jaunty. Swanepoel sat at the table next to the witness box. As David began to question him, the change was even more dramatic—he was confident and self-assured, and looked directly at the defendants. I wanted David to object to Swanepoel's presence at the table right next to the witness box but felt it was better not to interrupt him.

Having obtained reluctant admissions from Golding on such general subjects as his membership in and support of the British Labor party, which in turn supported trade unions and Socialism, and his support of the defendants' plans to improve conditions for black South Africans, David quickly moved on to question him about his experiences at Compol, security police headquarters in Pretoria. Golding said he was taken to a "questioning room" where he was questioned by Major Swanepoel, Lieutenant Ferreira, and others.

Liebenberg rose to object to this line of questioning but he was off on his timing. It was too early and Judge Bekker overruled his objection. A crucial decision had been made. We were through the gate and David hurried on.

Golding said he couldn't tell how many people were questioning him but said he thought about half a dozen. Then David asked:

Q. What did they want from you?
A. They wanted answers.
Q. How long were you in the interrogation room?
A. About two days.
Q. Were you allowed to leave?
A. No.
Q. And when you didn't talk what happened to you?
A. I really don't see the relevance of these questions.
JUDGE: Well now, the state is objecting—the witness is objecting—and [speaking to defense counsel] I trust you will bear in mind the relevance of this.
David proceeded:
Q. When you didn't talk, what happened?
A. I was asked to stand. I was kept standing.
Q. For two days?
A. Yes.
Q. And did you eventually give information?
A. Yes.
Q. Rather reluctantly?
A. Yes.
Q. Was this a painful procedure?
A. What do you mean by that?
Q. Emotionally or physically painful?
A. I wouldn't say emotionally particularly.
Q. Were you slapped?
A. No.
Q. Not at all?
A. No.
Q. Be candid please.
A. I am being candid.
Q. One of the defendants in the room next door heard the assault on you.
A. I wasn't slapped.

Q. What did happen?

A. I believe I was being assaulted in some way.

The judge intervened:

I beg your pardon?

A. I said I believe I was being assaulted in some way.

Q. In what way?

A. I was punched.

Q. On your left cheek?

A. Yes.

Q. Any other part?

A. No.

Q. Were there no other assaults?

A. I was kicked a bit.

Q. You were kicked a bit? On what part of your body?

A. On my back.

Q. Often—or only once?

A. I can't remember.

Q. You can't remember?

A. I can't remember. Say four or five times.

Q. At what stage were you kicked—were you still standing or had you fallen down from exhaustion?

The judge intervened again:

Well, he hasn't said it yet, that he fell down from exhaustion.

From then on, Golding said again and again that he could not remember anything more, but did say that he went through quite an ordeal at Compol. This was enough—we had made the breakthrough in less than an hour. Cross-examination had revealed the truth; Swanepoel's strenuous efforts to hide it had failed.

Golding had steadily lost his self-assurance during the cross-examination. At first he stood up straight; as questioning went on he grasped the witness stand with both hands. Propping himself up with this firm grip, he became defiant for a moment but weakened as he lost control of his and

Swanepoel's efforts to hide what had really happened. He was forced to admit the assaults on him and his reluctance to do so underlined the terror he had been subjected to. With Swanepoel seated at his elbow, that terror was present even in the court. This was what was so horrible. Here was a man who had been cruelly assaulted and so terrorized that in his fear he now sought the court's aid to protect his own persecutors.

Swanepoel showed little obvious emotion during the exchanges; his red face darkened as the cross-examination proceeded. He fiddled with a pen in his fat, stubby fingers and kept his head down. He seemed to recognize this defeat for what it was and I was sure that inside himself he cursed his bad luck with this witness.

When the tea break came we gathered around David, full of congratulations. His cross-examination had been quick and sharp and he had discredited Golding. Now, having set the precedent, the judge could not stop us from questioning other witnesses about their maltreatment in detention; now the security police were in the dock. The morning tea tasted like the best champagne.

When we returned to court Liebenberg tried to repair the damage but succeeded in making matters worse. He couldn't attack Golding's credibility because then Golding's evidence for the state would suffer. So he didn't challenge Golding's statements about his assaults but simply tried to tone them down. His efforts could not succeed for either it was a fact that Golding was made to stand for two days or Golding was lying. When called upon to identify the man who had assaulted him, Golding said "Lieutenant Ferreira." (The same Ferreira, who, in the Looksmart case, was merely a sergeant.)

Q. Did you make a statement and if so, to whom?
A. Well, to all 6 people. They kept coming and going.
Q. Can you remember who punched you?
A. Yes.
Q. Who?
A. Lt. Ferreira.
Q. And who was the person who kicked you?

A. Lt. Ferreira.
Q. And did you make a statement to him?
A. Yes.

Thus, instead of improving his case, Liebenberg had increased the damage we had done. Realizing this, he sat down, a disappointed man.

At the end of his testimony, Golding was told by Judge Bekker that he could leave the box and if he wished to, return to England. Ignoring the defendants, and showing no sign of regret for his actions, Golding left the court. The British ambassador was satisfied and no further protests were made. In January, Golding returned to England and within hours of arriving, gave an interview to the British press. Next day a front-page story gave full and detailed accounts of his torture by the security police while he was at Compol. It was a much more detailed report than he had given to the court. In England, however, Swanepoel had little power to influence Golding.

At the next session of the court the state called a number of witnesses who entered the box to give evidence against the twenty-two and then, under cross-examination, corroborated Golding's testimony about torture. One of these witnesses was Nonyaniso Madikazela, Winnie's sister, who had been arrested shortly after Winnie's arrest. She told me after the trial that Ferreira, in the presence of Mendel Levin, had threatened her with prison for the rest of her life if she refused to give a statement. Levin had persuaded her that Winnie had agreed that she should make a statement to the security police and give testimony in any trial. But when she appeared in the witness box and faced her sister, her distress and anguish was pathetic. In a whisper, she told the court how she had been tortured. Rothwell, the prosecutor on duty, objected to the relevance of the line of cross-examination we were following.

Quietly, but firmly, Judge Bekker ruled: "It may be irrelevant but if these things happened, I wish to know about them." That simple sentence placed the security police on trial and it later led to a sensational decision that was to end the proceedings. Rothwell could only plod on, calling further witnesses whose testimony David turned to our own advantage under cross-examination. The significance of the successful gamble we had taken with Golding now became evident.

On the last day of the trial in December, when I was detained elsewhere on urgent business, Liebenberg called two women witnesses who had indicated to the court that they did not wish to testify against the defendants. Judge Bekker warned them that their refusal to do so, without just or lawful reason, would result in their being sentenced immediately and returned to prison convicted of refusing to give evidence. He also explained that until the case was disposed of without them or until they changed their minds and gave evidence, they could be recharged and convicted again and again. If they gave satisfactory evidence they would be freed from detention and allowed out of prison.

One of these witnesses, Shanti Naidoo, was a close friend of Winnie Mandela and other defendants. Although she had apparently given the security police a statement, when she appeared in court she refused to testify. She asked that I represent her. In my absence, George Bizos advised the court that I could not represent her and act for the twenty-two defendants, too, and asked that the matter of her evidence wait until another attorney and counsel could act for her. Judge Bekker agreed to this procedure.

As soon as I learned what had happened, I arranged for an attorney and counsel to be briefed for Miss Naidoo and the other witness, Brycina Nkala. When their counsel arrived at court, I heard that the two women had been returned to their solitary-confinement cells. In the meantime, Liebenberg was rushing the proceedings in the hope of reaching the Christmas adjournment before they could be called as witnesses again. Since they would be kept in solitary, under complete control of the security police, it was terribly urgent that the court deal with the question of their evidence before the adjournment. It would be infinitely preferable for them to be convicted for refusing to give evidence, sentenced and sent to jail as prisoners, rather than for them to remain in the custody of the

special branch of the security police as detainees. It was
ironic but true that the only way they could escape the
security police would be to become convicted prisoners. As
sentenced prisoners they could receive mail, write letters,
receive visitors, and it was most unlikely that they would be
subjected to torture.

In the absence of their instructing attorney, who only
arrived later, I urged their counsel to appear for them and was
much relieved when the court reconvened and Shanti Naidoo
was called to the witness box. Her counsel was permitted to
lead her in evidence as she told the court what had happened
to her while she had been in solitary for the past six months,
and why she could not give evidence against her friends.

Q. Could you tell His Lordship briefly, under what
circumstances you came to make the statements?

A. I was interrogated; I was forced to make certain
admissions because I couldn't stand the strain of
standing on my feet for hours and hours.

Q. Can you estimate for His Lordship, the approxi-
mate period that you were made to stand?

A. I lost track of time completely—it is difficult to
say. My mind went completely blank at times
. . . and as a result . . .

Q. Yes?

A. Also, I was threatened with detention of my
whole family.

Q. Now, as a result of the prolonged period of
standing, can you describe the particular events
that took place and that affected you, to His
Lordship?

A. My mind went completely blank and I went to
sleep standing . . . I had a sort of dream in which
I was actually speaking to the officers who were
interrogating me, in my sleep, and afterwards
when I had sort of regained my senses I was
interrogated on this dream I had which was
complete nonsense. It had absolutely nothing to
do with any. . . .

Judge Bekker intervened here and said: "I am afraid I am not
with you at the moment. You fell asleep standing and you had
a dream?"

A. My mind went blank—I had a sort of dream . . .
   and in this dream I was speaking with the officer
   who interrogated me. When I regained my senses
   I was interrogated on this dream.
Q. Can you tell His Lordship—if it is at all possible
   by way of estimate or otherwise—how long this
   interrogation was?
A. The interrogation went on for five days without
   any sleep.

She then went on to tell the court that she could not live
with her conscience if she ever gave evidence against her
friends. She had not willingly made a statement, she said, and
she was not willingly prepared to give evidence. Judge Bekker
explained to her that this was not a good and sufficient reason
(he did not say what was a good and sufficient reason) and
sentenced her to two months in prison. I was relieved for at
least she had been sentenced and some of her misery would
end. The other young woman, Brycina Nkala, who also
refused to testify, gave similar evidence about the torture she
had undergone and received the same sentence. Thereafter,
our case was adjourned and to my surprise, Liebenberg
agreed to a postponement until February 15, 1970.

By this time, the initiative was firmly in our hands. We had
already succeeded in obtaining admissions about police torture from five state witnesses. This was the corroboration we
required and police torture was now the important issue in the
trial.

George, David, and Arthur concentrated on obtaining statements from the defendants in answer to the particular charges
filed against them and consultations with the prisoners proceeded in a routine fashion.

An informal transportation system had been set up by
sympathetic whites and the defendant's relatives visited them
regularly. A young minister, Ian Thomson, had worked with a
number of other people to help the families of the prisoners.

He was a sincere, down-to-earth, hard-working, and completely dedicated Christian. He won my unending admiration and through him I met many other people who lived their Christianity. On certain occasions, when they knelt in prayer, giving thankfulness and praying for hope, I had no hesitation in joining them, despite my agnosticism. We were at one and we all wanted the end of the terror and a just society.

Shortly before Christmas, they approached my wife and said they wanted to give me a gift for Christmas. They wanted to know whether I would like a Bible or would I prefer a bottle of Scotch. I chose a Bible and asked that it be inscribed by each of the group. Jeanette invited them all to the house for coffee one evening. The Bible was presented to me by Ian, who spoke movingly and sincerely and offered a prayer. I was deeply touched by their friendship and support.

For years I had pursued my course without being aligned to any group or organization and this simple expression of faith was warm in its embrace. I thanked them and reminded them that the courage they had shown in the face of danger set an example for others to follow. I told them that I would keep the Bible by my bedside. Should I be detained I would take it with me to the loneliness of my cell where it would hearten and perhaps strengthen me.

It was near the end of the year—a year which for me had been a long and trying one. Earlier, I did not think I could survive it but like the defendants, I had somehow managed to see it through. I did not show the exhaustion and the anxiety I felt but Jeanette and a few friends knew that I had just managed to hold out. I told both my counsel and the defendants about my plan to accompany my family to the coast and they all agreed that I should go.

On Friday evening we drove through the night. The midnight air was cold as we traveled along the empty highway through the vast semidesert of the Karroo. The bright lights of the car cut a white tunnel through the darkness all around us. The hum of the engine was warming. Our children slept and all was quiet as we sped along. It was peaceful but I wondered how long this peace would last. I realized that living in such insecurity I had learned to enjoy every moment for I never knew at the beginning of every day where I would be or what I would be doing by the next sunrise.

We arrived in Cape Town early Saturday morning and I fell into a long and heavy sleep and then took a swim in the sea. I loved returning to this False Bay coast where the salt sea air blew off the crest of the waves and into my face. Cape Hangklip points the far end of the wide bay. Edging that shore, robed in blue and purple hues, range the rugged slopes of the Hottentots Holland. On the near side, sheer cliffs rise up from the wild coastline to Cape Point, the fabled southernmost tip of the great African continent where warm Indian Ocean currents flowing into the bay are cooled by the icy South Atlantic seas. But the beauty of the place is marred by signs posting "whites only" areas along with desolate "nonwhite" spots.

Table Mountain rises above the mother city, overlooking its own bay. Behind it, stretching down the peninsula, the mountain range binds the rock base of this buffeted land strip. Bordered by tall oak trees, the sun-drenched valleys of the Constantia vineyards caught me in their spell.

I was tempted to stay on, but Sunday I returned to Johannesburg to complete the few tasks left for that year. That evening as my plane turned northwards, I watched through a porthole the pink clouds unfold their cloth over Table Mountain as the golden sea rolled at its base. Back in Johannesburg, I consulted with counsel and visited my clients in prison, collecting from them the statements about their torture by the police. After three days I flew back to Cape Town. Foolishly, I read the defendant's statements on the plane. I read until I could read no more of the horrors in them and put them away in my briefcase. I wondered how I could relax and have a holiday knowing what these people had gone through. I knew, though, that if I was to go on I had to take a break or else I would collapse.

At the airport, my wife and children already had a tan. Their embraces and smiles were so warm, and the children's chatter so incessant, that I managed to forget for a while the horror a thousand miles away. I wanted to enjoy this holiday—it might be the last we all took together.

XVII
THE NEW YEAR
BEGINS

Too soon, the holiday was over, and shortly after the New Year we were back in Johannesburg. I immediately visited the twenty-two prisoners in Pretoria. Their spirits were high and they told me of the great fuss made by the security police over the Christmas cards I had supplied them with so each of them could send greetings to their families and friends. The regular prison officials had posted the cards before the security police could stop them.

We discussed the progress we had made with their statements and they expressed their great confidence in the defense team. Winnie asked me whether we planned to see Nelson on Robben Island as he had been named as a co-conspirator in the indictment. Certainly we were entitled to see him and take a statement from him and I told her so.

Some years back, after the Gabriel Mbindi exposure, I was banned from visiting prisons for eighteen months. My banning order had expired and I applied to see Nelson. The prison authorities refused to permit me, and to our surprise, also refused permission to counsel. This was an obvious and clear interference with the conduct of the defense case and we decided to apply to Judge Bekker immediately after the resumption of the case, to have Nelson subpoenaed and brought to court in Pretoria. Had we succeeded in this application, it would have been a sensational achievement. Since his conviction six years earlier, little had been heard of Nelson but without doubt he was the leading figure in the underground resistance movement and the security police would move heaven and earth to prevent him leaving his island prison. We advised Liebenberg of our intention to have Nelson subpoenaed and we were only to learn later what plans the state made to avoid this potentially embarrassing situation.

A week after my return from holiday I went to bed one Friday at about 1 A.M. I was tired after a long day and fell into a heavy sleep. Was I dreaming or was it real? Someone was firing at my house. I heard a loud explosion. I had better get up and see—or was it all a dream? Next morning as I went to my car to drive to my office, I was shocked to see that the car and the walls of the carport were pockmarked with gunshot and the rear window of the car shattered. Suddenly I recalled my dream—it was no dream, it was all real. In a rage my first impulse was to call the security police and give them hell. I held my temper and by the time I had walked to a friend's house to use the telephone, I had regained control. I spoke to George and Arthur and they came immediately. While we agreed that I should make a full report to the local police station, I saw the danger of alleging that the security police or their willing helpers had been responsible. Such an allegation would have enabled the security police to detain me for questioning and once in detention I could be interrogated endlessly. Although I honestly believed that they were responsible, I could not say so. Soon after my report to the local police, a detective sergeant appeared at my house and we found shotgun pellets and cartridges. He determined that the shots had been fired from the street and suggested looking for other evidence of damage.

Outside the study we stopped. The window was black and coated with a slimy substance. Suddenly the sergeant leaned down to study the hydrangeas that grew profusely under the window. I saw that all the leaves were covered with gasoline and some were charred. I watched him pick out of the flower bed the neck of a large gin bottle. Around the top was wired a rag that had been soaked in gasoline and the wall beneath the window was covered with the substance. This accounted for the explosion I had heard in my sleep. A Molotov cocktail had been thrown at the study window but had hit the stone wall underneath and exploded against it. I stood silent—a cold fear running through my mind. Had the bomb gone through the window it would have set fire to the most flammable room in the house. The study was crammed with papers and wooden bookshelves, stretching from the floor to the ceiling, were full of papers and books.

The attack on the car was damage to property—the bomb endangered our lives and in a very real way. The study was the last room in the bedroom section and had this section been set alight it would have cut off our escape through any door. A frightening picture of escaping through broken windows flashed through my mind, but there was no point in even verbalizing my fears. We had to play down the danger for the sake of the children.

We put bulletproof plate glass in the windows and I made plans to build a great iron door to the garage. The police sergeant gathered all the available evidence—the gunshot pellets and what remained of the Molotov cocktail—and left with it. I was then visited by a series of detectives who questioned me and insisted that I tell them whom I suspected. What they wanted me to do was to accuse the security police for if I made such an allegation, the matter would have been reported to them for action. That afternoon I had an informal visit from a security policeman in the person of Tiny van Niekerk. He asked to be shown around and expressed his regret at what had happened. The Sunday papers carried the story as a front-page news item and many people, some of them strangers, telephoned me to express their sympathy.

On Monday when I arrived at prison the deep concern of the prisoners was very moving. They welcomed me as a comrade into the ranks of government opponents and I realized that it was becoming almost impossible to maintain the lawyer's aloofness from his client's cause. I was being drawn into an emotional involvement with these people. Each one of them shook me by the hand and each one told me how thankful he was to see me well and unharmed. I was gratified by this aspect of our relationship but I was disturbed as well by its implications. However, there was little time to give it much thought as we hurried with our preparations for the trial.

We were preparing some of the defendants for their defense as a group as they had, in fact, acted as such. With the others, it was necessary to take long individual statements and prepare them singly for giving evidence in their own defense. Under the difficult conditions in which we worked in the prison it was an arduous task. But by February 16, when the trial was due to resume, we had completed most of the necessary work and were nearly ready. We expected to continue the successful course we had followed in December.

Monday the trial reconvened after a two-month recess. The first day was again a dramatic occasion with the police putting their special show of force before the gathered crowds. As on the opening day of the trial, when the police truck turned the corner toward the courthouse, the singing of the prisoner was heard—loudly and clearly—and there were shouts of approval and gestures from the crowd. Africans are warm and excitable people, not given to hiding their feelings, and African crowds are always vociferous and enthusiastic in their response to any particular situation.

When I arrived at court the black galleries were full and the white galleries were filling rapidly. The prisoners, having passed through the gauntlet of police, were already in the dock. We were approached by Liebenberg, the senior prosecutor, who said he wondered if we could help him figure out the number of witnesses that would be required for a full day's hearing. He asked George Bizos, who was due to cross-examine the first witness, "George, how long will you be cross-examining Nhlapo?"

George replied uncertainly, " About two hours, I think, but I can't be sure."

"That's okay," said Liebenberg, "I just want an indication, that's all," and he returned to his side of the court. Only minutes would pass before we realized how sly he was being. His question was designed to test the air and try to find out from us if we had any knowledge of the events that were to follow.

After the entry of Judge Bekker, I was placing the many suitcases holding all our papers in order, when I noticed Mr. Kenneth Donald McIntyre Moodie, the attorney general, entering the courtroom by the same side door through which Major Swanepoel usually brought in his witnesses. He was a tall, thin, hawkish-looking man, an appearance which his long black robes emphasized as he walked over to the prosecutor's table. If he had come only as an interested spectator, he would not be wearing his robes but neither we nor the judge had been advised of any change in the prosecutor's team, which already consisted of three senior men. It was normal procedure to do this in order that the judge, at least, would not be taken by surprise, but Liebenberg had just been speaking to George and had not mentioned it.

As Judge Bekker sat down, the attorney general rose and stood at the prosecutor's dias. The judge looked at him, raised an eyebrow in surprise, and invited him to begin the day's hearing.

"May it please Your Lordship," he said, and he went on to refer to certain numbered sections of the criminal code and to quote the number and years of the legislation. Then he announced to the court that it was his intention, as attorney general, to withdraw the prosecution.

I could not believe that I had heard correctly. The judge, at a loss to understand this sudden move, immediately drew his attention to the obvious fact that he had already entered a plea of not guilty from all the twenty-two defendants to the charges filed against them. To withdraw at this stage would entitle all the defendants to an acquittal.

The attorney general had remained standing throughout. He said in reply, "Yes, My Lord, that is so." Judge Bekker quickly turned his head away and for a moment his face flushed. He was obviously flustered and annoyed that he had not been taken into the attorney general's confidence beforehand. It took a moment before he could regain his calm.

While all this was happening, the defendants were looking to me for an explanation. I was simply stunned. An acquittal was just not possible; it was a victory too easily won.

But now Judge Bekker was asking all the defendants to rise, and I was hearing his words as he addressed them: "The charges against you have been withdrawn. You have all pleaded not guilty to these charges and you are, therefore, entitled to an acquittal. You are all acquitted; you may go." His head nodded and he then said the final words: "Court adjourned." He rose from the bench and walked out while the orderly jumped up and called for silence, the last words of these court proceedings.

There was no silence—there was madness in court. As the door closed behind the judge, I suddenly realized what this was all about and I whispered loudly to my clients, "You will not be released; you are going to be redetained—you are going to be redetained!" At the same instant the police had barred all doors to the court. More than a score of security policemen surrounded the prisoners and began marshaling them out of the door leading to the iron cage. Standing in front of me was the huge form of Lieutenant Dirker. I jumped over the table and tried to reach my clients but Swanepoel stopped me on the other side next to the door.

"I wish to see my clients," I demanded, "move out of my way."

He blocked my path and said threateningly to me, "You cannot."

"Why not?" I said. I knew his answer before he gave it yet his words hit me as if his own fat fist had punched me in the gut.

"They are all detained under the Terrorism Act."

I refused to accept this and protested again, "My clients have in their possession the defense statements prepared for this trial which you are not entitled to. As their attorney I demand the return of these documents."

With all the power his voice could command he replied, "What is in their possession is in my possession."

By now all my clients were outside. The police moved in front of me, blocking my view, my steps were barred by their Sten guns and my words were lost. Sadly and bitterly I realized we had failed. The twenty-two were back in detention.

In another part of the courthouse, another drama was taking place. While I had rushed after my clients, George and David, acting with great speed, had approached Judge Bekker in his chambers to advise him that we, too, had been unaware of what was about to happen and had been taken by surprise. George asked the judge to prevent an injustice by ensuring that the defendants' statements, which they had taken with them into court, be returned to the defense lawyers immediately. The security police were not entitled to these documents.

Judge Bekker asked his registrar to call the attorney general, and counsel repeated in front of him the necessity for the defense statements to be returned to us. Both the judge and the attorney general agreed and the latter left, promising to do what he could. When he returned a few moments later, he said to Judge Bekker, "I am afraid the defendants are all removed from the courtroom. They are now in prison trucks and are beyond my jurisdiction. I cannot assist further."

The security police had won—they had demonstrated where the real source of power lay. The judge, the attorney general, the prosecutor, all were but puppets to be manipulated. Defense lawyers would be tolerated or, where necessary, dealt with. The police accepted the law only when they were able to twist it to ensure that their state survived intact. Only a confrontation with a greater force would change this situation.

On the way back to Johannesburg there was silence and bitterness in the car. Outside the court I had talked briefly to the relatives and suggested that they come to see me at my office. Naturally, all of them were anxious and uncertain— how would it all end, they asked. I had no answers.

I dropped George and David at their chambers and returned to my own office. I was not expected and various clients, whom members of my staff were looking after, expressed their pleasure at seeing me. Their own troubles were as important to them, and the injustices that they complained of, as tragic as the events I had just witnessed in Pretoria. Even so, I could only give them rather absentminded attention and was relieved when the last one left. I desperately needed time to think and to be on my own.

I wondered whether we had erred in our attack on security police methods. Should we instead have ignored this and played the trial straight, countering allegation with allegation, proceeding to a normal end, trying to obtain some acquittals and for those not acquitted, sentences as light as we could hope for? At least the convicted would then have been able to start serving their sentences. Would this have been a better course to adopt? What was happening to my clients at that very moment? I wept at my helplessness. We had to find some way of helping them—but how, how? The law was in favor of the police and monstrous as their actions were, they were legal.

Suddenly I had a flash of inspiration—we had to bring an urgent court petition, the same kind as we had brought for Gabriel Mbindi, seeking a court injunction against security police torture. All the relatives were anxious about what would happen to the detainees and had every reason to fear security police methods. I jumped up—I was sure I had the answer but before I gave out any false hopes I wanted to check the reaction of George, David, and Arthur.

I arrived at George's chambers just as he and David were returning from lunch. George welcomed me with the words, "I've got a solution." Since the security police had illegally removed the defendants' statements, he recommended that we apply to court urgently to have them returned to us so that we would not be prejudiced by the state having advance knowledge of any future defense that would be based on these statements now in security police hands.

"I have another idea," I said. I told them what I had been considering and they thought that my plan could give more protection to our clients. After discussing the matter further, we agreed that we would make an urgent application to court, based on the fears that the relatives reasonably entertained.

We would ask the court to issue an injunction to prevent the security police from further practicing any illegal methods of interrogation. We would also approach Sidney Kentridge, a senior counsel at the Johannesburg bar, to lead the attack.

The one disadvantage to this plan, said George, was that we would lose a lot of time preparing all these papers. We would need each relative to sign an affidavit setting out the reason for his own apprehension about the safety of the prisoner. Then I remembered that I had obtained handwritten statements from all the prisoners about the torture they had suffered at the hands of the security police during their last detention. All of these statements, however, would have to be photocopied and typed to avoid any possible objection by the court as to their legibility in their original form. This would take days of typing and careful checking because the written and typed statements would have to be identical to avoid any allegations that they were inaccurate. Furthermore, to attain an element of surprise, all of the work involved would have to be done with the maximum secrecy possible. I did not intend to have a security police raid on my office and the original handwritten statements removed. Since my office and my telephone were bugged, we would have to exercise great care to maintain secrecy. Could this be done and the work completed in the next few days?

It was our experience that the security police usually took a few days to prepare for whatever action they were going to take and then, if they wanted to break the detainees in a hurry, the torturing would all take place during the first week of detention. I assured all the counsel that as far as my side of the work was concerned, I would handle everything and be ready for court three mornings hence. George had his doubts about this but was sure we could use the defendants' statements.

Sharply I said, "You prepare for the legal arguments and see that you're ready—don't worry about me. The job will be done." I regretted my touchiness but I think George understood my feelings.

Walking back to my office, I wondered if I had not been too confident. I had no idea how I was going to have all this work done beyond the ears of the security police. Then I remembered a number of good typists I had used before for part-time evening work. Without difficulty, I was able to line up several who would help with the typing.

Back at my office, a group of the relatives were waiting for me. Taking a few at a time for a walk down the long passage outside, I told them of my idea and they wholeheartedly endorsed it. All of them agreed to make themselves available to me at any time and promised to call in every day to see if they were needed. Those who had come from far away rearranged their return trips so that they could stay in Johannesburg and help.

Although my own staff was familiar with the conditions under which I worked, I stressed to them that nothing must be discussed aloud in my office or on my phone about the work they were to do. If any problems came up, they should put their questions in writing and I would reply in the same way. If necessary, we would ride up and down in the elevator and solve the problems there. To complete the maximum work in the minimum time, I worked out an order of priorities to ensure that both copying and typing could be carried on simultaneously. It was obvious that a lot of night work would have to be done.

When I arrived home my wife and I took a walk around the block and I asked her to line up a number of friends to help check the documents. Fortunately, one of our friends had just rented a new apartment but had not moved in and there was no telephone so bugging would not be easy. We brought in a few chairs and tables and made it our checking headquarters. The only disadvantage was that it was at one end of the town while the typists' homes were scattered all over the city and suburbs. It meant much running back and forth but I developed a routine. As soon as one batch of typing had been done, I would pick it up and rush it back to be checked and then fetch the next lot from another typist. By then, the first documents would have been checked and if any corrections needed to be made, I would return them on my next trip out to the typist.

We worked until one o'clock the first night and all day

Tuesday and into the early hours of Wednesday morning. On Wednesday afternoon, I sent messages to the relatives, telling them to call in at my office that evening. But by 4:00 there was so much work still to be done that I worried about their having to stay until late at night and not being able to get back to the townships in Soweto and elsewhere. There would be no public transportation at that hour and it would certainly be too far for them to walk. In addition, it would be after curfew and we could not run the risk of their being arrested. I contacted a number of my devout Christian friends and they agreed to help with the driving. Finally, I had to arrange for food to be brought in since there were no eating facilities open nearby for blacks and they would not be served in any of the white restaurants that were open. My staff had consented to remain working for as long as it was necessary and a young typist who had been caught up in the intensity of the effort offered to work through the night if necessary. My office was a typing-copying factory, producing affidavits and statements by the score. Meanwhile, I continued on as messenger, running around the city picking up final copy and dropping off work to be done.

At about 10:30 P.M. George returned the petition I had drafted with his comments on it and I asked him to be at my house at 8:00 in the morning to collect the documents in final form and then to go on to Pretoria without me. I would have to go earlier because there was one affidavit that had to be signed there. He agreed to be there but shook his head doubtfully when I told him of the volume of work that still had to be done.

At about that time I realized that I had forgotten to provide for a commissioner of oaths to attest the signature on each affidavit. I called a number of my colleagues and without giving any details, asked if they could stop in at my office that night to sign some affidavits for a very urgent matter. One young attorney promised to cut short his evening's entertainment and he arrived within the hour.

It was now nearly midnight and throwing caution to the winds and hoping the security police had gone to bed, I gathered all the relatives together in one group and read and explained the petition to them. I feared that the day might come when they might have to face cross-examination in the witness box, so despite the rush, I was anxious that everyone who signed the papers understand exactly what the petition and their own affidavit said. When all of them had indicated that they understood both the contents and the procedure, and when the young attorney had arrived, they signed the papers before him.

When they left, we got down to the remaining portion of our work. One complete set of papers had to be prepared for the judge, and two copies for the state attorney, as well as a copy for each of my two counsel and a few more copies for the clients and one for myself, making about ten in all. In addition, we had to complete an index and put each set of papers in order in terms of the index. It was after 5 A.M. when all the work was finally completed. The papers filled a suitcase, which I took home with me, immeasurably grateful for the willing cooperation of my staff and the others who had gladly put in so much time. I arrived home shortly before 6:00 and decided to drive my car right around the house and park it outside the bedroom where I hoped it would be safe. I could not afford the time for any security police diversions.

I was awakened at 7:15 by my wife who told me that there was a client waiting to see me who had a 7:00 appointment. I couldn't remember making any such appointment but when I saw him I recalled that he was a client who had been having such difficulty seeing me at my office that I had told him to come to my home early in the morning. He had traveled a great distance and I just had to give him twenty minutes and then I arranged to see him again. I phoned George to tell him that I was on my way to Pretoria and that the papers were waiting for both advocates at my house.

"I can't believe it," said George warmly, "congratulations!"

On the way, I stopped under the bridge in Alexandra Township, an old black ghetto, to pick up an elderly lady whose seventy-four-year-old husband, Douglas Mvemve, was one of those redetained. Two other people got in my car with her and I shouted to all of them, "Hold tight, we are going to go very fast." About twenty minutes later I had covered the thirty miles to Pretoria and was showing my passengers how to get to court, saying, "Wait for me there, I'll come later."

As soon as I had the missing signature, I went to the office of the state attorney, which was next to Compol, security headquarters. The man on duty, Mr. MacGregor, was the same man who had tried to negotiate a settlement of the first habeas corpus application of Nelson Langa that I had brought to court some thirteen years previously. I remembered well how he had tried then to persuade me to believe in the veracity of his senior state officials rather than accept the simple common sense and truthfulness of my black clients. I remembered, too, how even as a state attorney, he had not disclosed fully to the court the papers he had. Now he was arguing with me and taking technical points on me.

Speaking in Afrikaans, while I spoke in English, he said, "I am not accepting your documents, you have no right to serve them on me. Only a sheriff has the right to serve documents. This is set out in the rules of court."

"The matter is an urgent one," I replied, "and insofar as service is concerned, we are asking that strict compliance with the rules of court be waived by the court in view of the urgency."

Saying he was not interested he handed my documents back to me. I told him that whatever his attitude, I was leaving the documents on his desk and would advise the court accordingly; then I turned around and left. I knew he would use whatever arguments he could. But I also knew that if I left the documents with him, he would have to respond. He would brief an advocate to represent the state in court and together he and the advocate would be in court when the matter was called.

The petition I filed in court, brought by fifteen relatives of the twenty-two, cited as respondents the minister of justice and the minister of police. We sought an injunction directing the ministers to produce all twenty-two defendants before the court to give evidence on allegations of torture. Failing this, we asked that an attorney be appointed to take affidavits from them in detention. We further sought an order directing the ministers to take adequate steps to protect the twenty-two from assaults, enforced standing, and the performance of any act calculated to induce fear or prolonged discomfort, or to degrade them while they were being detained.

The first applicant, Winnie Mandela's sister, alleged that she and the others rightly entertained reasonable fear that the twenty-two who had been previously tortured by Major Swanepoel and his men would now, having been redetained by the same policemen, be tortured further in order to make them sign statements. She further alleged that the cruelty meted out to the detainees constituted an integral part of an interrogational method adopted by certain members of the security police under the direction and control of Swanepoel, and that it was common knowledge that a number of people died while in detention under the Terrorism Act.

In support of these allegations we not only attached the handwritten statements and their typed copies, giving particulars of the torture, but we also handed in to court the full record of the proceedings against the twenty-two and drew its attention to the five state witnesses who, under oath, had testified as to the torture they had undergone. The record showed that the prosecutors had not been able to challenge this testimony nor had they contradicted it. I was convinced that the court could not ignore such substantial evidence and that our case was strong, and that we were sure to receive a court order, however weakly the order was framed.

As I had seen to it that the press knew of these proceedings, I also knew that in addition to any court order, we would also obtain wide publicity and that might protect my clients. Once it was publicly alleged that the twenty-two were again faced with torture by the security police, these men might think twice about any further torture.

When I arrived at the courthouse, a number of the relatives had gathered in the foyer and I asked them to remain where they were until I found the court to which we were assigned. Sidney Kentridge and George Bizos arrived and while they were changing into their gowns, I reported to them on my confrontation with MacGregor over serving the papers. They suggested that I have a further copy served by the sheriff, which seemed a good idea. I rushed to his office and he promised to serve within the hour.

When I got back to the courthouse the foyer was filled with the security police gang. They might not be taking official notice of the service, but nonetheless, eight of them had come to stare and intimidate those people who had dared to challenge them. After I arrived on the scene they concentrated all their efforts on me. I ascertained from the registrar which courtroom we would be in and then guided my clients to it. Kentridge had learned that Advocate D. J. Curlewis, a senior counsel from the Pretoria bar, had been instructed by the state attorney, and had asked that the matter be postponed until 11 A.M.

Just before 11:00, I was called to the phone by the deputy sheriff. The state's attorney had refused to accept the papers from him as he said he had not seen the original documents and he was not prepared to accept the papers served by the sheriff as a true copy. I asked the sheriff to file his return accordingly.

"But where is the original document?" he asked.

"The judge is reading it now and the matter will be heard in ten minutes," I replied.

By now, Curlewis had arrived and wished a further delay but we insisted that the matter be called. I noticed that the papers I had left with the state's attorney were in his hands.

We had been assigned a small court in the west wing of the building. The only audience were the relatives of the detainees and the security police. When Judge J. K. Theron, a ruddy-faced man in his fifties, with a shock of white hair, entered, Kentridge rose to address him.

All we were asking the court to do, he said, simply but forcefully, was to order that no illegal treatment be used on the detainees. This would cause no harm to anyone; the police would not suffer from being forbidden to do what the law did not permit and that they would deny doing anyhow. On the other hand, the detainees could suffer irreparable harm if they were tortured. He concluded by saying: "I do submit that if this relief is not granted, it would mean, in effect, that persons in this situation are helpless; they are at the mercy of their interrogators because if this application, on this evidence, does not qualify for interim relief, it is impossible to conceive of any circumstances in which interim relief could be granted." The court also was referred to three other recent orders that had been granted in similar circumstances.

Our opponent submitted that there was no need for urgent relief. The police would deny that they were indulging in any kind of torture, and even if the handwritten statements of the detainees alleging torture were true, that torture was over and done with and subsequent to the event, the detainees had been brought to court and tried. What may have happened to them in the past could not be used as a basis for asking the court for relief for what might happen to them in the future. He said that he opposed an interim order, even one made without prejudice, as it would only cause the government bad publicity.

Judge Theron agreed with Curlewis and refused to make any order. What he was prepared to do was to grant a postponement so that affidavits could be filed by both sides and the matter could then be heard by the court in the ordinary way. That court would then decide what order should be made.

This would take weeks, maybe months. Earlier, in the Gabriel Mbindi case, I had at least succeeded in obtaining an interim order and subsequently the state refused to face a confrontation in court and settled the matter. The ruling of Judge Theron showed me how the court had now turned away from enforcing the minimal rights of detainees and from giving them any aid and had clearly ruled in favor of the security police.

We launched an appeal immediately but the judge indicated that we were wasting our time. He said the appeal would take as long to hear as proceeding with the original application. The court adjourned—the security police were triumphant. I told my clients not to worry for I would keep the matter on the roll as long as the detainees remained prisoners and this would act as a brake on the security police methods of interrogation. The facts alleged in the petition were given full coverage in the local and overseas press; editorials appeared at home and abroad. Although we had failed in court, we had placed white justice in the dock.

Knowing that any letters of mine to the International Commission of Jurists in Geneva would be opened, and knowing, too, that the police would never admit to interfering with this mail (subsequently, interference with the mail has been legitimized by a special law) I wrote them a scathing report on Judge Theron's ruling in court. I also kept up the pressure on the security police. By letter I demanded permission to see the prisoners so that I could take affidavits from them on whether or not they were being tortured. I demanded that they comply with the assurance given by the minister in parliament that relatives of the detainees would be informed of the whereabouts of those held by the security police. None of the relatives of the twenty-two had, in fact, been told what had happened to them or where they were being held. I also demanded assurances from them that all the detainees were in good health and I said that we were prepared to provide them with medical attention. I reminded them that Mendel Levin had been allowed to provide a doctor for Winnie Mandela and I wanted the same right. Finally, I demanded to know when any detainee changed his status and was either charged, in which case I would prepare for the trial, or became a state witness.

Receiving no reply I wrote again, enclosing a photocopy of the previous letter, and demanded a reply. I told them that I had ascertained from the post office that my first letter had been delivered. I blamed them for causing unnecessary delays in furnishing me with the information I requested and said that their failure to reply prevented the court from hearing the pending application as I was unable to complete my papers.

Finally, my nagging produced results. The head of the security police wrote to tell me that all twenty-two prisoners were detained under the Terrorism Act and he emphasized that under the terms of this act no person could have access to them, nor was I entitled to receive any information about them. He went on to give me assurances that the prisoners were all in good health, a fact that was not true as was proved later. He said the relatives had all been informed of the prisoners' detention and arrangements would be made for food, clothing, and the like to be delivered. Finally, he said, until such time as the detainees were released or their cases dealt with, no further correspondence would be conducted.

The Monday following the redetention of the twenty-two,

the Black Sash organization mounted the first of a series of all-day demonstrations and stated that they would demonstrate every Monday thereafter until the detainees were either released or brought to trial. Women stood silently holding posters at a particular street corner throughout the day, under constant surveillance both by police and security police. Their stand was a continual reminder of the events of February 16. Members of the public were invited to join this protest and I often took my place there.

Since it was an election year, there was much activity on the Witwatersrand University campus in Johannesburg, an English-speaking institution in a predominantly antigovernment city. I was the last of a series of speakers invited to address the students on election issues. The subject I chose was the abrogation of the rule of law in South Africa and I called my talk, "Arbitrary Detention and Its Implications." It was a challenge to deliver a speech on such a controversial subject to students in the presence of security police but it was a challenge I greatly enjoyed. I chose my words carefully and I made sure that my facts were entirely accurate and that every statement could be substantiated. I talked about the pass laws, the arrests under them, the illegal farm labor scheme, the abrogation of the rule of law, the unlimited power of the security police, the allegations of torture, the effects of sensory deprivation, and the number of deaths in detention. I spoke of how the courts themselves had bowed to the unlimited power of the security police. I concluded by calling on all students to resist and protest but to do it within the law.

The reaction to the speech was enthusiastic. Most of the information in it had not been put together before and much of it was entirely new to this audience. As a result, Neville Curtis, the president of NUSAS, a national student organization opposed to *apartheid* and the government, and by law an all-white body, asked me to talk to English-speaking campuses around the country. At the same time, the editor of the student newspaper asked me to write a long article which would show the distinct similarity between the events in Nazi Germany from the Reichstag fire at the beginning of the 1930s to Hitler's rule under emergency proclamation, and the events in South Africa over the last twenty years. This I did and I suggested that South Africa was fast following in Hitler's footsteps.

Then it occurred to me that on May 12 it would be twelve months to the day since the twenty-two were first detained. It would also be the beginning of the twelfth week of their redetention. An idea began to form. I discussed it with the Anglican chaplain of Witwatersrand University, John Davis, a man whose dedication, courage, and good sense I had come to know and respect. I suggested to him that if I went on a tour of campuses around the country, it might be possible to have all the English-speaking universities join in a national protest against the redetention of the twenty-two. The Black Sash had already said that they would continue their protests, and there was a growing body of opinion among the English-speaking universities and some churches and other organizations, as well as the press, which was concerned about the application of the Terrorism Act. If we could weld all this opposition into one mass protest on May 12, 1970, it would not only focus attention on the twenty-two, but might generate further protests, which if strong enough, could possibly put pressure on the minister to bring the detainees to trial more quickly, or even to release them. The chaplain agreed that the idea was feasible and our first step was to call on local student organizations. There were only five days left before Monday, May 12, and one of those days was a public holiday.

Luck was still with me. We discovered that representatives of five of the six universities were in Johannesburg at that moment for a meeting and I was able to put my plan before all of them that evening. They promised to let me know the next day and subsequently, they advised me that their universities would join the protest. The Black Sash were asked to move their protest from the street corner in the city to their usual stand, which was outside the university, to tie in with the huge demonstration the students would hold immediately opposite on university property. John Davis said he would take care of briefing the various church organizations, which I hoped would support the protest, and I contacted the editors of the local newspapers and offered them short articles on the detention of the twenty-two and on conditions in detention. The response from the press was gratifying. On Saturday, the afternoon English newspaper ran one of my articles; the Sunday paper took note of Monday's anniversary and supported the protest; Monday morning's newspaper carried excerpts of my speech, which dealt with the effects of sensory deprivation on detainees. Throughout the country, editorials were written in the English press urging the state to charge or release the twenty-two and to control the application of the Terrorism Act.

I led off the speakers at the protest meeting that Monday in Johannesburg. Supported by many of the academic staff and by many prominent South Africans, thousands of students gathered during the day to hear speaker after speaker come out against what was happening, and then stood silently throughout the night until the awful anniversary was over.

As protests continued throughout the country, I took a week off from work and went to Cape Town to begin my tour of the campuses. When I arrived at the place where the first meeting was to be held, I was told that a tear-gas bomb had earlier been planted in the hall. Fortunately, a strong southeast wind was blowing and this cleared out most of the fumes when the doors and windows were opened, but there was much sniffing and nose-blowing all evening. In spite of this, my speech was heard by a large and attentive audience and greeted with tumultuous applause. For the next week, at meetings throughout the country, the response was the same.

Before the last meeting in Durban, we heard that the minister of justice had called on the attorney general to expedite the bringing of charges against the twenty-two. He promised they would soon be brought to trial. The protests undoubtedly had had their effect.

While I was in Cape Town, the students in Johannesburg were planning a protest march. At the last moment the minister issued an order canceling the right to hold a procession. Nonetheless, twelve hundred courageous students, teachers, ministers, and others defied the ban and marched in a peaceful and orderly fashion through the streets of Johannesburg. Once the procession had gone past City Hall, many left the march but some four hundred students continued toward security police headquarters. There they were stopped by uniformed policemen so they sat down in the street, and 354 students were arrested. This was the first time that a mass arrest of whites had been made. The police had no facilities to accommodate so many whites and within hours most were released on their own recognizance.

Although the march had been peaceful and without incident, there was no doubt that it was illegal. In the end, after the police had harassed many students, and called them in for interrogation, and threatened them about their passports, they only prosecuted thirty. Many attorneys came forward to represent them and finally an arrangement was made with the prosecutor that in return for a plea of guilty to a municipal bylaw punishable by a fine, the serious charges originally brought against them would be withdrawn. They had first been charged under a law that permitted a punishment of whipping, or imprisonment, or heavy fines. The question of indefinite detention was now a subject of wide discussion in the press, in the pulpit, and in groups large and small throughout the country.

Early one morning, soon after these demonstrations, Vivian, my clerk, called me. He was almost incoherent in his agitation. "You had best come to the office right away. It's been shot up."

Fortunately, no one was injured. When I inspected the damage, I found the bullets had smashed the windows and some were imbedded in the doors and walls opposite at about five to seven feet from the floor. This showed that they had been fired from a height and not from the street five floors below. The only building opposite mine was a government building and it was obvious that the marksman had fired from there.

I reported the matter to the police, who were not helpful. They sent a fingerprint expert over and I told him he was welcome to take whatever prints he could find around the holes made by the bullets. Saying he would send the right man, he left. A week later a firearms expert called and spent

an hour looking for empty cartridges in the street below. Later
he told me that he found none but assured me that the shots
had not been fired from the building opposite!

The police later told reporters that they had reason to
believe I had shot up my office as a publicity stunt. I was
interviewed about this, and denying it, told a reporter exactly
where I was when the shooting occurred.

"Ah," he said, "but you could have arranged for someone
else to do the shooting!"

The rumor continued to circulate and some gave it cre-
dence. I believed that the whole incident was designed
primarily to harass me since whoever had fired the shots had
picked a time when no one was in my office. I took this as a
further warning from the security police to desist from my
activities.

The next attack was more frightening. A brown-paper
parcel tied with string and carrying a Zambian postmark,
arrived in the mail. It looked like a book. I cut the string and
tore the paper open to find a large volume of the complete
works of Mao Tse-tung. I opened it in some amazement and
was horrified to see that the inside had been hollowed out to
hold some kind of explosive contraption. Holding the book
gingerly in the same open position, I called Vivian to pass me
two heavy law volumes, which I placed carefully at the
corners so that it was held steady. I felt the sweat on my face.

"You are lucky, sir," said Vivian, "what will they do next!"

The other staff members came to the door hesitantly and
one said, "This is terrible, Mr. Carlson, thank God you're still
alive."

I was very shocked. I kept thinking of the threat to all of us.
Any one of my staff could have opened my mail and I didn't
know what I would have done if the bomb had gone off and
one of them had been harmed. When the police bomb expert
finally came he told me how lucky I had been that the device
had not detonated. He carefully disconnected it and took it
away. Later the security police phoned me to tell me that the
bomb was no more than a firecracker and would only have
given me a fright had it gone off. Again the rumor was spread

that I had devised the whole scheme myself in order to get publicity.

At home, Jeanette and I played down these incidents and encouraged the children to accept the police story that the bomb was a firecracker. But we were worried and tense as we waited for the next attack. How long could we go on in this way?

XVIII
RETRIAL: MY LAST
MASS TRIAL

On Thursday, June 18, 1970, at 9:30 A.M., Lieutenant Dirker phoned to tell me that my clients would be taken to court in Pretoria at 2 P.M. that day. Hurriedly, I sent messages to all the relatives, asking that they try to be there, and arranged transportation for them. Just before 2 P.M. I was again outside the court in Pretoria. Relatives, friends, sympathizers, and the reporters almost outnumbered the security police. The small room was packed as we waited for the detainees to appear. Half an hour passed and there was no sign of them. After nearly an hour the security officers arrived, the armed police closed the doors of the court, and up from the cells the prisoners came. But only eighteen were present. Winnie Mandela and three of the others were missing. Pleased as I was to see them all, I was anxious about Winnie and the others. Joyce Sikakane and Rita Ndzanga told me Winnie was in the hospital but they were less certain about the three men.

I turned accusingly to the prosecutor's table: "What has happened to Winnie Mandela?" I demanded.

Rothwell, one of the prosecutors, replied: "She is ill and in the prison hospital. I'll hand in a medical certificate about her."

"And what's happened to the other three?" I asked.

"They will be state witnesses," he told me.

Two were young men. The third was rather elderly and had a suspended sentence for a previous political crime hanging over his head; if convicted, he would have been doubly punished. At least now he would not go to jail.

Even after the arrival of the prisoners, the trial did not begin. I talked to my clients and in spite of the fact that some of the group were missing, they were in good spirits. They told me they had not been subjected to torture by the security police during this period of detention. Our application had had successful results after all. As we continued to wait, I asked the prosecutors what the delay was and was told that we were waiting for another defendant.

Turning to my clients I asked them whether they had any idea who the new defendant would be, but they did not. They had not received a new charge sheet and the prosecutors confirmed that the charges had in fact not yet been drawn. We had forced the state to bring the defendants to court before the charges were ready. When I asked them if they had any idea what the new charges were, they rightly said, "We have been in detention for over a year. What new charges could there possibly be?"

Finally, a stocky, powerful built man was led up from the cells and placed at the head of the line of the defendants. Before I could speak to him, Judge Strijdom walked in and the orderly shouted *"Stilte in die hof."* The prosecutor applied for a postponement to August 3 and handed in a certificate from the attorney general prohibiting bail for any of the defendants. He said that the new charges would be under the Terrorism Act and that the new defendant, Benjamin Ramotse, would be the first defendant. This was the surprise that the security police had for us.

Once again I rose to address Judge Strijdom and told him that I appeared for eighteen of the defendants present and for Mrs. Mandela who was in the hospital. I did not appear for Benjamin Ramotse as neither I nor any of the other defendants knew anything about his appearance in court that day. I suggested that if the court adjourned I could have an opportunity of speaking with him and could then advise the court what the position was.

When the court did adjourn, Ramotse and I conferred. He had been arrested and detained in May, 1968, two years earlier. In fact, I had received many messages from him over the past year when he was in prison. He had asked me to come to his assistance, but as he was a detained terrorist, I was not entitled to receive any information about him and could not accept the instructions he sent me. There was nothing I could do unless I received proper instructions. He now told me that he wished me to act for him.

I knew that Benjamin Ramotse had exploded a bomb in a post office in Dube Soweto, Johannesburg, in 1961, and had then fled the country. I did not know that he was working for the ANC beyond South Africa's borders until he had been kidnapped by Rhodesian police while he was in Botswana, a neighboring territory, and taken to Rhodesia where he was questioned and tortured. Eventually, the South African security police had come for him. He was blindfolded, handcuffed hand and foot, and brought back to South Africa, where he had been held under the Terrorism Act for seven hundred and two days.

The court reconvened and I informed the judge that Ramotse wished me to act for him, that he alleged that he had been kidnapped and held in detention for over seven hundred days. Naturally, the prosecutor objected but the facts were already on the record. Court adjourned until August 3 but stories about Ramotse and his long detention appeared in the papers and editorial writers raised the question as to how many others there were still languishing in detention who had been there as long or longer. A new trial, now of twenty defendants, was about to begin. I wondered whether it was really a new trial or just a continuation of the old one, with the addition of Benjamin Ramotse. I was soon to find out.

Three weeks after the eighteen were brought to court, Liebenberg phoned me to say that the indictment was ready. I was anxious to get hold of it immediately and so agreed to his suggestion that I come to Pretoria to have it served on me.

The charge sheet that he handed to me comprised fifty-eight pages, two pages more than the previous charge sheet. Whereas the first indictment was brought under the Communism Act, the new one was brought under the Terrorism Act, but the substitution of the word "Terrorism" for "Communism" seemed to be the only thing different about them. The specific acts complained of were identical in both cases. There were minor differences—Nelson Mandela was not mentioned in the new indictment and Benjamin Ramotse was made the first defendant in place of Samson Ndou.

Benjamin had been in captivity for over a year before any of the twenty-two were arrested. The state sought to use the joinder provision of the Terrorism Act to join him to the others by saying that all the defendants were members of the ANC and, therefore, irrespective of where and when any criminal act was committed, all members were held responsible for any criminal act committed by any other member. Some of the young men who were now charged with Ramotse were in elementary school when he escaped the country in 1961. Ramotse did not for a moment deny the part he played until his capture and arrest, but it was clearly ridiculous to hold the other accused guilty with him. Many of them had never heard of him and none of them knew what he had been doing for the last eight or nine years.

It was obvious that the state had had a difficult time in producing a new charge sheet. The prosecutors had charged the defendants under a different law and tried to weave a new pattern of criminal actions. However, the charges now made of "acts of terrorism" were of a much more serious nature than they were when called "acts of Communism." Conviction could result in death or life imprisonment and the minimum sentence was five years, none of which could be suspended. Whether the prosecutor could make the charges stick remained to be seen.

Our first task would be to mount an attack on the indictment. We would have to show to the judges, even of these courts, that the defendants faced double jeopardy of the kind that even the Terrorism Act (which expressly permitted double jeopardy) did not provide for. A careful and meticulous study was made of the allegations in these two indictments. The more we studied the indictments the more we were convinced that we could make a strong and successful double-jeopardy plea for all of the twenty defendants except Ramotse. But this was a new field as far as the Terrorism Act was concerned and there was no certainty of achieving an acquittal. If we failed we would have to proceed with the trial.

George Bizos, David Soggot, and Mike Kuper worked with Sidney Kentridge, our senior counsel, to make a precise breakdown of the old and new indictments. Every single allegation was classified, one set next to the other, and excluding Ramotse's part in the second indictment, we found that of the 540 allegations in the new indictment, 528 were identical to the allegations in the old indictment, with only the substitution of a different adjective here and there or the juxtaposition of the words in a different order.

While the defense team was busy working up the legal aspect of the case, I concentrated on the prisoners. The women, particularly, had suffered terribly in their redetention. The white matrons had sought revenge for all the battles I had conducted on their behalf over the last five months. It was a wonder that they had survived at all.

The elderly men had felt the detention more severely than the young men but their condition was still not as bad as the women's. Although the security police had carried out further interrogations and had made dire threats against all of them, they had not practiced any further assaults on them. One of the young men, Manke Paulus Matshabe, who had not appeared in court. had suffered a mental breakdown and had been taken to a mental home. The remaining two of the original twenty-two, I was told, were being held in police stations in Pretoria.

Paulus had previously been employed by the morning Johannesburg newspaper. I suggested to reporters from this paper that they check his whereabouts with the responsible officials. They did this and the newspapers carried a daily report of their search. Alert, bright reporters interviewed officials from various government departments, none of whom were prepared to tell the truth about either Paulus or the other two "missing men."

The response from the attorney general was that the three men had been released and he had no knowledge of their whereabouts.

The minister of justice was even more cynical and said, "If released men do not return home it's their own business."

The three men did not return home and no word was heard of them by their relatives or friends. The reporters persisted in their search and approached the commissioner of prisons.

Enigmatically he said, "I have no information to give," and referred them to the security police.

In turn, the security police referred them back to the prison commissioner, saying he should know if they were in jail—or, they said, they should try the commissioner of police. It was the same old runaround I was so accustomed to.

The newspaper then reported that Paulus had been found wandering in the street near his home. He had no idea where he was or why he had been brought there. A neighbor said the police had dropped him off and that he and others had guided him to his home. The paper had him examined by doctors and psychiatrists who pronounced him mentally ill. Later he often came to see me in my office and when he was lucid and asked me about his comrades, I would try to explain what was happening to them. He really did not understand any more what it was all about. He was beyond any help that I could give him.

The next missing defendant, Victor Mazitulela, suddenly appeared in Johannesburg. He talked to a friend and telephoned his father to say all was well. Having established that he was "free," he was then returned by the security police, who had taken him to Johannesburg, to the police station in Pretoria where he said he was "staying." Later in the year, he came into my office and disclosed to me the real fraudulence of the police action. He had never been released, he said. He was only permitted to communicate with his relatives and friends and was then immediately returned to police custody. It was clear that the police had reacted to the harassment they had been subjected to by the reporters and had done everything they could to deceive and falsify reports concerning these missing men.

The third man, Livingstone Mancoko, was still "missing" until one day, about two weeks after the trial recommenced, when the police arranged for him to meet me in extraordinary circumstances designed to appear as a coincidence. I had been visiting my clients, and from the prison, where the telephone was probably bugged, I had telephoned a Johannesburg newspaperwoman at her Pretoria office, offering her a lift home. I arranged to pick her up outside her office building in the center of town. When I arrived there she was not outside and I parked my car and went up to her office. We came downstairs and were about to cross the road to my car when suddenly Livingstone appeared in front of me. I was stunned, for his home was a thousand miles away and he was a complete stranger to the city of Pretoria. I asked him what he was doing and he pointed out a black security policeman standing nearby.

He made it obvious he was reluctantly acting under orders. He said to me, "I don't want to say anything that would harm you." I introduced him to the reporter and then I could see he was anxious to leave and we parted.

I felt the web of security police movements being spun but could see no real purpose in this maneuver other than that of making me aware of their presence.

My three counsel painstakingly completed all the paperwork and drew all the schedules, showing beyond doubt that the two indictments were identical in substance and in fact. We were increasingly convinced that the court must uphold a double-jeopardy plea and acquit the nineteen for the second time.

The Lawyers Committee for Civil Rights under Law flew out its dynamic executive director, Peter Connell, to observe the trial in Pretoria, where it reconvened in August. After listening to our arguments on the first day, he asked me what would happen if the nineteen defendants were again acquitted. I told him it was no longer possible to predict with certainty what would happen. That evening he cabled his committee in Washington, asking them to alert the American Bar Association to the possibility of the defendants' further redetention. I knew the cable would be read by the security police and thought it was important that they know in advance that massive international opposition and protest would arise if the defendants were subjected to a further period of detention. The following day, Connell met Judge Gerrit Viljoen during the tea adjournment and described to him who the members of the Lawyers Committee were and the work it did in the United States. He explained also why an American body was dedicated to upholding the rule of law in South Africa.

A number of other foreign observers also attended the trial. This was particularly important as we were arguing a special plea, objecting to the jurisdiction of the court insofar as Ramotse was concerned. We maintained that the court had no jurisdiction to try him for there was no doubt that the South African security police had obtained him from the Rhodesian security forces without any extraditing formalities. This was not even denied. It was public knowledge that the two forces cooperated closely in dealing with guerrilla activity on the Rhodesian and South African borders. Both regimes were equally dedicated to upholding white supremacy.

Ramotse was able to show that he had been in the independent country of Botswana, which had common borders with South Africa and Rhodesia, and that Rhodesian forces unlawfully crossed the border after their informers had appraised them of his presence in Botswana. Using a special spotter plane, the Rhodesians tracked Ramotse down, kidnapped him, and took him into Rhodesian territory.

In the celebrated case of Adolf Eichmann, his kidnapping by the Israelis was eventually condoned by the Argentine government. Otherwise, it would have breached international law. We now argued that to avoid contravening such law, the South African authorities should hand Ramotse back to Botswana or negotiate with Botswana on the matter. Until such time as this was done, Ramotse should not be tried in a South African court.

When Major Swanepoel entered the box to give evidence

about Ramotse's capture, he said he was unable to admit to or deny Ramotse's allegations of torture by the Rhodesian security forces. He did, however, emphatically deny that he or any of his men had tortured him. Ramotse had given me a long statement telling how he had been tortured, first by the Rhodesian security forces and subsequently by the South African security forces, and had drawn graphic diagrams. However, the issue of torture was, as before, strictly irrelevant to the legal issues before the court. While we could raise the issue, we could not pursue it without an invitation from Judge Viljoen. He refused to consider that aspect and we could take the matter no further in his court. Once again, the court remained silent in the face of torture allegations and thereby condoned these practices.

Having dealt with the issue of Ramotse, Kentridge spent the next three days carefully and methodically spelling out to the judge, word for word, all the hundreds of allegations made against each of the nineteen defendants. The proceedings dragged on, hour after hour, only lightened occasionally by some of Kentridge's ironic comments: "It is inconceivable, My Lord, that by merely re-arranging the sequences of allegations as they applied to the defendants numbered 2 to 9 in the first indictment, and having them now apply from 9 to 2 in the second indictment, the prosecutors hoped to deceive the court and the defense, for such a deception would be too patently obvious and could not even have entered the prosecutor's mind."

Late on the second day, Judge Viljoen began to get the message and asked Kentridge to dispense with lengthy comparisons of the two indictments. He agreed to accept the written comparisons we had drawn in support of our oral submissions. It was becoming obvious, even to this judge, that our arguments carried substantial weight and it was unnecessary to argue the matter further. We merely had to draw his attention to the facts.

Liebenberg, the state prosecutor, had difficulty replying. He struggled to answer the arguments, stressing the few dissimilarities. His main argument was based on the law and he showed that the first indictment was a charge under the

Communism Act and the second indictment, a charge under
the Terrorism Act. But he failed to convince the court that
both these "statutory evils"—"Communism and terrorism—
"had objectives other than the violent overthrow of the
state." Therefore, the defendants were in jeopardy for substantially the same crime. It was clear that in both charge
sheets the state could have used either statute.

While Liebenberg continued to stress the dozen new allegations in the second indictment, I suddenly recalled his opening
remarks to the court in the first trial. These remarks did not
form part of the official record so none of my counsel had
considered them before. I rushed up to the records room of
the Supreme Court and found the wax record which had these
opening remarks recorded. I then made special arrangements
to have a transcript typed right away. By the time I got back to
court, reading as I ran, Liebenberg had completed his argument and Kentridge had risen to reply.

I drew junior counsel's attention to the fact that in the
previous opening address, the prosecutor had included in the
first indictment almost all the twelve allegations which he was
now using to stress the differences between the two indictments. In substance and in fact, we had now established
beyond all doubt that the defendants were being placed in
double jeopardy of a kind that not even the Terrorism Act
permitted. Kentridge, in calling for a second acquittal of the
nineteen prisoners, emphasized the overwhelming similarity
of the two indictments. The judge adjourned the case for two
weeks to consider his judgment. Once more the prisoners
were returned to prison.

While we felt very confident as to the outcome of our
special pleas, I did not want the defendants to be overin-
fluenced by our confidence. It was not difficult to think of the
words that the judge could use to dismiss our submissions and
permit the trial to proceed. His record in matters where there
was a conflict between the races was not a happy one.
Sometime before he had convicted four young white men of
brutally assaulting and raping a black teacher. The sentence
he imposed was a nominal fine. Had the races been re-
versed, the sentences would have been immeasurably more

severe. I was convinced that if our special plea was lost and the trial proceeded, this judge would not permit us to expose security police brutality and those convicted would receive severe sentences. Thus, we continued preparations for the trial as usual, and I held out little hope to my clients for the success of our point of law. I gave the same impression to their relatives.

When court reopened in mid-September, I arrived early to watch what I hoped would be the last security police parade of force. After Judge Viljoen took his seat on the bench, the first matter on which judgment was delivered was the question of Benjamin Ramotse. Quietly and without emotion, the judge said he would read only the concluding sentence of his decision which was: "I have, therefore, come to the conclusion that his seizure was lawful and his trial should proceed." Not unexpectedly, we had lost the point of law for Benjamin Ramotse. I gave him a sympathetic glance and he shrugged his shoulders. He was much too important a catch and we would all have been extremely surprised if we had succeeded on his behalf.

My attention was quickly drawn back to the judge who was now giving judgment on the double-jeopardy plea. Again he said, "I am handing down my judgment as I do not intend to read it out but for the last sentence which reads as follows—I have, therefore, come to the conclusion that the plea taken on their behalf is a proper one and they are acquitted. All nineteen for whom the plea succeeds may go." He rose to leave the court.

I looked at George Bizos' face—his mouth was open, his face was white, and he registered stunned amazement at our success. Turning to the prisoners, both my hands clasped in joy, I gasped, "You are acquitted, you are acquitted." The audience upstairs was shouting excitedly. The security police moved in then, jumped on Ramotse, and dragged him off to the iron cage behind the court. Kentridge and the other advocates moved to interpose themselves between the security police and our clients and escorted them out of the court where I asked them to wait for me while I packed my bags.

When I got outside there was pandemonium—everyone

was milling about, there were cries and tears of joy and high-pitched laughter, shouts of recognition as friends and relatives found their loved ones and congratulated them. We had won! We had won!

The security police were still on duty taking pictures and moving through the crowd but nobody cared. Then the captain of the uniformed police came up to me with a number of his men, all carrying Sten guns. He complained that this was an unlawful gathering and said that the crowd must disperse. I remonstrated with him—the prisoners had been in detention for nineteen months and he certainly could not blame them or their families for showing their jubilation. "Leave them," I said, "they will soon go home."

"They must disperse immediately," he said gruffly. "I am going to order them to disperse." He picked up his megaphone and shouted to the crowd, "This is an illegal gathering; you must disperse immediately."

I jumped on the wall next to him and shouted, "Go home, go home." I did not want any shooting and with the police bitter and thwarted, I was very afraid that it would happen. I particularly feared the Sten guns. The crowd ignored the captain, ignored me, and continued to talk among themselves, wildly and excitedly.

I turned to the captain and begged him, "Give me five minutes and they will start moving—just give me five minutes." I knew the crowd wanted to be together and did not want to break up. A solution would be to invite them all to my house. I moved among them saying, "Leave here, go to my house; leave, go home to my house."

Soon people began to move off. In less than five minutes they had more or less dispersed and I sighed with relief that the danger had been averted.

As my counsel came out of the courtroom, having changed out of their gowns, I saw Swanepoel and Coatzee move up to them and offer their hands in congratulation. This was the time for Swanepoel to play the gentleman and all three counsel reluctantly shook his hand. He wished to build an image of a bona fide opponent. I walked back into the courthouse to find Ramotse but he was gone. I took a last look at the courtroom and at the iron cage. I hoped it was the last time I would see this court. After telephoning my office and giving my staff the good news, I left the building to return to Johannesburg.

As I came out I saw the prison van going back to the jail with its sole occupant, Benjamin Ramotse. Suddenly, he spotted his wife and nine-year-old son, a son he had not seen since he fled the country, standing on the sidewalk. He jumped to the bars and shook them and shouted, "My son, my son," as the van sped up the street. Mrs. Ramotse was in tears. Among all this jubilation, her distress was the greater.

I told her to follow me to the prison as I was a familiar sight there and had established good relations with the guards. At my request they allowed Mrs. Ramotse to go into the prison. They seemed genuinely puzzled by the turn of events, noting that Ramotse had been the only man returned to the prison in a prison van that had been filled with prisoners that morning. They asked me if it was not unjust that all the others were acquitted and yet this man, who had been in prison the longest, was still on trial. I could only tell them that it was the law and I didn't expect that we would succeed in getting him acquitted because his case was a tough one.

Then I said, "I want to ask you a favor—I have his wife here. She saw all the others acquitted and her husband taken back to jail. Can I see Ramotse for five minutes to set up our future consultations and would you permit his wife to see him in your presence for a few minutes?"

The guards had no objection and Ramotse was brought down. Although he knew that the case against him was entirely different, the taste of his captivity was bitter on his tongue as he saw the other nineteen acquitted and freed. All I could do was give him a few words of encouragement and assure him that we would do our best for him. I promised to see him on the following day. The guards then allowed Ramotse to have a few minutes with his wife. We turned our backs as she cried on his shoulder. He wanted to see his son but I knew that prison regulations would not permit this.

It was after all a sad journey back to Johannesburg. I could not dismiss from my mind the picture of Ramotse grabbing the bars and crying for his son while on the other hand, I knew that at my house awaiting me were all those whom we had been successful in having acquitted again. At last they were free. This society was at war and in the conflict there would inevitably be much suffering.

At my home there were almost a hundred people—clients, their relatives, friends, sympathizers, reporters, and a Swedish cameraman all swarming around the house and out on the lawn. My wife and her friends were making endless cups of tea. No one could have expected that this beautiful spring morning would have been spent in this way. The sunshine was filled with laughter, excitement, and gaiety. Winnie Mandela, Joyce Sikakane, Rita Ndzanga, Venus Mngoma, and Martha Dlamini, all dressed in two of the ANC colors, posed for press photographers, defiantly raising their hands to give the ANC salute. I ran for my camera so I, too, could record this dramatic occasion. However, I warned the reporters not to print any such pictures as it was an offense to give this salute and realizing this they promised that they would not.

I took pictures of the different groups among the defendants—there was no generation gap here. Douglas Mvemve who had turned seventy-four in detention and was soon to celebrate fifty years of marriage, stood hand in hand with his wife, Violet. Next to them stood George Mokwebo, David Motau, and Joseph Zikalala, all young men in their late teens and early twenties. None of them could quite believe that they were not, within the hour, to be led back to their cells, that at last they were free to go home. When the celebration broke up, one of the last to leave was Mrs. Ramotse. I watched her walk away sadly, her arm around the shoulders of her young son.

We were all uncertain about the future. Neither I nor anyone else knew what move the security police would make next, but they would not let matters rest—inevitably they would devise new ways of harassing the men and women just freed. I also expected action to be taken against me, greater harassment than before, but I was also sure that I would have a few weeks' respite. Anything done to me immediately after the second acquittal would be too obviously vindictive and would give rise to too much protest at home and abroad. I had no idea, however, how subtle and pervasive their future actions would prove to be.

At the end of the farm labor campaign, I had given a party for all those who had helped contribute to its success, and I decided now to give a *braaivleis* (barbecue) for all the prisoners and their families, and for all the many people, white and black, who had assisted our latest effort. I wanted to celebrate our success, to reunite the prisoners, and to introduce them to all the people who had given them succor and support throughout the long struggle. I knew that such a party might provoke the police but I decided to take that chance. It had to be held quickly before the security police took any action against anyone and no liquor might be served to avoid any possible charge that I contravened the law by supplying blacks with alcohol. But for those who had suffered so long, going without liquor at a party would be no hardship. Our spirits would be high enough.

Invitations went out on the bush telegraph and on Friday night carloads of people came to the house. I did not fear the security police or the uniformed police as much as the off-duty police—the vigilantes. It was they who could cause heavy damage to cars and to other personal property and threaten people's lives. In the afternoon and early evening I went around the split-rail fence surrounding my house and stuck pieces of broken glass on top. I installed arc lamps to light up the grounds. All the cars were parked in front in one small area, which left only a narrow entrance through which people could come and made it easier to guard the cars and give warning of any attack. A watch was kept throughout the night. Inside my house, black and white mixed freely, enthusiastically and happily. There was eating and laughter; there was singing and stamping; then there was dancing which could have gone on and on, but the curfew hours had to be obeyed and transportation to distant townships had to be arranged. The party broke up before midnight. What a happy, joyous occasion it was! It proved to be a historic one, too, for never again were we all to be together.

XIX
THE TRIAL OF
A SOLDIER

Benjamin Ramotse was now brought to trial. He had been more active than any other accused I had defended and there was no defense for him; the death sentence was a real possibility. In consultation with counsel, I decided that the best interests of Ramotse would be served by allowing the state to conduct a very speedy trial. It was on a Saturday morning that I introduced Nami Philips, a senior counsel, to Ramotse. Ramotse had been trained as an officer overseas and had spent considerable time in Cairo. Philips had served in Egypt in the South African army as a colonel during World War II. They exchanged views on matters of interest there and I left the guerrilla fighter and the army man together in their new roles as defendant and counsel. They understood one another and Philips handled a difficult case excellently. I limited my own role to being present at consultations and to seeing Ramotse on his own occasionally. I attended court throughout the trial.

Ramotse was convicted—which really came as no surprise. We were surprised, though, at the stupidity of one of the state witnesses, a Rhodesian security officer, who foolishly tried to convince the court that his forces had not kidnapped Ramotse. Under cross-examination, he had been obliged to admit that the map of the area he produced for the court was one drawn especially by the Rhodesian government recently, and the border lines marked in this map differed from those shown in other maps of the area. Nor was he able to deny Ramotse's version of the episode involving the spotter plane and Rhodesian security forces, or that they acknowledged that Ramotse's car was found in Botswana. Through the British high commissioner I had drawn the kidnapping of Ramotse to the attention of the Botswana authorities, and a protest was made by the Botswana government to the South African government. Although nothing further was done, I hoped that sufficient pressures had been placed on the court by the raising of this point of international law, by the interest of a foreign government, and by the attendance of foreign observers at the trial, to ensure that Ramotse would not hang. Relieved when he heard this, Ramotse accepted my advice that since he was a soldier and not a politician, he should not make any speeches in court and should neither plead for mercy nor attempt to justify his actions to the court.

When the judge asked whether he had anything to say before he passed sentence, Ramotse said, "I have nothing to say."

On the day of his sentence I brought Winnie Mandela and three of the other ex-prisoners to court to give him moral support. Philips briefly addressed the court in mitigation of sentence and Judge Viljoen returned an hour later to give his final judgment. Although I was expecting a minimum sentence of at least twenty-five years, the sentence was fifteen years. While Ramotse was still in court, and before he could be removed to the prison cells below, I went up to him and shook his hand. He thanked me and counsel for our efforts. Then, in front of the security police, he turned to the four women with me and bade them farewell, raising his hand in the ANC salute.

The next day a house-arrest order was served on Winnie Mandela, and on the following days, each of the nineteen who had been acquitted was served with a similar banning order, preventing them from attending any gathering. This meant they could not make any formal plans to meet one or more persons, anywhere at any time, during the next five years. Never could we all meet together again. Furthermore, a number of them who were employed had to give up their jobs, and I knew they would have a difficult time finding work elsewhere. This harassment of these people would extend to their would-be employers as the security police now exacted their punishment for our victories in the courts.

The security police then turned their wrath on the families of the nineteen and pressured the state's attorney to proceed against all those relatives who had been party to the urgent application that we had brought to court to protect the detainees from being tortured. The state's attorney issued a writ calling on each of them to pay the sixteen hundred dollars' costs and attached the few pieces of furniture they had in their homes. This was so obviously and patently an act of revenge that only if I exposed it would there be any chance of stopping it from going further. With the help of the press, stories were carried about this vindictiveness on the part of the security police and it had the desired result. The state's attorney dropped the action.

I then learned of a new kind of malice inspired by the security police. Just before midnight one night, I was telephoned by a woman reporter who got me out of bed to ask me whether I had kept the money raised by university students in Johannesburg to help the relatives pay the costs demanded by the state's attorney.

The facts of the matter were that without my knowing it, the students had collected about five hundred dollars for me to give the relatives to help them pay these costs. Since the money was no longer needed for this purpose once the state's attorney failed to proceed further, I approached the students through one of their leaders and explained the position. I told them that the money should not be given to me and it was not. It was pure spite to infer that I had been given the money and had then failed to pay the state.

I was annoyed at being awakened but even more annoyed at

the impertinence of the reporter's questions. My relationship with the press had always been good and this attitude was something new and obviously inspired by the security police. Rudely, I denied the allegation and demanded to know the source of her information. She was evasive and then hung up.

Half an hour later, she telephoned again, giving me a slightly different version of the allegation. Both of us knew that my telephone was tapped and I realized how happy the security police would be to know that I had been called upon by the morning newspaper to account for monies I had allegedly received and not paid over. Again I denied the allegation.

When the phone rang a third time I lost my patience and was determined to put an end to this. "Look here," I said, "if you have this information then I suggest you take it to the security police, who will surely be interested in it, and if you don't, I will."

The reporter said she would report the matter to her editor.

"You do that," I said, "and leave me alone," and I heard no more about it.

The smear techniques intensified and some reporters from both the English press and the Afrikaans press sought interviews with me to get me to comment on a number of anonymous poison-pen letters that had been circulated among editors, lawyers, and the staffs of foreign consulates. All the letters alleged that I was a Communist, as well as a capitalist, a publicity-seeker, a rogue, a thief, a Jew, and an atheist, and on and on for three or four pages. I invited the reporters to tell their editors that if they believed what was in the letters, they should publish them, but none was ever published.

The next form of attack was one with which I was familiar, for it had been practiced on me before. At a time when I had difficulties in employing staff, a nineteen-year-old black secretary came to work for me as a receptionist. She was a very quiet, pleasant, self-effacing person, slightly built and frail. Being black, she and her family were particularly vulnerable to police intimidation and could have housing and other permits withdrawn. She was picked up by the security police and subjected to interrogation. In an effort to induce her to cooperate with them, the security police offered her large sums of money to inform on me. They also made veiled threats of retaliation if she refused and warned her not to tell me anything about their approaches to her.

I noticed that something was wrong and pressed her for an explanation. She called me out of the office and tearfully revealed what was happening to her. She shook with fear as she told me how each time she left the office, or walked home from the railway station, she was accosted by men in a Volkswagen who insisted that they take her home. They followed her if she refused. Intimidated, and fearing detention, she was persuaded to enter into conversation with them. They visited her home and waited for her in the morning. They persisted with their demands that she become a police informer. I suggested that she give me notice immediately and leave me but she was afraid to do this. She had been warned not to.

I told her to tell her story to an advocate and later held consultations with him. We discussed the possibility of obtaining a court injunction. However, she could not prove the harassment and the security police would certainly deny that they were in any way involved. Furthermore, court action could result in her being detained for questioning about these "false allegations." I was helpless and unable to protect her.

I sent her away on paid long leave as she was not well. She returned two months later and had only been back in the office one day when the security police moved in again. I insisted that she stop working for me and helped her find another job. Even after this, she was still pestered by the security police but there was nothing more I could do to protect her. We just had to wait for them to divert their attentions elsewhere. I wondered who would be next on my staff, or among my few remaining friends, to suffer so.

This latest maneuver of the security police, coming so soon after the double acquittal and then the banning and house arrests of the defendants, made me question seriously the validity of my work as a lawyer in South Africa and whether I should continue. No matter how many times a case was won in court, there was no stopping the security police from exacting their own punishment and their own retribution. They were above the law—they had become the law.

Furthermore, it became clear to me that my opposition to the regime, carried on within its framework, helped to maintain the status quo. The irony of the situation was that my work was assisting the regime to present an overall image, at home and overseas, of judicial integrity and a fair legal system. I was, in fact, part of the facade of democracy in South Africa. I began to think in earnest above leaving the country. In the past I had rejected the ideas I had entertained of living in exile, because I had been convinced that the work I was doing was worthwhile. This, however, was no longer true. The basic truth was that the structure of the system in South Africa was beyond repair. It was too rotten, too unjust, too cruel to be salvaged. The violence it perpetrated on people every day could be abolished only by overturning the regime, which then would have to be totally rebuilt.

Toward the end of January, 1970, the Very Reverend Gonville ffrench-Beytagh, the Anglican dean of Johannesburg, was arrested and detained. He and I had been friends and were closely associated in some of our work together. When mutual friends asked me why his offices had been raided and he had been detained, whereas my offices were left untouched and I was still free, I knew that some of them did not believe my explanation. Had the security police wanted to detain me they could have at any time. Even though I was satisfied that if I survived detention, and was subsequently charged, I would have been acquitted, I knew that the security police had boasted to some of my clients during their interrogation, that I would be dealt with, that I was not to be martyred by arrest or detention: I was to be destroyed by smear and suspicion, so that people would lose confidence in me and cease to trust me. There was already evidence of these techniques being employed.

In February, there was a rash of countrywide searches, arrests, and detentions. Church organizations were raided; student and Black Sash offices were searched and documents removed, but once again, my office was left undisturbed. I remained untouched by any kind of police action.

Distrust of me grew and very few people saw through the sophisticated and shrewd attack on me. At the same time, I was becoming a menace to my friends, my family, and my staff.

Jeanette and I took long walks and discussed all of these problems at length, over and over again. If we left the country, where were we to go and what was I to do? Neither of us had passports, nor was there any likelihood that I would get one. It was obvious that even if we were finally permitted to leave, we, like many others, would not be allowed to take our assets with us.

At last I made the difficult decision to leave my homeland and to continue my work beyond its borders. Jeanette wholeheartedly supported me and we now had to plan how this was to be done.

Something else the security police had told my clients was that they planned to drive me into wanting to leave the country. I would then be forced to apply for an exit permit, which was the only lawful way a South African without a passport could leave the country. The minute I did this, they said, they would make their moves to break me totally.

Somehow, I had to outwit them this last time. Before I took any action I asked the advice of friends abroad who were familiar with the whole situation. I wanted to know whether I was misjudging or overemphasizing the dangers. These friends, who had inside information and expert knowledge at their disposal, emphatically told me that I was, in fact, underestimating the dangers. They begged me to move with greater urgency.

However, the dean had been brought to trial in early February. If I left so soon afterward it might give the impression that my departure had something to do with his trial and I did not want that to happen. I made inquiries from his advocate repeatedly over the next few weeks and months, asking whether I would be involved in the trial in any way and whether I could help in any way. I was told that my pressence and assistance were irrelevant and it did not matter whether or not I was in Johannesburg.

I then received in the mail an empty envelope with "The

Center for International Studies, New York University," as the return address. Inquiries were made and I discovered that the security police had removed the letter and that it was an offer of a university post. The offer then arrived again in cable form. I cabled back accepting the post—"subject to the South African authorities returning my passport." I was, by now, determined to leave.

An item about the offer was published in the paper and reporters called me to ask whether I was accepting it. I said I would be happy to provided I received my passport, but I did not expect to receive it and this was just as well, as I had no intention of leaving the country. This last part was said only for the benefit of the security police. In addition, I purchased new carpeting for my office and bought a new car and deliberately gave no impression of preparing to leave.

At this point, a number of wives whose husbands had been arrested and detained in a new nationwide mass arrest, instructed me to act for their husbands in detention. I accepted their instructions and did whatever I could at the time but I also, at an early stage, tried to form a team of lawyers who would handle the case when it came to court. If the trial commenced within the next two or three months I would stay with the case for its duration. I would then postpone my plans for departure. However, my guess was that the trial would not begin for another five months and I hoped to be out before then.

I asked my member of Parliament, Mrs. Helen Suzman, to speak to the minister of the interior about the return of my passport and I gave her copies of the invitations I had had to go to the United States. Neither of us was optimistic. Mrs. Suzman, who was once my university teacher, was elected to Parliament in the mid-1950s and since the formation of the Progressive party, has been reelected time and again to Parliament as its only member. She is a painstakingly thorough worker. Her speeches are precise, relevant, and courageous and her questioning of ministers is a constant embarrassment for the government. Her lone fight is respected by all, and at all times in her career, she has been approachable by all South Africans. Nevertheless, she, too, is a part of the façade of democracy in South Africa. Toward the end of February, she told me that the minister had refused to return my passport and she stressed that he was most emphatic about it.

The major decision I had to make was whether to risk an application for an exit permit. Taking this step would bring about one of two results: Either I would be arrested and held in detention or the application would simply be delayed indefinitely and neither granted nor refused. But once I took the step, I would have officially alerted the security police of my intention to leave. This would mean that my only other alternative, a back-door escape attempt, would be practically impossible. So I decided that before I approached the authorities for an exit permit, I would fully investigate all possible escape schemes.

There were two prerequisites: My family and I all had to escape from South Africa safely, and we had to escape to a country where there was little or no danger of our being kidnapped by the security police before we were able to go on to England or America. We pored over maps and considered various plans, including the use of hired airplanes, and we even considered a friendly hijacking, but ultimately we abandoned these as too risky.

When I discussed my predicament with a trusted friend from overseas, he said he could obtain a faked passport for me but I knew that my face was too well known. I was sure that I would be recognized at the airport and the police would then legitimately arrest me for unlawfully attempting to leave the country.

At this point, the consul for one of the foreign countries sent me word he wanted to see me urgently. When I went to his office he told me bluntly, "Your plans to escape are known. Give them up, for you will be caught." He told me enough to convince me that the security police were indeed well informed. Then he went on to say that he was in a position to offer me a way out. "You and your family," he said, "will be able to leave the country with valid passports and make whatever travel arrangements you wish. However, you will not be able to return to South Africa. In addition, we

are aware that you have accumulated enough capital to make
you secure for some years overseas or until you are able to
reestablish somewhere. You will be allowed to take all your
money with you and exchange-control restrictions, which
normally apply, will be waived in your case."

I really could not believe it. I smiled at him and asked,
"What's the catch? It's too good to be true."

"There's no catch," he replied. "For ten, fifteen, twenty
years, you have done more than ten other men to further your
ideals and to bring about justice in this country. You have
done a great job—your work is recognized here and overseas.
Now you are a thorn in the government's flesh. Be satisfied
with what you have done—you have done enough. Retire and
live happily with your wife and family. This must be the end
of your work. You must realize that as far as South Africa is
concerned, you have no further interest in it. You cannot
write about it; you cannot talk about it. Your retirement must
be complete. You will have to agree to these terms and we will
accept your word for it. However, if you break your word,
such a liberal offer will not ever be able to be made to anyone
else again."

Before I could speak, he added, "Let me tell you, your wife
knows of this offer, and approves of it. In the interests of your
family, you should accept this and remember you have a duty
to them."

What an astonishing proposal this was. I could not believe
that Jeanette had approved it and rushed home to ask her. As
soon as we were out of the house and walking, she told me
that yes, the proposal had been made to her.

"Well, let me tell you how it was put to me," I said, and I
repeated the conversation in the consul's office.

She gasped, "Is that what they meant by retirement? I did
not understand. It's ridiculous—how could we live with
ourselves? We are leaving here to seek peace of mind. If we
accepted this we would never have it."

"Good," I said, "I'll tell them that tomorrow."

Next day I saw the consul again. I thanked him for his kind
interest and concern and politely refused his offer.

He was not perturbed. "I understand," he said. "You will

now be applying for an exit permit. Well, I wish you good luck. However, do tell your wife this—if, after you apply for an exit permit, you are detained, she should come and see me here. My door will remain open. It will, of course, not be as easy, nor will the conditions be as favorable, but we will do our best."

I saw that it now had become imperative that I leave soon. I had the feeling that now that I had rejected the way out offered to me, I might be detained that very night. I got my bag and toilet requirements ready, but morning came and all was still quiet. I decided to abandon any hope of getting a South African passport, nor did I think I would apply for an exit permit in the near future.

Late in March, I hit upon a new plan. After carefully investigating the law and satisfying myself that it was legally possible, I ascertained that if Jeanette and I obtained British passports, to which we were entitled because our parents had been born in Britain, and we then renounced South African citizenship, the law compelled the authorities to register this renunciation. Once registration was complete, I could leave the country legally without further permission. This was under the terms of a new section of the law and no one I consulted knew the procedure. Carefully studying what procedure was to be followed, I asked different friends to make different inquiries concerning each step without disclosing my plans to them.

However, once the renunciation had been made it would be official and I did not know how efficient the bureaucracy was in passing such information on to the security police. They could still detain me while I was in South Africa despite the fact that I was a British subject. My judgment was that the officials in the immigration department would not have been briefed that all such matters were security matters. Therefore, after the renunciation had been made and I had managed to obtain its registration, my guess was that I would have about two weeks to make our arrangements to leave before our plans became known.

Jeanette and I applied for British passports immediately. I obtained one set of forms of renunciation and made exact replicas for Jeanette. I carefully filled them in, attending to all the details meticulously, had them sworn to, and went into action.

I decided to go to Pretoria myself to hand in the renunciation papers, anticipating that I would not have too much difficulty with the junior officials who would attend to me. At that time, all the senior officials of the various government agencies were down in Cape Town where Parliament was sitting. Those civil servants left in Pretoria would be far from the top rung of the ladder.

I arrived in Pretoria shortly after lunch on a Friday. By a stroke of luck I could not find a parking place. As a result, I got to the government office in question just ten minutes before it closed. Naturally, the civil servants were anxious to go home on time and they dealt with me and got me out in a hurry.

Early Monday morning I went to a pay phone booth and telephoned the official in Pretoria. Cheerfully he told me, "You can come and get your papers. They are all in order and have been registered." Since I had to attend to a postponement in a divorce court matter in half an hour, I hastily telephoned a colleague in Pretoria and asked him to pick up my documents. This was my one mistake. When I got back to my office from court my colleague phoned me there.

"Joel," he said, "these papers you asked me to pick up concerning your departure—the passport officer wants to know where you will be living in London or wherever else you are going. What address will you have?"

The cat was out of the bag. It would now be reported on the tape attached to my telephone. The best thing to do was to make no fuss and just give him an address, which is what I did.

It was nearly 11 A.M. I knew that the security police would now be alerted to my plans but I was not sure when the telephone call would be monitored. Would they replay the tape that night or the next morning? Clearly, the two weeks that we had counted on were now out of the question. Jeanette and I had discussed this possibility already and we had decided that if any snags cropped up, I should leave immediately, and Jeanette and the family would follow as soon as possible. The threat of detention was directed against me and once I had escaped, it was most unlikely that any action would be taken against Jeanette.

If I left immediately the chances were that I would be gone before the security police realized it. I had to make up my mind quickly. After thinking about it for half an hour, at 11:30 that morning I decided the only thing to do was leave that day. Jeanette was at home but I could not telephone her and neither could I take the time to go home to tell her of the change of plan. There was little enough time in the next few hours for me to try to put my affairs in what order I could, and get a visa and a plane ticket.

I told my staff to distribute my case files among three attorneys, which would avoid having any one colleague being questioned or detained about my affairs, or being solely responsible for them. I signed the necessary powers of attorney and arranged for payment of all outstanding debts. Once these matters were taken care of, I concentrated on getting the necessary documents for leaving. First, I collected my own British passport and one for Jeanette. Then I saw about the visas. Next I arranged for my departure papers to be picked up in Pretoria and brought to my office where I had them copied. Finally, at 4:45, I dashed out to get a plane ticket. Now I was ready to go home.

As I came out of the airline office, I realized I did not know where my clerk had parked my car. I started to run back to my office, convinced that he would already have left and I would not have time to go home and still catch my plane. But my luck held. As I turned the corner I was nearly knocked over by him. Realizing that he had forgotten to tell me about my car, he was coming after me. It was pure chance that we had bumped into one another and I took this as an omen that things would go well. The car was parked in a towaway zone but it did not even have a ticket on it.

Twelve minutes later I was home, after a mad dash through town. Hurriedly, I told Jeanette of my plans, saying I would fill her in on the details on the way to the airport. She was completely taken aback. "But the children are not here," she said, "you can't leave without saying good-bye to them."

"I'll get the kids; can you pack?" I asked. "Just throw some things into a suitcase, I'll be back for you in a few minutes." I picked up the children, and Jeanette was waiting for us when we drove up to the house.

On the way to the airport I gave Jeanette an infinite number of instructions. There was still so much to be done and there was no longer any time to do it. Once I was out of the country, though, the heat would be off and she would be able to leave in a more organized way. I suddenly realized that I would probably not see my home again and that this was the last drive I would take in South Africa. I wanted to turn back but there was no time for indecision and we had too many questions to discuss in the little time left. At the back of both our minds was the uncertainty as to whether I would be stopped at the airport.

When we got to the airport, I kissed Jeanette and the children good-bye and headed toward immigration. The security police sat behind a one-way glass panel opposite, carefully scrutinizing all departing passengers. With my back to this panel, I approached the immigration officer. At that moment, neither Jeanette nor I knew whether I would be sleeping that night on a plane or in a cell in Pretoria. The officer was young and, I realized, somewhat of a rookie. I showed him my British passport and the departure form I had filled in.

"Where were you born?" he asked.

"In South Africa," I said.

"But you have a British passport," he exclaimed.

"That is so," I answered. "I am a British subject."

"But then you need a permit to leave the country," he said .

"My dear man, no doubt you mean this," and I produced the registration form with the fresh new blue stamp and signature from the office of the secretary of the interior. He gave it only a quick look and I regretted that I had gone to all the trouble it had taken to get it.

"Carry on," he said, and I moved into the departure lounge. As I entered the lounge I met an acquaintance.

"Good God, Joel," he exclaimed, "what on earth are you doing here?"

"Shut up," I hissed, "are you crazy?"

Then, appreciating my anxiety and uneasiness, he said, "Relax, they've gone for a drink." By a stroke of good fortune, three planes were scheduled to leave within a span of eighty minutes, a rather unusual schedule for a Monday night in Johannesburg. The first plane leaving before mine had been heavily overbooked and it had a full complement of passengers which the security police had had to scrutinize carefully. The plane after mine was also similarly overbooked and my flight was a stopgap to take the overflow. In between the takeoffs of the two planes, the security police had gone off to have a drink, and during the ten minutes in which I was in the departure lounge, they remained absent.

My nerves were tested once more that evening. The airport bus broke down en route to our plane and a police constable came up to us and said, "You will have to take another bus. This one is broken."

My friend said again, "Relax. It will all be all right," and he was right. We changed buses and, without further incident, boarded the plane.

While the plane was warming up I sat tense and jumpy in my seat and thought that it was still possible that some alert security policeman could discover that I was on it. Even after we were airborne, I considered the possibility, albeit an unlikely one, that if the airport security police, checking through the papers, saw my name, they could still recall the plane. My friend offered me champagne but I shook my head. "It's too soon, it's too soon," I said. It was only when we made our first stop ten hours later, two thousand miles up in Africa, that I began to believe that I had done it all.

For four days in London, I remained in hiding while I tried in vain to have my wife and family join me immediately. I learned that there was no pressure on her, and in fact so carefully had we prepared, that the newspapers were unaware of my departure. When they did learn of it the story received banner headlines. I then gave a statement to British newspapers and appeared on TV and the BBC. I hoped that the favorable publicity would deter the South African government from taking action against Jeanette.

The minister of immigration and the security police issued

conflicting statements about my departure and it was clear that they, too, were taken by surprise. The security police chief, when interviewed, said, "Who is Mr. Carlson? We have no interest in him."

Later, the minister of immigration gave my wife official notice to leave the country with the children, within a month. He also stated that my family and I would not be given permission to return to South Africa. This did not upset me for I do not expect to return during this government's rule—which will not last. Once the new society has been established, I will go back and I hope I will still be young and energetic enough to continue practicing law. For as long as a few exercise power over many, there will always be injustices. I wish to do no more than seek to restore the balance and to help to apply simple justice for all people.

INDEX